Harry Ritchie

Harry Ritchie was born in Fife in 1958. He was Literary Editor of *The Sunday Times* from 1993 to 1995. His two previous books are SUCCESS STORIES and HERE WE GO. Harry Ritchie lives in London.

SCEPTRE

Also by Harry Ritchie

Here We Go
Success Stories

The Last Pink Bits

Travels Through the Remnants of the British Empire

HARRY RITCHIE

MECHANICS' INSTITUTE

SCEPTRE

Copyright © 1997 by Harry Ritchie

First published in 1997 by Hodder and Stoughton
A division of Hodder Headline PLC
First published in paperback in 1998
by Hodder and Stoughton
A Sceptre Paperback

The right of Harry Ritchie to be identified as the Author of
the Work has been asserted by him in accordance with the
Copyright, Designs and Patents Act 1988.

10 9 8 7 6 5

All rights reserved. No part of this publication may be
reproduced, stored in a retrieval system or transmitted,
in any form or by any means without the prior written
permission of the publisher, nor be otherwise circulated
in any form of binding or cover other than that in which
it is published and without a similar condition being
imposed on the subsequent purchaser.

A CIP catalogue record for this title
is available from the British Library

ISBN 0 340 66683 8

Typeset by Hewer Text Composition Services, Edinburgh
Printed and bound in Great Britain by
Mackays of Chatham PLC, Chatham, Kent

Hodder and Stoughton
A division of Hodder Headline PLC
338 Euston Road
London NW1 3BH

JUN 1 7 1999

MECHANICS' INSTITUTE LIBRARY
57 Post Street
San Francisco, CA 94104
(415) 393-0101

Acknowledgements

I am greatly indebted to all the people who helped make this book possible by giving me their time, expertise and hospitality. In addition to those who appear by name in the following pages, I would like to thank Nigel Bowden, Rachel Calder, Sukey Cameron, Tony Cross, Karen Geary, Basil George, Stetson George, Graeme Gourlay, Angela Herlihy, Peter James, Jane Memmler, Roland Philipps, Jonathan Rose, Maria Strange, David White and Angela Wigglesworth. Heartfelt thanks also to the captains and crews of the RMS *St Helena* and HMS *Endurance*. Three books in particular provided invaluable background material – *Britain's Dependent Territories* by George Drower, *The Rise and Fall of the British Empire* by Lawrence James, and *Outposts* by Simon Winchester.

MECHANICS' INSTITUTE LIBRARY
57 Post Street
San Francisco, CA 94104
(415) 393-0101

JUN 17 1954

Contents

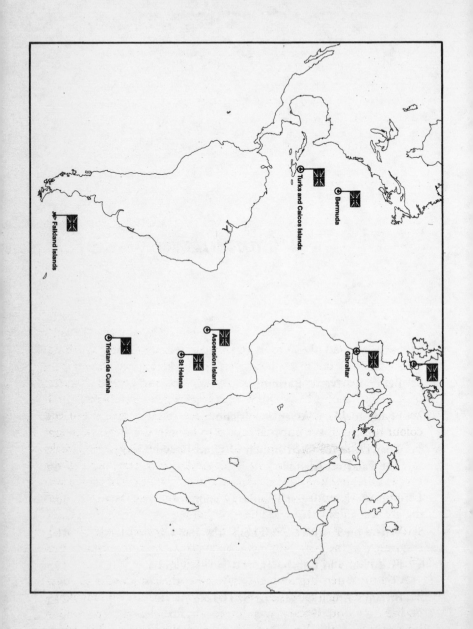

Introduction

It was a vast and magnificent extravaganza, arranged to pay tribute to the ruler of the greatest empire the world has ever known, an empire that covered a fifth of the planet's land surface and a quarter of its population. There were speeches, parties, exhibitions and, above all, mighty military parades. Subjects of every race, creed and colour flocked to the imperial capital to honour the great sovereign.

It sounds like a scene from the long-vanished heyday of the Greeks or Romans. But the ruler wasn't Alexander the Great, nor did the people watching those parades speak Latin. The imperial capital was London, the Empress was Queen Victoria, the year was 1897, and the greatest empire the world has ever known was British. And those celebrations for Queen Victoria's Diamond Jubilee were so awe-inspiring that the *New York Times* and even *Le Figaro* concluded that Great Britain and its empire were invincible.

A century later, Britain had to give away the last jewel in its long-battered and much tarnished imperial crown. Its lease on Hongkong having run out, Britain was forced to flee, leaving six million inhabitants in the hands of China and the People's Liberation

Army. By chance, what was an inevitable humiliation for Britain and could well be a disaster for those six million inhabitants took place in a year fraught with galling anniversaries in addition to that of Queen Victoria's Diamond Jubilee. The handover of Hongkong in 1997 happened exactly 500 years after John Cabot spotted Newfoundland and thereby started Britain's imperial adventure, fifty years after India won the independence that proved how astute was Lord Curzon's judgement: 'As long as we rule India, we are the greatest power in the world. If we lose it, we shall drop straight away to a third-rate power.'

Third-rate power it may now be, but Britain is still an imperial one. Even after the loss of Hongkong, it still possesses the largest empire in the world, at least in the number of its overseas posses-sions. Like a lot of people, I used to assume that Britain had lost or deliberately mislaid all its last imperial territories by about the time the Beatles were splitting up. The post-imperial reality first dawned on me while I was visiting Hongkong, nine years before the handover. I was meandering around in Central one night when, amid all the Cantonese hustle and jostle, a tram appeared, full of blonde, screeching Sloanes. They belonged to a category, I was told, known by the acronym FILTH – Failed in London? Try Hongkong. Barely restraining myself from slapping my forehead, I realised that these Sloanes could try Hongkong because Britain still owned and ran the place, if on a leasehold basis. To the backing track of cogs cranking creakily round in my brain, I then realised that, if Britain owned and ran this country, that meant that the locals didn't.

Some years later, with a deadline imminent and people screaming at me for a newspaper article I had yet to start, I found myself idly flicking through *Pears Cyclopaedia.* Having read through the Coun-try Code and checked on the phases of the Moon, I reached the last entry in the book – the Members of the Commonwealth and, below, a list of Britain's dependencies. And it was a surprisingly long list – seventeen countries, counting Hongkong and allowing for places that were uninhabited or dependencies of those dependencies.

Whenever I mentioned this fact, friends would invariably nod thoughtfully and embark on an attempt to name them. 'Okay, there's the Falklands, right?' they would say. 'And Gibraltar, yes?' After a long pause, they would then, with an air of no little triumph, come up with a third name. Puzzled though I am by the apparent need to do so, I'd like to stress that Belize became independent on 21 September 1981. In fact, as well as the Falklands and Gibraltar, the Union Jack still flies over Anguilla, Ascension Island, Bermuda, British Antarctic Territory, British Indian Ocean Territory, the British Virgin Islands, the Cayman Islands, Montserrat, Pitcairn, St Helena, South Georgia, the South Sandwich Islands, Tristan da Cunha and the Turks and Caicos Islands. A cynic might point out that, with the loss of Hongkong, the combined population of Britain's overseas possessions fell from roughly 6,158,053 to 158,053 (noting the crucial contribution to that total of Pitcairn – pop. 53), but it can still be claimed that, from Bermuda to Gibraltar to the archipelago of the British Indian Ocean Territory to Pitcairn in the Pacific, the sun never sets on the British Empire.

It was what seemed to be the anachronistic absurdity of section Z:12 in the *Pears Cyclopaedia* that gave me the idea to write a book about what remains of Britain's possessions after the loss of Hongkong, a book that would offer an answer to the question George V whispered on his deathbed: 'How is the empire?' I'd be sixty years too late to be of any use to George V, but there would be appealing compensations in travelling to these far-flung but Britishly safe countries: no hassle with visas, no language problems, no ghastly insects or other sources of terror. So I thought, blithely unaware that ahead of me lay some bureaucratic misery, many strangely accented or downright incomprehensible locals, and far, far too many causes of panic and horror for my wimpish liking.

There was one problem I faced right at the start. Where to go? First of all, there were other countries apart from those listed dependencies that might be thought of as colonies. I mean if I was going to get picky about it, I might include the Isle of Man and the Channel Islands as overseas territories, since they aren't part of the United Kingdom. And what about Northern Ireland? There are many people there who think they do live in a British colony, and Derry certainly makes for a more convincing site of imperial oppression than Douglas or St Helier. Come to think of it, many Scots and some Welsh feel that they are the victims of the imperial oppression of the bastard English.

There are few political developments I would welcome more than the creation of an independent Scotland, but the harsh reality is that Scotland, like Northern Ireland and Wales, is a part of the United Kingdom. So they didn't count. Nor did the Isle of Man or the Channel Islands – they are part of the British Isles, they feel integral to Britain and, besides, the *Pears Cyclopaedia*, and the *Dictionary of the British Empire and Commonwealth*, didn't list them as, to use the current term, 'dependent territories'.

With those quibbles conveniently batted aside, I still had a list of countries that represented what threatened to be far too much hard work. First to be crossed off the list were those territories without any inhabitants, or whose only inhabitants were visiting scientists or troops. So that was a big, black line scored through British Indian Ocean Territory, British Antarctic Territory and the Falklands' dependencies of South Georgia and the South Sandwich Islands, along with a variety of unpeopled dots on the map, including the most recent acquisition to Britain's empire, Rockall, a small lump of granite far west of the Hebrides that was officially claimed by Britain in 1955 when a Royal Navy expedition hammered in a plaque to announce that this small lump belonged to the crown.

Next to be deleted from the list was Pitcairn. To prove that this book offers an impressionistic and whistle-stop tour of Britain's remaining empire – certainly not a comprehensive or definitive survey – I chose not to go to Pitcairn on the persuasive grounds that I didn't want to. A jaunt to the airstripless island halfway between New Zealand and Peru would involve hitching a lift on a supply ship whose infrequency of visits would consign me to spending either two hours or six months on a colony whose fifty-three inhabitants are all Seventh-Day Adventists descended from Fletcher Christian's muti- neers from the *Bounty* and whose one means of transport until fairly recently was the wheelbarrow.

As I am writing this, I am looking out at a lifeless, leafless, cold, grey December and I cannot for the life of me recall why I then decided that I would visit just one of Britain's five possessions in the Caribbean. Perhaps it was something to do with lack of time or, more likely, money. I have an inkling that I might have wanted to focus on one territory rather than scoot haplessly among all five. Maybe the prospect of sunbathing for six months didn't square with my Presbyterian *joie de vivre*. Having restricted myself to one territory among Anguilla, the British Virgin Islands, the Cayman Islands, Montserrat and the Turks and Caicos Islands, I selected the last because it had a funny name and I'd never heard of it before I read section Z:12.

The variously whimsical deletions left me with travels up and down and across the Atlantic, to Bermuda, the Falklands, Gibraltar, the Turks and Caicos, Tristan da Cunha and St Helena. Plus Ascension Island, which I visited by mistake.

I assumed that what I'd find in these outposts would be an odd, touching and farcically inappropriate Britishness, or what the natives mistakenly thought of as Britishness – gin-swilling nobs toasting Charles and Diana, pith-helmeted exiles who pined for farthings and Arthur Askey, EIIR pillar boxes in the middle of the tropics, cricketing Falkland Islanders shivering in five layers of whites, bekilted folk tossing cabers along Bermudian beaches, Tristanian cottages wallpapered with the *Picture Post.*

I discovered that baked beans and bitter are popular in Gibraltar, I found a bleached, pealing phone box in Grand Turk, and I was bored senseless in St Helena by a drunk who was not to be persuaded that Ian Rush no longer played for Liverpool. And, of course, people in the colonies do drive on the left (though not in Gibraltar), the Queen's head features on their stamps, wigged barristers can be seen in their courts, many children follow the English national curriculum, there is a high incidence of royal-family mugs, and each colony has a British-appointed governor equipped with a silly plumed hat and powers which are, in theory and sometimes still in practice, dictatorial.

But, instead of finding them out of touch, tune or step with Britain or the rest of the world, I soon appreciated that the people in each country entertained no delusions about themselves or the supposed motherland. Britain was reluctantly pitied in wealthy, sunny Bermuda, Tristanians and Falkland islanders shook their heads at a country where people lived in fear for themselves and especially their children, Gibraltarians knew that British politicians were not to be trusted, the Turks and Caicos islanders would much prefer to be Canadian, and in St Helena a devotedly loyal people wondered why they had been betrayed, abused or ignored.

In fact, it is Britain that suffers from delusions and uncertainties.

Britain still doesn't know what its place and status in the world are. Does there linger any kudos in its imperial past or none? Is Britain European or not? Is it an important country or a fairly ridiculous one? By the end of the century it seems that Britain matters very little in global politics and tends to inspire not respect but derision, that the Great in its title resonates with as much power as the Great in Yarmouth's. It's not patriotism that makes this difficult to accept; 'British' and 'patriotism' are two words that do not sit easily together, because national identity in the not very United Kingdom is precarious and the two categories of people who like to wrap themselves in the Union Jack are manipulating politicians and English football hooligans. No, it is sheer force of habit that makes many Britons suspect their nation is or ought to be, in some way, important. Such is the legacy of the Victorians' theory that the Supreme Being had equipped the British with the qualities that made them fit to rule the world – courage, resolve, self-sacrifice, a sense of duty, of decency, of fair play.

Nine years after India's independence, the majority of people in Britain were delighted to see the Anglo-French invasion of Suez, interpreting this not as the dreadful, humiliating nonsense that in truth it was but as an obviously justified – because British – action to teach Johnny Arab a lesson. Twenty years after India's independence, as a child, I treasured a little plastic globe that still coloured a quarter of the world pink and I counted myself extremely lucky to have been born British and not some poor benighted foreigner. The fact that Britain was an uninvaded winner of the Second World War (and continues to be a particularly insular island) may have helped this feeling of racial self-assurance, but the fact that Britain had so recently been the world's greatest power, and even the apparently gracious and gentlemanly disposal of the empire, helped maintain such increasingly mistaken self-esteem.

That the delusion of importance lingers explains the content of the truly immoral British Nationality Act. This denies inhabitants of all but two of Britain's colonies the right of abode in Britain and was created to prevent Britain being overwhelmed by the six million people who, it was thought, would invade the country before the Chinese takeover of Hongkong. What price principle? Well, £200,000, to be precise, for that was the sum that someone from

Hongkong had to invest in the UK to be granted full British citizenship. The delusion, shared by both Conservative and Labour MPs, was that people from Hongkong would want to come to Britain in the first place. They didn't. Hongkong has a higher per-capita income than Britain, a third of Britain's unemployment level, lower infant mortality and higher life expectancy. What was supposed to be a flood-tide amounted to a trickle of 5,000 immigrants in five years.

Hongkong's last British Governor, Chris Patten, nobly stated that he wanted to see Britain walk out of the colony with honour. How on earth could that be done, when British diplomats admit that Margaret Thatcher oversold China's promises and reassurances, and when the little effort Britain has made to introduce anything resembling a democracy in the colony has been token and last-minute? (At least the handover to an avowedly totalitarian regime would not constitute a great culture-shock.) Looking at Britain's mean, shabby and stupid treatment of Hongkong, it can be very difficult to acknowledge that this same country was once an extremely self-righteous superpower.

But it was self-righteous and it was a superpower. However, Britain's empire was not acquired according to any great masterplan. Initially, in the seventeenth and eighteenth centuries, British foreign policy amounted to the need to expand to survive, since France was so much bigger and richer. Thereafter, most official energies were spent fulfilling the desire to hold on to India. Many of its overseas possessions Britain gained through the private enterprise of, among others, the Virginia Company, the Hudson's Bay Company, and then Cecil Rhodes' British South Africa Company, the North Borneo Company, the British Imperial East Africa Company, until well into this century when the Anglo-Persian Oil Company ensured that even an eventually independent Iraq would be part of Britain's unofficial empire. The greatest outfit of them all was the East India Company, whose military as well as commercial power in India and China was so great that it just had to be brought under parliamentary control.

Other territories were roped into the empire unofficially at first, by trade agreements and British offers of protection (of which a mafioso would have approved). The classic instance of unofficial imperialism at work is provided by Egypt, which was given money by Britain and France, couldn't pay back the debt, was rescued from bankruptcy when Britain and France stepped in to take control, saw violent protests against this move, was helped to restore law and order by the British military, and was then annexed by Britain to safeguard the Suez Canal. And, since it was technically a province of Egypt, the Sudan became part of the British Empire as well.

Further south, Lord Lugard surveyed Britain's influence in what is now Kenya and concluded that he was seeing a 'Pax Britannica' which was 'the greatest blessing that Africa has known since the Flood'. Nowadays, the automatic reaction to such a judgement is to stamp it HUMBUG, and it is undeniable that the Pax Britannica was often brutally imposed, that it involved slavery, disease, prostitution and all manner of destruction, that missionaries converted people to a religion that conveniently demanded respect for white rulers and the need to buy British, that the empire gave to some profoundly troubled men enormous scope for violence, that the undoubted courage of British soldiers was not hampered by those soldiers being equipped with Maxim guns and confronted by enemies equipped with spears or, in the case of the Chinese Boxers, the knowledge that their magical powers rendered them immune to bullets, and that the British public was fed a strictly controlled diet of *Boys' Own* tales of imperial derring-do while atrocities remained unreported.

However, it is also undeniable that Britain ruled with benevolence as well as brutality, inspiring tributes not only from mavericks such as the Indian writer Nirad C. Chaudhuri (who dedicated his first book 'To the memory of the British Empire in India . . . because all that was good and living within us was made, shaped and quickened by British rule), but from the greatest man of our time, Nelson Mandela. And, now that the empire has been dismantled, Britain can find causes for pride as well as horror in its legacy: the withdrawal from India, for example, involved the catastrophe of Partition, which saw the deaths of untold thousands of people (half a million? nobody knows), but it also happily bequeathed independence to a country that immediately became the world's largest democracy.

At first sight, it seems obvious that Lord Curzon was right and that the beginning of the end of the empire can be dated to 15

August 1947, when India gained its independence. However, the empire was already on the rocks by the time Queen Victoria accepted the tributes of her grateful subjects fifty years earlier. There was a prevalent fear around the turn of the twentieth century that Britain was in danger of losing its empire because of a lack of moral fibre or because of ill-fed, ill-educated, ill proles (hence the invention of the Boy Scouts, the Boys Brigade, the League of St George and the Anti-Smoking League). The threat to the empire came not from slackers and smokers but from two uncomfortable realities. One had been pointed out some time earlier, in the fifth century BC, by Cleon to his fellow-Athenians: 'A democracy is incapable of empire.' The second had arrived in 1890 when Britain dropped to second-richest nation in the world, having been overtaken by the United States of America. So another key date in the empire's decline and fall is 1776, when America declared independence from Britain (and Adam Smith asserted in his *Wealth of Nations* that Britain's colonies prevented the development of a free market). More writing on the wall was provided by the Durham Report of 1839, recommending local self-determination for Canada. And, much later, but six years before India's independence, there was the Atlantic Charter drawn up by Churchill and Roosevelt which stated that the new world order would ensure 'the rights of all peoples to choose the form of government under which they live'. At the same time, the Lend–Lease agreement ensured that Britain's war would be financed by America in return for Britain giving America access to imperial bases such as Bermuda and Ascension Island.

So it is no wonder that the empire was dismantled so quickly after the war. Now, with Hongkong gone, Britain is left with colonies that are either uninhabited but retain strategic significance or are inhabited by people who remain colonised because they want to. The inhabited dependencies share the common feature of being just too small to become independent, but there are various other reasons for this desire – fear of rival claims to ownership (Gibraltar, the Falklands), cachet (Bermuda), cash (St Helena, although it sees precious little), emotional attachment (everywhere bar the Turks and Caicos) and having someone to blame (everywhere).

'Colonialism' is such a dirty word, connoting as it does other nasty nouns like 'racism' and 'exploitation', that this rejection of independence is rarely understood. It certainly isn't understood at the United Nations, where Gibraltar's Joe Bossano was suspected of being a British stooge, where the ringingly patriotic speech of the Falklands' Councillor Wendy Teggart was greeted with bafflement, and where anti-colonial ideals have been put into typical practice – the UN declared the 1990s to be 'the International Decade for the Eradication of Colonialism' and set up a Special Committee to mull things over. Tyrants tremble.

Nor is this desired dependence, or any other aspect of the colonies, properly understood or appreciated in Whitehall or Westminster, where Britain's dependent territories are viewed as a nuisance. Foreign Office high-flyers steer well clear of the likes of St Helena. When, with the zeal of a parliamentary new bug, the MP George Walden wrote several articles in *The Times* about colonial affairs, he was taken aside and told this was in no sense a good career move. Looking back on his time as Foreign Secretary, Geoffrey Howe sighed, 'I never thought I would have to spend so much time on the bloody Turks and Caicos Islands.' The Falklands War is reminder enough that, for pragmatic as well as moral reasons, Britain should pay far greater attention to its overseas possessions.

Before I started my grand imperial tour, as I flicked through my atlas and played spot-the-British-colony, I could only think of the prophetic lines Kipling wrote (in 1897, intriguingly): 'Lo, all our pomp of yesterday / Is one with Nineveh and Tyre!' But, as I would discover for myself, these neglected territories are much more than dots on a map, embarrassing reminders that Britain once owned its lion's share of that map. Little did I know that I was about to visit a series of extraordinary, fascinating, perplexing countries – the last pink bits.

Chapter One

Better Believe It: Bermuda

From the top. Having thought long and hard, I decided that, yes, this was the most beautiful ten square yards I had ever seen. It was a secluded, sub-tropical grotto at the bottom of a sumptuous garden in Bermuda and it looked like a scene from Heaven as illustrated in a Jehovah's Witness pamphlet. To my left, a path led up a small slope and on to a clipped lawn that prostrated itself before a house with walls the colour of raspberry mousse, a gleaming white roof and a pedigree stretching back to the eighteenth century. To my right, the path led past ferns and foliage down a small slope and on to the white sand of a deserted beach and to the sea, spangly in a shaft of hot sunshine. Perhaps I'd go for a swim later. I sat down on a smooth rock and sighed.

'Can I get you anything?' asked my host. 'Perhaps another iced tea?'

'Perfect.'

Three days I had been in Bermuda and it hadn't let its guard down once. The people were more than friendly, they lived prosperously in gorgeous white-roofed houses, the landscape was wonderful – and now it had come up with this paradisical grotto. The temperature was a perfect 88 degrees, which it remains, courtesy of the Gulf Stream, almost all the year round. (Januaries are a tad damp.) Hurricanes were devastating parts south and east but, as usual, they'd had the good grace to avoid Bermuda. There were no ghastly creepy-crawlies; I had found one devilish furry thing in my shaving brush but, since I didn't have my glasses on at the time, I'm willing to admit that it might have been a wodge of fluff. So charmed is this country that allergy-stricken flower-lovers can breathe normally as they marvel at the orchids and hibiscus, for the breeze sweeps pollen out to sea. If Bermuda didn't exist, Walt Disney would have had to invent it. But Bermuda could wheel on all the sub-tropical idylls and warm hospitality it liked. I wasn't going to be taken in. I was ready and waiting to spot the snake on the lawn, the sneer behind the smile.

My host smiled as he asked if the iced tea was still cold enough. 'It's perfect.'

Just for the moment, with the coast clear and the grotto to admire, I could relax and gaze at the foliage and, through the ferns' gauze, at the sea, shimmering and calmed by the coral reefs that protect Bermuda's shores from any nasty big waves.

'This is', I said, spreading my arms and pausing to find the *mot juste*, 'perfect.'

'The garden?' asked my host.

'That too. It's all . . . perfect.'

I noticed that as my host pondered my insight, his eyes betrayed the slightest flicker of pain. It wasn't too difficult to guess the reason. He had confessed to me over our poolside lunch that he felt very much at home here, and he certainly looked the part, for he was an Englishman who met all the requirements of the old-fashioned stereotype of the Englishman – he was posh and blond, fey and gay. But that wasn't his villa or his garden and this wasn't his grotto. He was house-sitting for the Bermudian owners, who were off in some other agreeable spot on an extended holiday. They were the ones who were leading the lifestyle that he still couldn't accept hadn't been his by birthright. He came from a family of empire-builders who had once lorded it over East Africa and now lived in comfort but no splendour in the East Midlands. He was too intelligent and too self-aware not to mock himself for it, but he still longed for the good old days when his family had belonged to an English upper class which could remain sublimely indifferent to economic realities and puzzled by the idea of work – yes, one's family is rather well off, so one does have money. And then one, well, one spends it. D'you see?

So here he was, hired to keep the villa and the garden and the grotto warm for someone else. I tried to distract him by ineptly remarking on the vivid colour of some anonymous bloom, how it contrasted, er, perfectly with the green of the lawn. He tilted his head to see if my clumpingly heterosexual observation passed aesthetic muster. 'Yes,' he murmured wistfully. He ran his fingers through that lush, obedient hair posh people have. 'Yes, it is veh pretty.' He bowed his head, defeated, dejected, yesterday's man.

It seemed too good an image of post-imperial decline to be true, but then the whole of Bermuda seemed too good to be true. That is not what I'd expected. Given the choice, I'd rather have resat a school Chemistry exam than spend any time in Bermuda. Everything I'd read about the place had confirmed my notion that it was not so much a country as a country club, enjoyed only by rich American golfers. Britain's oldest, wealthiest and, with 57,000 inhabitants, most populous remaining colony was obviously suspect. The locals had been delighted to hand over 10 per cent of Bermuda's meagre land surface to an American military base and were dismayed when that base had closed down. The Queen's Birthday was a public holiday. The men wore Scout shorts. And how boring did a country have to be for Anthony Trollope, as far as I know a stranger to orgies or discos, to have complained about Bermuda's 'immunity from the dangers of excitement'?

I had flicked through my two guidebooks in a sulk. Lists of hotels decorated with lots of dollar signs, of shops that appeared to sell only cashmere and crystal . . . tips on the best cruise ships . . . the greens were slower than those in the US and putts tended to break less . . . Admittedly, one of those guidebooks was Fodor's, which, no matter what the country covered, can be relied upon to induce dismay in any non-millionaire under the age of eighty. And, fair enough, the other was called *Bermuda Past and Present,* published in New York in 1910 and written by Walter Brownell Hayward, who, I confidently imagined, had been an ex-Harvard man with a private income and a furtive, tingly interest in shoes. He was also very keen on Bermuda, recommending it to Americans 'who desire to exchange the rigors of our northern winter for blue skies and a balmy atmosphere'. Party on.

While I was busy postponing my trip, things suddenly looked up. Bermuda was to hold a referendum on independence. It looked as if Britain might lose its oldest, wealthiest and most populous remaining colony, and I wouldn't have to put in any more practice with my rusting seven-iron.

No cigar. By a thumping three-to-one majority, Bermudians voted to remain colonised. Gloomily, I shopped for suntan lotion, new trunks and David Leadbetter's video on how to improve my swing. Alas, there was space on the plane and, wouldn't you know it, a hotel did have a room available. There was no way out. Since my flight was due to leave Gatwick at two-thirty in the afternoon, I took the opportunity the night before to stock up on the enjoyment I wouldn't be finding in a country which prided itself on its afternoon teas.

This accounts for the truly dreadful state I was in when I shuffled queasily into Gatwick at one-thirty the following afternoon. Of all the varieties of hangover – the sluggish, the mad, the randy – this was by some distance the worst. This was the Samuel Beckett. It was the sort of hangover that allows all-day access to the feeling you get when you lie resolutely awake and it dawns on you with terrifying clarity that there is no hope and love is only need.

According to Walter Brownell Hayward, Mark Twain had commented, 'Bermuda is Paradise but you have to go through Hell to get to it.' What did Mark Twain know? He only had to survive a journey by boat across a storm-tossed North Atlantic. He never had to endure five hours, waiting for a delayed flight, in the departure lounge at Gatwick with a Samuel Beckett. Children screamed and bawled. Parents yelled. Oasis thumped and whined out of Our Price. The tannoy was full of information it wanted to share with us all: 'Beeng-bing-bong. In the interests of security . . . Would Mr Beelzebub, meeting Mr Heseltine . . . last and final call for . . . passengers are reminded . . . beeng-bing-bong . . .'

Finally, the tannoy decided to call flight BA 233 to Bermuda and I slouched off to the gate, two crimson marks on my brow where I'd been pressing my hands for five hours. I joined the line of people waiting to board and saw that I was the only person in that queue not wearing a linen suit or a blouse with a gold slogan scribbled across the bosom. Ah, not quite the only person. There was one elderly couple who were wearing sky-blue anoraks, and who were now rummaging frantically in bags for elusive boarding passes. They must have won a competition.

I looked out of the porthole and spotted in the dusk a clutch of white roofs amid a splash of greenery. This was the first sight of land since the plane had left Southampton behind six hours before. There is a common misconception that Bermuda lies somewhere in the Caribbean. It's a mistake that horrifies Bermudians, who hate the idea that they might be associated with the riff-raff of the Tropics. As locals like to stress, Bermuda is a thousand miles north of the Caribbean, in the middle of the Atlantic, 3,500 miles west of Britain, 600 miles east of Cape Hatteras in North Carolina. Since Cape Hatteras is its closest neighbour, the 180 islands and rocks that comprise Bermuda's twenty square miles constitute the second most isolated bit of land in the world. (The most isolated bit of land in the world is another British colony, St Helena, far off the coast of Angola.) By rights, Bermuda shouldn't exist. It does so only because a primeval underwater volano once spewed up some rocks, most of which didn't quite break the Atlantic's surface. But they did attract coral, and less than 100 million years later the coral had turned into limestone: Bermuda had been created by mistake.

Another popular misconception about Bermuda is that it is American. Bermudians earn and spend dollars, they speak in American-ish accents and watch American TV, 80 per cent of the tourists are American, and the otherwise comprehensive *Dictionary of the British Empire and Commonwealth* has forgotten to carry an entry for Bermuda, so it's an understandable error. But Bermuda is British. A fact that seemed particularly strange as I stepped out of the plane and into an alfresco nighttime sauna. Immediately moist with sweat, I joined the parade, sponsored by Louis Vuitton, of the linen-suited and gold-sloganed.

There was a queue at passport control, where we were inspected by a bleached portrait of a young and unimpressed Queen. The hold-up was caused by a middle-aged fellow who looked respectable enough, in a linen-suited sort of way, but who seemed to be in real danger of being refused entry to the country or allowed entry on condition that he went straight to jail. Was his face on local Wanted posters? Had he packed his colon with sausages of heroin? No – he hadn't made a hotel reservation.

During his lengthy interrogation, it occurred to me that the suitcase trolley being hauled by the woman in front of me was still squeaking even though she hadn't moved for several minutes. Then it occurred to me that the squeaks were actually coming from some nearby trees. That's odd, I thought.

The squeaking continued while I queued, cleared passport control, marched through customs, was driven to the other end of Bermuda (the journey took about a quarter of an hour), checked in at my hotel and enjoyed a saunter round the pool. Squeak, squeak . . . squeak . . . squeak, squeak, squeak . . . squeak . . . There was no mistaking this racket for one unoiled suitcase trolley. A thousand suitcase trolleys, yes, at a rave recording organised by Stockhausen, but since this explanation seemed unlikely, I asked a waiter.

'That's the tree-frogs, sir.'

'Do they make that noise all the time?'

'Only at night.'

'All night?'

'Sure thing.'

'Don't they keep you awake?'

'You get used to it.'

'So you brake with your left hand, control speed with your right, press the left-hand brake at the same time as the start button to get going, twist the steering to your left and press the key in to lock. Traffic's on the left, you should be okay with that. Always wear your helmet. And whatever you do . . .'

'Yes?'

'Never look behind you. Okay – take her round the block.'

Mothers, they're like policemen. Never there when you need them. Exhausted after a night spent listening to the tree-frog chorus and now suffering the heart-rate of a novice newscaster, I lurched off on my moped, reached the hotel car park ten yards up the hill, turned round and, still without serious incident, wobbled back to my instructor, who was trying to look encouraging.

'You'll be fine,' he lied. 'Off you go, then.'

I flicked a salute off my helmet and kangarooed down the hill, negotiated the first corner and stopped behind a hedge. I waited for a minute, then peeked over the hedge. He'd gone. I squirmed out of my helmet, heaved the moped on to its stand, failed to lock it and tiptoed back to the hotel where I ordered a taxi to take me into Hamilton, the capital.

Only residents are allowed to drive cars in Bermuda and even they are limited to one car per household – which is, I need scarcely add, marvellous. The downside is that visitors are expected to zoom around on these wee moped things. The speed limit is, theoretically, 20 miles an hour and Bermudian drivers are said to be wonderfully cautious and courteous, especially to those Americans who, having turned right, immediately regress to puttering along on the right-hand side of the road. So riding a moped here was, everyone agreed, not only the best way to see the islands but terribly safe. Uhuh? In that case, how did everyone explain away the fact that yesterday, a couple of hundred yards down the road, a guy on a scooter had slammed into a van and died? I was getting a taxi, me.

The cab-driver dropped me off outside an Italianate building with an overgrown clocktower – the Sessions House, home of Bermuda's Supreme Court and parliament, the House of Assembly. Since today wasn't a Friday between October and July, the House wouldn't be in session, so I contented myself with taking a very dull photograph of the exterior before tussling with the map to get my bearings. These were, I saw, very easy to get indeed, since Hamilton is tiny (est. pop. 3,000) and is laid out on a neat grid system. I was on Parliament Street. If I walked up the hill and turned left towards the big church, I'd be on Church Street. If I walked down the hill towards the waterfront, I'd be on Front Street. Now what kind of trees might I find on Cedar Avenue?

It was three in the afternoon, and it was hot and humid, but almost everyone who passed by did so at pace and in very smart clothes. These people clearly meant business. Taking the easy, downhill option, I headed for Front Street. This was a picturesque bustle with the harbour on one side and on the other an array of shops sprouting flags. How very strange it was to see the Union Jack flutter above such prosperity. The shops themselves contributed to the festive display, for they were all brightly painted in white, blue, peach and pink – the colours of the leisure shirts sported by the richer American tourists. The high-fashion notes, however, were struck by the local businessmen, who really were wearing Bermuda shorts, always with sturdy black shoes, dark knee-length socks, blazer, shirt and tightly knotted tie. I have to admit that, after I'd smirked for a couple of minutes, the outfit began to look rather good. Nevertheless, in both senses of the verb, I'd be sticking to long trousers.

Several minutes' slow walking later, I'd reached the end of Front Street, so I turned left towards a little park at the harbour's edge for a well-earned rest. The sun shone. The water sparkled. Yachts bobbed.

This strangely urbane, semi-tropical tranquillity was threatened only by four grizzled old boys behind me, who had been shooting the breeze under a palm tree and were now arguing fiercely. Ah-hah. These would be members of Bermuda's oppressed black majority (three-fifths of the population is black, two-fifths white) drowning their sorrows or lamenting the injustice of lives lived under the post-colonial jackboot. I eavesdropped, eager to tune in to anecdotes illustrating honky supremacy.

'No, man. I said, *no*.'

'Hey, you want to believe that, I'm not saying you can't.'

'Not a matter of can or can't. Matter of the truth.'

'You say so, bro.'

'Not a matter of I say so. It is *written*. Isaiah, sixty-*fav*.'

The quartet interrupted the theological seminar to wish me a good afternoon and an enjoyable holiday as I walked back to do some window-shopping, the only kind of shopping I could afford here. Bermuda's shops have always catered for moneyed Americans. Hence the establishments specialising in tweed and kilts and Cuban cigars. Hence, too, the Yankee retailspeak of the larger stores like Trimingham's ('Open until 9 PM for Your Shopping Convenience') and even the little souvenir kiosks ('Shades – The First in Protective Eyewear since 1984').

The relentless demands of research obliged me to investigate a nearby pub. Since the cost of living and particularly drinking in Bermuda is so high that ordinary currencies like sterling can only peer up in awe at such Olympian prices, I chose Flanagan's because it was hosting its happy hour – or, in my case, slightly less mortified hour. In exchange for an American ten-dollar note, I received a pint of Newcastle Brown and a mere handful of Bermudian dollars. (The local dollar was pegged to the pound until 1972, when Britain allowed the pound to float, or rather sink. Since then, it has been on a par with the US$, although Bermudian notes come in different colours and still feature the Queen.)

Amazingly oblivious to the cost of doing so, two cheery sots were getting hammered at the bar and carrying out a wager.

'Twenny dollars says you wone make it.'

'Twenny dollars? To stand on one leg?' Laughing uproariously, the second sot began to slide down from his bar stool.

The barman shook his head. 'Man, state you're in, you couldn't stand on two legs.'

The barman was right.

After the rescue party – and it was a party, because of the second sot's infectious whoops of laughter – Flanagan's was suddenly filled with customers. Fit, good-looking, well-dressed, joyful customers, black and white. I felt as if I was in an advert. A fit, good-looking, well-dressed, joyful waitress placed a basket crammed with food on my table.

'Sir? Here we have a fish selection, freshly made deep-fried meatballs, I can really recommend them, chips, all sorts of stuff.'

'I'm sorry, there must be some mistake. I can't afford, I mean, I didn't order this.'

'It's complementary, sir.' She blessed me with a stunning smile. 'It's happy hour.'

This particular happy hour lasted for 150 minutes, during which time I made the most of my free meal and was befriended by the celebrants at a neighbouring table. Like everyone else in Flanagan's, with the exception of Darren the barman, who hailed from Manchester, they didn't belong to the islands' tourist majority. These were Bermudians, office-workers who were having a few drinks before going on to what would evidently and gallingly be a fun-packed yet eminently civilised evening out at a neighbouring wine-bar.

Their departure signalled a change of shift among Flanagan's customers. With the joyful, beautiful people gone, a new set took over that was shabbier, poorer and very convincingly oppressed – the Brit guest-workers. I was harangued by a couple of blokes who were eager to tell me that they had multiplied their incomes threefold by coming here on a year's contract. To perform what job they didn't say. Since my role in this conversation was to nod in an enthralled manner while wiping stray flecks of spit from my shirt, I extricated myself as soon as I could and returned to the hotel, but not before noticing a poster on Flanagan's door: 'The Jock Stein Glasgow Celtic Supporters Club Bermuda – Motherwell v Rangers – Live by Satellite – Saturday 11 AM – Flanagan's'.

Well, that was tomorrow morning taken care of.

For once in my life I was almost glad to see Rangers win, because that was the one bit of normality in Flanagan's the next morning. It had been strange enough to watch a Scottish match live on a king-size screen before noon. But far more discombobulating was the clientele – I was standing at a bar with fifteen Glaswegian men and there wasn't a cigarette or a glass of alcohol in sight. Apart, that is, from the pint of Murphy's which I had ordered out of habit – okay, so I had fallen out of bed, knackered, courtesy of the tree-frogs, only an hour before, but I was watching football, for goodness' sake – and which I now sipped, telling myself that civilisation had clearly turned these men into cissies but knowing that I stood out like a pie-eating champion at an aerobics class.

My discombobulation was complete when Rangers scored the only goal of the game and four of the fifteen non-smoking, non-drinking Glaswegians shouted with joy while eleven slumped in disgust. Until that moment, given the absence of fistfights, I hadn't an inkling that the clientele came from both sides of the sectarian divide.

While the rest of us were gaping at the huge screen, one chap, who had been assigned to monitoring his radio, spent the morning squinting at the floor as he tried to decipher the latest scores from the crackle and hiss of the broadcast from Scotland. Every five minutes or so, he'd yell out updates – 'Celts one up, a Hibs own goal. Somebody sent off for Dundee United . . . Wait . . . Yeah – Celts gone two up. What's your team, pal?'

'Raith Rovers,' I replied.

'At home to Aberdeen?'

'That's right. You got any score yet?'

'Youse are one–nil up.'

But the Glaswegians' interest was not confined to the Scottish Premier Division, as the radio monitor's updates proved. 'Wimbledon beating Everton. Burley's scored for Chelsea at Sheffield Wednesday. Essex 36 for 5. Sorry, pal, half-time at Kirkcaldy and it's Raith one, Aberdeen three.'

I swallowed my misery and tried to distract myself by asking a man in a very unGlaswegian pink T-shirt how they managed to receive this TV broadcast from Scotland.

'Flanagan's arranges it. We all pay a sub. That's ten bucks, by the way, pal. Been doing it for the past four years. What we're watching is being beamed from Glasgow to the Canadian Sports Network and then I think throughout the States. At any rate, the Canadians broadcast the whole game but back home they won't show all this. They'll only use the highlights in the evening.'

'Which explains', chipped in someone wearing a Celtic strip, 'why at half-time like the now, you get crap like this' – he pointed at the screen, which had gone fuzzily blank – 'because the Canadians are getting adverts.'

'Aye,' said his friend. 'And wait till you see what happens after full time.'

What did happen after full time was that the four Rangers fans cheered the screen, the eleven Celtic fans celebrated the radio monitor's news that they'd trounced Hibs five–nil, I sighed at Raith's four–one defeat, and then the loudest cheer of the morning went up as the camera zoomed in for a close-up of Jock Brown, BBC Scotland's very bald football commentator. Several men who'd drifted off to watch the last minutes of the Sheffield Wednesday–Chelsea match on another screen hurried back.

'Oy! Quick! It's Jock!'

'Has he done it yet?'

'Nup. He's still on the mouth-stretching.'

Sure enough, the king-size screen was filled with the sight of an out-sized Jock Brown grimacing manically.

'You see, pal,' the man in the Celtic strip explained to me, 'what we are privileged to view, courtesy of this satellite facility, is Jock preparing to do his live link-up with the *Grandstand* studio in London. He'll start on his hair in a minute.'

'But he doesn't have any hair.'

'Aye, but Jock doesn't know that. Nor does he realise that he's on candid camera.'

'Who'll be watching Jock do all this face-pulling then?'

'Only us and everyone tuning in to this station everywhere in Canada and the States. Hello!'

Wild cheering reverberated around the bar as Jock Brown stopped impersonating an astronaut coping with the G-force of a botched re-entry and started licking down the wisps of hair above his ears.

'Way-hay! *Smooth* it down, Mister Brown!'

'Where's your comb, Jock!'

'Must've lent it tae Yul Brynner!'

All too soon, Jock was on live to London. The excitement over, the Glaswegians began to make arrangements for Wednesday's European Cup matches.

'You coming, pal?'

'I'm not sure. What time?' I asked.

'Seven-thirty kick-off back home, so it'll be half-three in the afternoon here.'

'Aye, but remember,' one guy warned. 'There's the Dutch league game on Channel 24 that morning. PSV Eindhoven, I think. Then the Brazilian highlights programme. And the Portuguese round-up.'

'Plus the American soccer league later on.'

'And then highlights of the other European Cup games after that.'

'You do all have jobs here, don't you?' I said.

'Sure. The only other way you can live here is by marrying a local. I'm an accountant. He works for a bank. Boy over there works in a hotel. Earning good money, the lot of us.'

'And do you like it here?'

'Be fools not to. Unbelievable place. They're into their football here too. The local season'll be starting soon, not a bad standard, but the main thing is we can watch all the football we like on TV.'

'So how do you find the time if you're all working?'

'There's ways to wangle it. Besides, why do you think none of us have got tans?'

Feeling like an elephant on a unicycle and trying very hard not to think about the time when my friend Bill left his Triumph Bonneville at 70 miles an hour and ended up spread-eagled on a garage forecourt on the opposite side of the road, having dived head-first through the garage's revolving Castrol sign, I lurched slowly but precariously on my moped down from the hotel to the junction with the main road, staying at that junction for some considerable time while I waited for the traffic to recede to the horizons, before revving wildly to execute a disgracefully inept left turn.

An hour later, I'd zipped through Hamilton and zoomed all the way up to Spanish Point, a good seven miles from the hotel. A patch of scrub featuring a couple of trees and a fair amount of litter, Spanish Point was to be one of the very few unbeautiful spots I found in Bermuda. But it made some sort of sense to start my historical tour of the islands with a visit to this particular tip, because it was here that a boulder was found with an inscription R and P or possibly T and F and the date 1543. Whoever RP or TF was, he must have been very lonely, for the first person known to have landed on Bermuda was Henry May fifty years later. May was one of several survivors of a ship which crashed into reefs near the islands because it was crewed by French drunks; the castaways stayed for several months while they constructed a makeshift boat.

The islands had been discovered in 1503 by Juan Bermudez and were sighted by various other Spaniards throughout the sixteenth century. None landed though, for the Spanish reckoned that the islands were inhabited by demons. This scaredy-cat assumption allowed the British to get their hands on one of the most prosperous and beautiful bits of the new world in 1609, when Sir George Somers' vessel, the *Sea Venture*, was battered by a storm and ran aground here just as the sailors were toasting their imminent deaths by drowning. The incident provided Shakespeare with material for Act One of *The Tempest* and Sir George Somers with the opportunity to spend a couple of months here chopping down cedar trees and building another ship so that he could continue his original mission to take supplies to the several hundred settlers who were dying of disease and starvation in Britain's new colony at Jamestown, Virginia.

Various memorials of Somers' expedition can be found in the little town of St George in the north-east of the islands, so I hopped back on the moped to putter along the North Shore Road, past the enticingly gorgeous beach at Shelly Bay, past the airport and over the little bridge to St George's Island. The roads were quiet enough for me to start risking some appreciation of the backdrop to my journey – palm trees, hedgerows full of hibiscus blooms, gleamingly pink and white and yellow villas, calm bays of green and turquoise water. It was like riding through a brochure.

St George turned out to be much smaller, older and prettier than Hamilton. In any other country, I'd have dismissed the town as a theme-park re-creation of itself, but two days in Bermuda had been long enough to persuade me that the place was for real. Sure, the stocks and the ducking-stool and the replica of Somers' Bermuda-built vessel, the *Deliverance*, were strictly for tourist use only, but locals were cashing real cheques in the period-piece bank and genuinely popping in for a drink at the beautifully preserved White Horse Tavern.

I parked the moped outside the White Horse with the aim of strolling around the little town. Ten very hot yards later, I made my first stop-off, beside a statue which depicted Sir George Somers flinging his arms aloft in gratitude at making his landfall on the islands. The poor chap didn't realise that this was to be his last piece of good fortune; less than a year later, when he returned to the islands from his mission of mercy to Virginia in 1610, the strain of all this adventuring proved too much and his heart gave out. That particular organ was buried on Bermuda in a grave which was subsequently adorned with a plaque bearing a verse by Governor Nathaniel Butler, a verse that makes a David Bowie lyric sound like Milton. 'In the year 1611 / Noble Sir George Summers went hence to heaven' are the first two lines. There are six more, but, as Sir George would agree, life is short and, besides, anyone who has to change the date of a death to get a rhyme, and a rubbish rhyme at that, doesn't deserve to be quoted. Anyway, as I was saying, Sir George's embalmed and heartless corpse was stowed away on board the *Deliverance* for its return journey to England, while three crew members remained behind to watch over the islands.

The three men, plus a dog, were left alone on Bermuda for a couple of years. They had no difficulty surviving until they came across several large blocks of ambergris washed up on the beach. At that time, the only things known about ambergris (it is actually a kind of whale sick) was that it was rare, smelled to high heaven and, paradoxically, was vital to the manufacture of perfume. So vital that, in early-seventeenth-century London, it fetched three quid an ounce. One of the blocks they had found was over eighty pounds in weight and therefore worth a then-socking four thousand pounds in money. The trio immediately agreed that they really ought to overlook the legal nicety that the ambergris belonged to the newly formed Bermuda Company, then immediately disagreed about how they should divide their spoils and then immediately started to fight among themselves. A year of fisticuffs later, they managed to come to a truce and were planning to sail off on a makeshift boat when a ship arrived from England with Bermuda's first proper settlers. The three thieves tried to conceal their treasure but, true to their haplessness, failed.

Under the disastrous governorship of one Richard Moore, these idyllic islands, previously inhabited only by very friendly and edible wild hogs and cahow birds, were just about destroyed. The tame cahows were eaten into near-extinction and rats, imported in a grain shipment, overran the place. In the meantime, the settlers had discovered that the local palmetto berries made a fine liqueur, and spent their days and nights appreciating it. During one bout, a settler drank so much he died on the spot.

While his colonists were drinking themselves into temporary or permanent oblivion and then starving to death, Moore concentrated on building a fort – a completely unnecessary project, as was proved by the arrival of two Spanish ships in 1614. Realising only at the last minute that these weren't British vessels bringing them food and party packs of malmsey, the persistently clueless colonists rushed around over the barrel-load of gunpowder they had spilled, somehow avoided blowing themselves to smithereens, and prepared to defend the islands. Moore managed to fire two shots in the general direction of the Spanish ships, which promptly fled, unaware that Moore's munitions now amounted to one cannonball.

After Moore went back to London to bluster to the Bermuda Company bosses about why loads more ambergris hadn't been discovered (the first find was to be the last, because whales are too busy frolicking in the Gulf Stream to be throwing up in these parts), the new colony descended into even more spectacularly drunken anarchy. Until the Bermuda Company sent a Virginian planter, Daniel Tucker, to the islands in 1616 to sort the place out. This he achieved by enforcing work programmes, ordering whippings and hangings at a whim, and introducing slaves from the Caribbean. Having tried to cure the rat plague by setting fire to the islands' superb cedar forests, Tucker divided the charred remains into 'tribes', later termed parishes, which still exist and still bear the names – Hamilton, Sandys, Smith, etcetera – of the lords and gentry who had invested in the Bermuda Company and who now owned these chunks of the islands.

Tucker's harsh regime was also corrupt and ineffective, and the tobacco crop was fated to be always inferior to Virginia's. By 1684, with the islands still failing to make a profit, the Bermuda Company was dissolved and its charter was handed over to the crown. Things soon looked up as some colonists used the islands' rejuvenated cedar forests to start a ship-building industry and others sailed down to the Caribbean to found a salt industry in the Turks and Caicos Islands. There was also money to be made in the rapidly expanding business of privateering – that is, mugging foreign merchant ships, an activity to be distinguished from piracy since privateering was regarded as legal, even patriotic.

As I walked sweatily around St George, I had to jettison my remaining suspicions about such a perfectly quaint town and accept that the whole place really was a living museum. Why, there was St Peter's, the oldest Anglican church in the western hemisphere. Just across the road was the former Globe Hotel, now a museum devoted mainly to exhibits from the time of the American Civil War, when Bermudians made a packet by running the North's blockade of Southern ports.

I returned to the moped to continue my historical tour. Now a moped expert, I reared my roaring machine up in a macho wheelie before shooting off through the town square, nought to sixty in five seconds. 'Liar, liar,' I hear you say. 'Pants on fire.' Oh, all right. I wobbled off at eight miles an hour on an epic journey. If you picture Bermuda as being shaped a bit like a sea-horse lying on its stomach, St George would be the sea-horse's eye, and I had to travel right the way round, through the parishes of Hamilton, Smith's, Devonshire, Paget, Warwick, Southampton and Sandys, all the way to Somerset at the tip of the sea-horse's tail, a good twenty miles away.

Hours later, I brought the moped to something resembling a stop and slithered off to have a look around my destination – the Royal Naval Dockyard. My epic journey had taken me past row after row of charming roadside houses and cottages, all painted in bright colours and topped by shining white roofs. Lots of freshly whitewashed churches, some grander houses set in well-appointed gardens, quite a few hotels, these I had also juddered past, giving me the clear impression that Bermuda was one of the most peaceable and least military countries on earth. So tramping round the vast acreage of the dockyard acted as a timely reminder that Bermuda has always been overly fortified, ever since Richard Moore constructed that first redundant fort in 1612.

Today the dockyard is just another tourist centre, with the whole complement of craft shops, restaurants, arts complex, Clocktower Speciality Retail Centre, museums and games arcade (Sparky's Family Fun Centre). But at the beginning of the nineteenth century, the dockyard was intended to turn Bermuda into another Gibraltar – providing security from a recently independent America and giving the Navy a base from which its patrols could protect imperial shipping routes. Ten thousand slaves and convicts laboured for forty years under a glaring sun to construct barracks, wharfs, warehouses, a dry dock, a fortified keep, the whole shebang. Huge and imposing as it is, the dockyard never did prove terribly useful. The Navy eventually abandoned it when the British military pulled out of Bermuda in 1951. By that time, the islands had already been a base for US forces for ten years under the Lend–Lease agreement. Having used Bermuda as their base for North Atlantic aircraft and nuclear submarine patrols, the Americans themselves pulled out in 1995, which means that the islands are no longer on the thermonuclear front line, and that for the first time in its history of human occupancy the country is not a military centre.

As bitter chance would have it, the day after my intrepid wobble round the islands on the moped, a nice lady at the Department of Tourism phoned to say that she had arranged a tour for me. At no small personal sacrifice, I rejigged my busy schedule, postponing until the afternoon my planned three hours' sleep beside the hotel swimming-pool, and went out to meet the taxi-driver whom the nice lady had assigned to my case.

'Good *day* to you, my friend, and how ya doin' this fine morning?' A tall, burly black guy who might have been in his early sixties and was definitely wearing a candy-striped shirt and vermilion Bermuda shorts ushered me into his taxi while I tried to summon up a reply enthusiastic enough to match his greeting.

'All right, thanks,' I said.

'That's *great*.' He held out his hand for what I just knew was going to be a wince-making handshake. 'Name's Custerfield Crockwell. Folks call me Crock. Harry, right?'

'Yes. Ow. Pleased to meet you . . . Crock.'

'Harry, I thought we'd start with a run up to St George, then maybe head over to the dockyard, what do you say?'

'Well, in actual fact, I've done that on—'

'Your moped, right? Hey, that's *great*. How about I take you to a few other places, we have a general look around?'

'Good idea.'

'*Excellent*.'

We set off down to join the main road, where Crock immediately demonstrated his skill as a driver because the demands on him were many. Not only did he have to steer and so on, he was obliged to wave, shout and peep at every car-driver or pedestrian he knew, and he knew each and every one. Too diligent to do otherwise, Crock persevered with his conventional approach to the tour for the first half-hour, pointing out all manner of hibiscus and oleander, taking me to see the Aquarium and the Perfumery, until he appreciated that, like him, I really was much more interested in just driving round the place and talking about more important matters.

'. . . Okay, I take your point, and it's real popular here, believe it, but I'm not so keen on football. Hey there, honey! Cricket, on the other hand, yes sir, that's my game.'

'Cricket's quite big here, isn't it?'

'Better believe it. You wanna go to the museum at Fort St Catherine? No? Fine by me. How ya doin', David? You heard of the Cup Match? Takes place every year, two days in early August, St George's versus Somerset. Good morning! Only sporting occasion in the world that's a national holiday. Twelve, fifteen thousand people turn up.'

'All locals?'

'We get a few tourists wondering what all the – hi there, Louis! – fuss is about. They've started to put up a special tent for the Americans, where someone can explain to them what's going on out there.'

I remembered the story of the cricket fan who sat down with an American and patiently explained the rules and intricacies of the sport, unable to believe that he was succeeding – to the extent that the American was asking about the wisdom of long-on retreating to the boundary against a slogger, thereby allowing an easy single – until, having shown a complete grasp of the difference between a googly and an off-break, the American sighed in wonder that such a fascinating game could be played on horseback.

We continued to bundle along a series of neat roads, all decorated with flowering hedgerows, while chatting, in between Crock's constant greetings, about the prospects of the Bermudian national side in their upcoming match against the Leeward Islands. We were somewhere to the east of Hamilton when Crock pointed out the house where he grew up as a kid and added that this was a poor area. Some houses didn't have gardens and a few hadn't been painted that year. I assured Crock that back in my native land these wouldn't be regarded as slums so much as prized holiday homes.

'Well, I tell you,' he said, shaking his head, 'we do have a bad situation in Hamilton.'

'You can't mean that there's a ghetto?'

'A problem area, yes. Wanna take a look?'

'Absolutely.'

A few minutes later, we were passing a series of warehouses and small factories on the northern outskirts of Hamilton. Shortly after that, we were cruising past a row of mildly dilapidated houses and shops. From what I had seen of Bermudian society, the inhabitants of this area should have been young, white, British guest-workers, but they were in fact *bona fide* victims of racial oppression. Not that Bermuda's black ghetto-children seemed very oppressed. Several guys were milling about outside a slightly mildewed off-licence. As Crock slowed to a halt at a set of traffic lights, a teenager sashayed in front us and chummily slapped the bonnet. Crock waved back. Five old chaps were sitting on a wall, swigging from a brown paper bag. The traffic lights turned to green and we moved off down the hill towards Front Street.

'Okay. Now you've seen it. Court Street.'

'That was *it*?'

Crock laughed.

'But it was only a bit run down,' I said, 'and it only lasted for about a block.'

'That's why it's called the Block.'

'And it looked all right to me.'

'Yeah, but. You was to go there on your own, you'd get people stopping you, asking you for a dollar, trying to sell you drugs maybe.'

'Marijuana? . . . For example.'

'Yeah, marijuana. And crack cocaine. Could have been stopped years ago, but – good to see ya! – I just didn't have the back-up.' Crock caught my puzzled frown. 'I was in the police thirty years, 'fore I retired. Did narcotics for a while. Fact, I *was* narcotics. Me and my dog. Now if we'd had more on the case back then, and maybe two, three more dogs, we wouldn't have this problem now.'

'How bad is it?'

'Nothing compared to the US, that's for sure, but we do have some junkies, a few girls who're walking the streets, more muggings. But, hey, back when I was in the force, we had some trouble too.'

'What, there was an outbreak of people not dressing for dinner?'

'No sir. Back in '72 the Commissioner of Police was shot dead. Hi there! Next year the Governor, Sir Richard Sharples, his assistant and his dog also shot dead. Man, we had a state of emergency declared.'

'Was it some kind of political action?'

'Nothing political 'bout it. Month after the shooting of the Governor, a supermarket was robbed, two guys who worked there shot dead as well.'

'What was going on?'

'We all knew who was behind it, but we never could touch the man. He'd get all these kids do the work for him, fire them up on drugs, let them do their worst. And a good morning to you! Still, we got the killers in the end. Buck Burrows and Larry Tacklyn. Both of them got the death sentence.'

'But this was the mid-seventies.'

'We still had the death penalty. Buck and Larry, both were hanged. Trouble didn't stop there, though, believe it. Protest riots after the hanging, arson at one of the big hotels. And it was a real serious fire. Two Americans staying there and one of the hotel workers died in it.'

'What about all the stuff in the guidebooks about this being a really safe place?'

'Almost all true. But that was a bad time. And it only takes a few robbers or muggers, whatever, can make a big impact. How ya doin', honey! This is a small place. What's the time?'

'Half-eleven.'

'What do you say we take a look around St George?'

'Fine, though as I said, I have been—'

This appeared to be one of the funniest things he'd heard in ages. 'Sure, sure, but I'm a member of the police club up there, take you for a drink. What you paying in Hamilton for a beer?'

'Four or five dollars.'

'Get you a beer in the club for two dollars fifty.'

'Deal.'

We headed back up a road I just about managed to recognise from my moped expedition and soon reached St George, which I also just about managed to recognise. The road was only intermittently familiar, because on the previous trip I had been concentrating on not killing myself. However, it was St George itself which had been transformed – by the arrival of a multi-storey cruise-ship. This had disgorged hundreds and hundreds of American tourists, who were now crammed into the little town. Had these been hundreds and hundreds of non-American tourists, St George would have coped with the invasion quite adequately, but the amount of room occupied by the average American was twice that of the average non-American. I do have qualms about making this point, since it's rather like reporting back from Moscow the startling news that lots of Russians drink far too much, but these people really were *massive*. Not for the first time, it struck me that there are two distinct kinds of American: one, the people who live and work-out in California and the thin people with lots of teeth and hair who appear on TV and, two, the rest. To be fair, there were a few non-fat Americans that afternoon in St George – an unremarkably proportioned baby in a pushchair, a couple of very frail octogenarians – but as for the vast majority . . . Even the slim ones were fat. And the fat ones were much more than obese. They were triangular. Some had been crippled by their weight and had to use sticks or walking frames to drag themselves about. One young man was so wide he was walking down a lane sideways. Granted, St George's lanes were old, had narrow pavements and could accommodate only one-way traffic, but they were still capable of accommodating traffic. The Americans themselves were evidently unconcerned that they looked like a crowd of mammoth weebles because they were all kitted out, preposterously, in sports gear not intended to conceal knees with the diameter of my head, thighs the width of my torso, arses the size of my flat.

Still waving and peeping at each local that passed by, Crock squeezed his taxi through St George's overwhelmed streets and uphill towards a small complex which was markedly unBermudian in that the buildings were just not pretty. They were, Crock informed me, the sometime barracks of the British Army, now used for a variety of purposes, which included housing the local police club. Save for the air-conditioning, this looked (and smelled) strangely like my secondary school — although, come to think of it, much though we would have appreciated one, Kirkcaldy High also lacked a cut-price bar.

Crock threw back a litre of coke, I downed a litre of beer, and we discussed matters of import. To wit, a letter in that morning's *Royal Gazette* from a New Yorker complaining about Bermudians' rudeness. It was a shocking complaint because Bermudians set great store by propriety. The dress code here is strict, to the extent that it is always advisable for men to wear jacket and tie to a restaurant, and, to avoid nasty looks while shopping, women should avoid wearing trousers. The following activities are illegal in Bermuda: consuming alcohol in public, topless sunbathing, wearing curlers in public, riding a scooter shirtless. And Bermudians pride themselves on having extremely good manners. Perversely good, said the New Yorker in the *Royal Gazette*, citing the experience he'd had when, in the middle of a downpour, he'd scampered out from under cover to ask a taxi-driver politely for directions. The driver had stopped, wound down his window and said, 'Good afternoon.' But that was all he said. Bemused and now very wet, the New Yorker had repeated his polite question, only for the taxi-driver to reply, more pointedly, '*Good afternoon.*' Realising the nature of the impasse, the tourist in the taxi had wound down her window and told the New Yorker to walk down the road and take a left.

Crock shook his head in mild despair and said that he'd heard about government receptionists who just hung up if you didn't bid them a good morning. Having agreed that there was no telling with some people, we finished our drinks and headed back to his car. As I followed Crock out, I noticed for the first time that he was limping. I asked if he was okay. He pulled himself into his seat and burst into laughter.

'Man, I am in constant, unbearable agony, twenty-four hours a day, every day of the year.'

'Are you kidding?'

'Better believe it, I ain't. Wish I was.' We moved sedately back down to St George, where Crock had to busy himself waving and shouting out yet more hellos while he steered and changed gear. 'Yes sir, I am in pain. Whatchoo got in that bag, darlin'? I have this neural problem. All the nerves and muscles in my legs – yo, bro, what's happenin'? – are destroyed. Hi there, honey!'

Crock's tour had allowed me a sight, at long last, of an unprivileged bit of Bermuda but I couldn't accept that the absence of privilege began at one corner of Court Street and ended at the next. There had to be a catch to this country, and my money was on institutionalised racism. Crock disappointed me terribly by remaining faithful to the conventional belief in Bermuda that racial discrimination had simply stopped here in 1959, when blacks boycotted the segregated cinemas for four weeks and the cinema-managers capitulated. I'd read that those dramatic crimes in the 1970s had been an expression of Black Power militancy, but most locals seemed to share his view that the murders were murders, not assassinations, and that the subsequent riots were in protest against the hangings, not against any white Establishment.

Try as I did to find evidence to the contrary, Bermuda really did seem to be as colour-blind as locals claimed. It was more likely that a street-sweeper would be black than white, but not inevitable, and there were also many black people in positions of power, blacks appeared in adverts and even featured (a good sign, this, of a well-integrated society) in non-racist cartoons. Just in case anyone infers that this is a legacy of British fair play, I should add that in the two centuries of slavery on the islands blacks were often subjected to the customary intense brutality (it was not an offence for owners to kill slaves while punishing them), and that, for example, during the Second World War, the Colonial Office in London campaigned successfully to persuade America not to send black GIs here, in case their affluence and confidence gave 60 per cent of Bermudians ideas above their station.

Despite the best efforts of the Colonial Office, many Bermudian blacks had made quick and effective progress up the social stairwell – to the level where members of the large and influential black middle class realised that the stairwell led up to a reinforced-steel door, which was bolted and locked and which kept out almost every person in Bermuda, black or white. Beyond that door there swanned around the (all-white) elite who owned the real money and power in Bermuda, and who were descendants of those first aristocrats who sliced up Bermuda in the seventeenth century. Nicknamed the Forty Thieves, these fabulously wealthy descendants, I was told amid nudges and winks, were the real rulers of the country, pulling all the important political and economic strings. My first reaction was that this was a daft conspiracy theory, but then I wangled a visit to one of the houses of one of those families. After an afternoon spent admiring vast reaches of rolling parkland, touring the stunningly beautiful house (with its slave quarters), and learning about the land that the family owned – tranches of real estate, chunks of Front Street retail facility – I changed my mind.

Unlikely though this may seem, Crock is only the second friendliest person in Bermuda. The friendliest person in Bermuda is so friendly he makes Crock look like a grouch – so friendly that, when I first heard about him, I could only assume that the poor fellow was not the full shilling. Far from it, Crock assured me: 'Believe it, Johnnie Barnes has *all* his scruples.'

Johnnie Barnes is in fact a living landmark because every weekday morning for the past twenty years he has stood on the same roundabout at the edge of Hamilton to wave hello to the traffic.

'Yes sir,' Crock had said, 'Johnnie will be at his roundabout, rain shine or blow. Even Hurricane Emily couldn't stop Johnnie. One time he wasn't there, folks went crazy with worry. Switchboard at the radio station was jammed, it was on TV, reporters running round, kids crying. Turned out Johnnie was having a hernia operation at the hospital. Well, Johnnie got more visitors and cards and flowers than the Queen of England. They had to move him to a private room.'

So one day, just after breakfast, I got on the moped, lurched down the road towards Hamilton, turned left at the roundabout and barely avoided steering into the kerb because a slight old black man with a fluffy white beard and a straw hat was waving delightedly at me and exclaiming that he loved me.

A little shakily, I parked the moped and watched Johnnie Barnes standing on the roundabout – specifically, the special bit of pavement which the Bermudian government had recently constructed for him on the roundabout – where he was blowing kisses and waving and shouting words of joy. It was as if each scooter and car were being driven by a best pal who that morning had been released from decades of captivity. 'God bless you! I love you, Margaret! Nicholas, good morning to you! God *bless* you, Janet! I love you, sir, I *love* you!'

Taking advantage of a brief pause in the traffic, I ran over to the roundabout and asked Johnnie if we could have a chat.

'Sure thing. What's your name?'

'Harry.'

'God bless you, Harry. What's the time?'

'Half-nine.'

'Be okay with you if you came back at ten? That's when I knock off.'

Half an hour later, when Johnnie had finished at the roundabout for the day, he led me across the road and over to a seat by the water's edge. While he was carefully laying down his bag and umbrella, I asked him about his routine.

'I aim to be there by twenty to five each morning, Monday through Friday. The good Lord and I are there until ten.'

'I hope you don't mind my asking, but how old are you, Johnnie?'

'I am seventy-three years of age. Yes, the good Lord has allowed me to go the first mile, three score years and ten. I retired ten years ago.'

'But you've been doing this for twenty years?'

'That's right.'

'So how did you manage to do it while you had a job?'

'I used to wave hello to folks for an hour or so early in the morning 'fore I started work. I was a bus driver. 'Fore that I worked on the trains we used to have here.' He laughed. 'You know, when I first started greeting folks, I didn't tell my wife.'

'And why? I mean, why do you do what you do?'

Johnnie beamed at me. 'When you accept Jesus as your personal saviour from sin, you are duty-bound to bring joy. And let your light shine.'

He would have been better off explaining photosynthesis to a baby. I nodded solemnly and tried to think of a vaguely sensible question. 'But don't you ever get a hard time from people who don't understand this?'

'Oh yes. A few have come here and shouted at me, saying I'm a disgrace to my race and so on. But my aim is to love each and every individual, no matter who they are, no matter what their colour, no matter even if I don't like them. I might not like someone but it's my duty to love them. When we will to do God's will, God himself will will to do his will in us.'

We both nodded solemnly at all these wills. 'And now that you're retired, what do you do after you've finished at the roundabout?'

'I'll go home now and work in my gardens. One at my house and another one I rent. See these?' He hoiked out a bunch of green bananas from his bag. 'Home grown. And I don't use no chemicals. Only horse manure. Because bugs have to eat too. God placed them here long before he placed us here.' He beamed at me again. 'That's the truth, they gotta live too. You know something?'

'What's that?'

'We all die, because death is the wages of sin. And we can't take anything with us. So why fight? Why not try to be happy? There's so much in this world to make us happy. So much that's beautiful.'

'In this place, yes.'

'Everywhere. Life is beautiful everywhere.' He smiled and spread his hands wide, catching happiness. He stood up. 'Got to go to my garden.' He gathered his bag and umbrella in one hand and held out the other to clasp mine. 'Where you from, Harry?'

'Scotland.'

'I thought I heard an accent.' He was still holding my hand. 'Will you do something for me?'

'Of course.'

He gazed adoringly into my eyes. 'You tell the folks in Scotland I love them.'

'I'll do that.'

'And Harry?' He gripped my hand tight.
By this time, I was croaking back tears. 'What's that, Johnnie?'
'I love you.'
Oh Jesus God almighty, I was in a mess.

Just as a seven-and-a-half-feet-tall pygmy would be considered by the tribe to be a freak of nature, whereas a seven-and-a-half-feet-tall Dinka would be thought by his mates to be a bit tall, it is a tribute to the general and genuine friendliness of Bermudians that Johnnie Barnes can stand at his roundabout, a rational man, and confer his blessings on the traffic. Were he the product of any other Western society, Johnnie would be marked down, quite justifiably and at the very least, as soft in the head. But, because he was Bermudian, he was completely sane, just noticeably more pally than the norm.

Another sign of the Bermudians' benevolence was their hand-wringing over a miniature crime wave in the islands. On the Saturday, the *Royal Gazette* led with the news that two masked men, one armed with a machete, had stolen $2,000 from a supermarket. Below that was a report that twelve handbags had been snatched in the previous three days. Monday's issue carried the scandalised reaction of Public Safety Minister Quinton Edness, who called the bag-snatchers 'hyenas'. By Tuesday, Public Safety Minister Quinton Edness had so thoroughly stoked his ire that he was calling for bag-snatchers and muggers to be birched.

The proposal was popular with cabbies. Why? Because they were cabbies, I suppose, and, besides, several had recently been robbed at knifepoint. It had reached the stage, one taxi-driver confessed to me, where he was thinking about maybe giving prospective passengers a once-over before allowing them into his cab. (When I asked if he'd have accepted me as a fare had I hailed him from the street rather than from my hotel, he looked me up and down and smiled regretfully.) During a discussion of the topic with another taxi-driver, I felt a sharp pang of nostalgia as he lamented, 'What can you expect? This permissive society . . .'

As Crock had pointed out, it only took a couple of criminals to inflict a lot of damage on Bermuda's crime statistics and, far more importantly, on its reputation. And locals were extremely worried that tales of snatched handbags and machete-wielding robbers on the islands would cross the water and spread throughout the United States. I could see the locals' point. Over three-quarters of Bermuda's tourists come from a society whose citizens are so suspicious or afraid of other countries that only one in seven people possesses a passport – and that adventurous minority will cancel any non-domestic flight at the slightest hint that there might be the merest touch of bother abroad. (Given that it was safer to live in Belfast at the height of the Troubles than any major city in the United States, this behaviour pattern might strike you as strange as well as feeble.)

Bermuda was beginning to suffer other ailments. One was the main cause of the growing crime-rate – drugs. Imported by a few crew members of cruise ships. Bought on Court Street. Consumed at some expense, one spliff costing an exorbitant $25.

A second affliction was unemployment. Just how many islanders didn't have jobs was hard to say, because Bermuda doesn't have the dole as Britons know it but a kind of state aid to the needy and deserving, and the traditional and expected way of coping without a job has been to pick up bits and bobs of casual labour, catch a few fish, hang on in there. According to union officials, 9 per cent of the population were without work, but the government pooh-poohed this, stating that the number of people actually registered unemployed was 686 – 2.45 per cent of the labour force. Even that figure was enough to worry islanders.

Most worrying of all was the decline of the tourist industry. Locals suspected that the government was massaging the figures to make the truth less painful, but all I can say is that I found the Department of Tourism so open and helpful that, after I visited its offices to ask for a few facts, I had to lug around a carrier bag bulging with surveys, year-on-year tables and pie-charts. I happily pass on the information that 13 per cent of Americans called the toll-free number when planning their vacation here. Having stared at the splurge of data for hours, with a level of baffled impatience I last experienced while attempting to build an Airfix bomber, I can assert with some confidence that Bermuda's tourist trade is not what it was.

More than half a million people visit the islands each year but the number of people actually staying in Bermuda has fallen, with the shortfall taken up by an increase in cruise passengers. The problem with cruise passengers, almost all of them American, is that they aren't very rich but merely middle class. And cruises tend to be all-inclusive, so the passengers tend to spend only a little time on dry land before heading back to the ship's cabarets, bars and – most importantly of all, as the high obesity rate indicates – restaurants.

To tell the truth, I was feeling a bit guilty about being appalled by the bulk of the Americans who waddled off their ship and into St George. The guilt started after I read an American problem page, syndicated in the *Royal Gazette*, which was devoted to outraged defences from very fat people who claimed they were victims of prejudice/glands/some chemical thing. But then I learned about the cruise-ships' meals – of which there are six a day. At this point, you exclaim, 'Six meals a day! Don't be silly.' And I reply, 'Full English breakfast, morning coffee with cakes and pastries, three-course lunch, afternoon tea with cakes, pastries and ice-cream, seven-course dinner, and supper. Plus a midnight buffet lest anyone feel peckish.' Which queasy revelation goes some way to explaining why cruise passengers comprise a third of Bermuda's visitors but contribute less than a tenth of the annual tourist spend.

The trouble is that Bermuda has, until recently, relied on attracting only visitors who threw money around the place. The trend started in 1883 when Queen Victoria's daughter Princess Louise wintered here, encouraging the American upper class to follow in her regal wake. Bermuda began to trade on its reputation as British and posh by selling posh British goods to wealthy Americans. 'Back in the fifties, Bermuda was the showcase of the empire,' one local boasted to me. 'Trimingham's had the reputation as the finest haberdashery in the Western world. And now look at it. A shitpile.' (Trimingham's actually struck me as all right, if you like diamond-patterned jerseys and pastel polo shirts, but I'm not a haberdashery aficionado.)

The man who was outraged by Trimingham's seemed to think that the islands had lost their rich fan base, but you still have to be well off to take a holiday here. Wages are high and everything bar the sunshine is imported, so this is no place for bargain-hunters. And even if some company were stupid enough to set up cheap-and-cheerful hotels for package-holidaymakers, the hotels would remain empty because the government permits only scheduled flights to land here. When I asked the nice lady from the Department of Tourism about this, she was horrified by my misinformation; didn't I know that a chartered flight had flown here from Gatwick not two years before? Yes, a group of people who wanted to celebrate New Year in London, then hop on Concorde, beat the clock and celebrate New Year all over again here. (Ibiza this isn't.)

Unused to self-doubt, Bermudians were beginning to fret over a variety of social problems. What about Aids? (The country's 100th Aids victim was buried as long ago as 1989.) And the homeless? (There used to be two people living rough on the islands; now there were over a hundred.) Wasn't the education system in a bit of a mess? Children followed British or American syllabuses in schools that were state-funded or private, religious or secular, good or bad. Why did the state school that was currently being built have provision in its plans for a metal detector at the entrance? Why had none of the last three Ministers of Education lasted the pace? Ah, because no politician in the country was any good. And what about the political scene? As is not the case with other colonies, Britain's role (technically that of ensuring internal and external security) was non-existent and the current Governor, David Waddington, was a nonentity; his wife was well liked as an enthusiastic fête-opener and charity fund-raiser, but Waddington himself was thought to be a shadow of his former self, a husk, a shell, a man broken by his long years of servitude to Thatcher. (I can't verify this for myself because, when I asked to meet him, I was snippily informed that that was quite out of the question – which makes me even more inclined to believe local hearsay.) Bermudians were even more scornful of domestic politics; the United Bermuda Party had been in power since 1968, so it was said to be stagnating, while the Progressive Labour Party were said to be untrained for office. And how could you cope with a right-wing party (the UBP) that was more liberal than the left-wing but religiously fundamentalist and therefore reactionary PLP? *O tempora, o mores*, oh dearie me.

Actually, I found it easy to share Bermudians' worries. With a good deal of luck and hard work, they had produced a society that was admirable and prosperous and it was depressing to come across any malaise that threatened to drag Bermuda downwards and make it just like anywhere else in the West, with most people achieving a comfiness and some joining a hopeless underclass whom the comfy people look down on in fear. Even so, most social ills here are, by the standards of normal countries, minor. Yes, the education system is a hotch-potch but the literacy rate is 98 per cent, the highest of any capitalist country. There are crack addicts, muggers and prostitutes, but most of them can be found on one block of one street. The departure of the American military had been a bit of an economic blow, but Bermuda was going to win that bout, since it had repossessed 10 per cent of its land surface, which was going to be the site of a business park maybe, or a leisure complex . . . something big and profitable.

Because they are minor, Bermuda could solve its social problems fairly quickly. Or so I reckoned. Throw money and expertise at the new state school and the Block, legalise and control drugs, and – tah-rah! – no more tiny underclass, no more small crime-wave, and everyone could go back to fretting about the quality of Triming-ham's haberdashery. But that won't happen. Not unless Bermudians have the audacity to hire me as a policy guru. And not with a government that is underfunded (there's no income tax here), conservative and challenged by a supposedly left-wing opposition party whose reactionary instincts can be inferred from the fact that most of its members think that God created the world in 4004 BC, on 26 October, at nine o'clock in the morning.

So here's what will happen to Bermuda in the foreseeable future: the state school will be studiously avoided by the country's middle-class majority, the Block will acquire more crack victims (not many, but enough), and the *Royal Gazette* will run lots of stories about tourists being mugged, tourists complaining about being pestered by the occasional beggar, tourists avowing that next year they'll be spending their cash in the Bahamas instead. And the Department of Tourism's pie-charts will get that little bit smaller.

But economically that won't matter a jot. Bermuda has been good at making money ever since its first colonists stopped drinking and started working. And, these days, it can cope with a bit of a decline in tourism because tourism is no longer the only or even the most important industry in the islands. That honour now goes to high finance. Over half of Bermuda's GDP of $2 billion – the fifth highest per capita in the world with a (no pun intended) mean wage of with the same population as Keighley possesses the world's second-largest reinsurance market, larger than Lloyd's of London and bested only by New York. As for the captive-insurance market (captives being companies that are established to underwrite parent companies), well, you could say that Bermuda is the world's biggest, with 1,400 captive management companies and, in second place, the Cayman Islands, which has 60.

The big-business boom explains why Bermuda doesn't want independence. By remaining a colony – albeit a colony that could just about buy up its owner – Bermuda can boast about its olde-worlde reliability and its sophisticated legal system, based on English common law and with recourse to English courts. So appealing are these features, I was confidently informed, that on the day of the independence referendum the airport runway was chock-a-block with private jets ready to whisk company execs and their files out of the danger zone.

I was rather thrilled by this image of corporate melodrama, but when I asked local businesspeople about the jets they tended to be less excited. In fact, they tended to burst into laughter. One of the sceptics was Wendy Davis Johnson, who works for the Bermuda International Business Association and who was kind enough to point out, slowly and gently, that every politician on the islands had been at pains to proclaim guarantees during the independence debate that, no matter what the outcome, business would be as usual. She then went on to list the advantages Bermuda has apart from having the Queen on its dollars and the Privy Council as a legal safety net: (1) no tax on income, capital gains or profit, (2) state-of-the-art communications with fibre-optic technology, (3) political stability, (4) a dedicated workforce which includes (5) the highest proportion of people educated to tertiary level of any country in the world, and (6) an unrivalled reputation as an offshore centre that has always been well regulated and untarnished. It also has the attractions for visiting business types of (7) a fabulous climate, (8) beautiful scenery and, clinching the whole deal, (9) the greatest concentration of golf courses of any country in the world.

I conceded the argument.

It was time, finally, to give up. I'd tried to find one but Bermuda really didn't have a hidden, hideous flaw. It did have those bloody tree-frogs at night, it did have the Block, and I wouldn't recommend the country to mountaineers or disco-groovers, but there really were no snakes on the lawn and the smiles really didn't conceal sneers. Since she was every bit as friendly as every other Bermudian, I binned my (very short) list of financial questions and asked Wendy how she rated the quality of her life here. Tilting her head to see if she could come up with a con to set alongside the pros, she admitted that she was occasionally irked by the humidity, but then she too gave in.

'No, it's an absolutely charming, *charming* place. I was thinking about this when I came into the office this morning. I started early today, at seven, because I wanted to get on the phone to London – that's another thing, we're in a great time zone, I can call London while I wait for New York to open up an hour behind us, and at the end of the day, I can fax Hongkong and have their fax waiting for me the next day . . . Anyway, there I was on my scooter, coming into Hamilton after dawn with the lights still on all over the cruise-ships in the harbour, and the freshness of the morning around me, the smell of the hibiscus in the hedgerows, and I said to myself, "This is heavenly." Then I reached the roundabout and, to cap it all, there was Johnnie telling me that he loved me.'

I checked but Wendy said she didn't need another secretary, so I traipsed off to the park by the waterfront where I'd overheard the seminar on Isaiah 65 and where I now sorted out my notes and surveyed for the last time the shimmering water and the boats bobbing in the harbour. The *Coralita* looked nice, as did the *Elizabeth*, but I much preferred a trim little yacht whose name was elaborately flourished across a freshly painted hull. My heart, it soared like an eagle, for I could now say, in all honesty, that I had seen *Anarchy* in Bermuda.

Irony's heavy hand was to give me another swipe that evening back at my hotel, where I dined under the stars. Refreshed by a pre-dinner sampling of Bermuda's speciality cocktail, a black-rum and ginger-beer combo called a dark 'n' stormy (actually, it was three dark 'n' stormies, but they tasted as strong as Lucozade), I joshed merrily with the waiter and, toying with my *amuse-gueule*, tiddlywinked it neatly into my vast glass of perfectly chilled Chablis. It didn't seem to affect the Chablis too much, so I swigged it back, ordered another half-pint of the stuff and settled back to enjoy the surrounding susurration of opulence. The soft chink of cutlery on china, the tinkle of laughter, the soothing serenade of the resident calypso crooner, the honed mahogany back of a haughty German temptress, the chilled perfection of another glass of Chablis to accompany my grilled fish – ah yes.

It was after I had managed, with very little difficulty, to order a port to accompany my cheese, that I got a bit sad. Waste being here on my own . . . hammered – four–one at home to Aberdeen . . . how come all these people had so much money . . . in couples and with lots of money . . .

The calypso crooner strummed his guitar and launched discreetly into another number. Since that evening I have tried to think of a song that I would have found even more heart-rending and inappropriate in that state and in that setting, but 'Love Is in the Air', 'White Riot', 'You Cannae Shove Your Granny off the Bus', none of them competes with 'The Banana Boat Song'.

Somehow still doing so with joined-up letters, I etched my name on the doubtless astonishing bill and weaved off to order a taxi. High time to get out of here, have a last look at Hamilton, maybe a nightcap in Flanagan's.

The cruise-ships had left and Front Street was empty. So was Flanagan's. I think I had a chat with Darren, the barman from Manchester, and I do suspect that more strong drink may have been taken as well. After an unspecifiable time, calling on the wisdom of my years, I decided to leave and find a taxi that would take me back to the hotel. This proved to be more difficult than I had found in the past, as several taxis with for-hire lights ablaze inexplicably ignored me.

'You had a good evening?'

A youth had joined me at the street corner. Small, white, eighteen maybe, baseball cap, mildly soiled T-shirt.

'Good splendid.'

'Could you spare a dollar so that I can buy some fries?'

'Fries dollar sure.'

'Thanks. I'm Andrew.'

'Pleased to meet your acquaintance. Crack?'

'Ain't got none, man.'

' 'Snot what I meant. Meant if you were on crack not to spend. The dollar on it.'

'Man, you seen brain scans of crack addicts? I'd never take that shit. You enjoying your time here?'

'Last night shame great.'

'Well, I hope you had a good time.'

'Andrew fine person take care.'

'And you, man.'

He shook my hand and walked off. Now where else would a beggar be so sweet? And genned up on junkies' brain scans? He really was going to spend the dollar on fries. Dollars . . . did I have enough dollars left for a taxi? My hand went inside my jacket. The pocket was empty. My wallet had gone.

Suddenly sobered by a wild adrenalin rush, I took a couple of very deep breaths, reflected that I was a special kind of klutz, and scanned the street. No sign of the little bastard. I took a chance and sprinted up Parliament Street. Yes! There he was walking quickly round the corner. I ran after him as quietly as I could, resolving to control my fury and do what I had to do coolly and calmly. Soon he was only ten yards in front. He spun round just as I reached him.

'Piece of fucking shit, give me my fucking wallet back or I'll fucking—'

'No, man, no! Get off me! I didn't do nothing!'

Grateful that he was small, I pinned him against the window of Marks and Spencer and repeated my request.

'Honest, man, I ain't got your wallet.' His eyes were wide and his mouth was quivering. 'Please, man.'

'Fucking little—' I had a terrible thought. Still holding him against the window, I sneaked a look down at my side pocket. A leather rectangle was sticking out of it.

Oh.

'Andrew, I am really, really, really sorry.'

'I ain't no pickpocket, man. I wouldn't pinch your wallet.'

'I know and I'm really, really sorry. God, are you all right?'

'I'm fine, man. How you feeling?'

'Very bad.'

'You'll be fine in a minute. Take it easy, you'll come down soon.'
'Okay.'
'How you feel now?'
'Bad.'
'Know what'll make you feel better?'
'What?'
'You give me another couple dollars.'
'You are absolutely right. Here. Take this.'
'Generous of you, man. Hey!' He flagged down a taxi for me and ushered me inside. 'Safe journey.'
'Thanks, Andrew.'
'Good to meet you.'

Well aware of the dire symmetry in all of this, I prepared to leave the following day while nursing a hangover. Fortunately, it wasn't a Samuel Beckett. Tedious, dim, with an undercurrent of gross lust, this was only a Terry-Thomas.

It was windy, so I had to have breakfast indoors. I didn't complain. This wasn't the first time I'd had to hew at the coal-face of research and it wouldn't be the last, so I made light of the appalling inconvenience and tried to keep down some coffee and grapefruit juice while flattering the haughty German temptress with an adenoidal leer.

Stupid with the Terry-Thomas, I required an hour of pottering back in my room for it to sink in that the wind really was strong. And that this strong wind might not be unconnected to yesterday's television reports about Hurricane Hortense, which had just left twelve dead in Puerto Rico and was moving up the Atlantic to make, it was feared, landfall in New England. I dug out a map and traced a path from Puerto Rico to Boston. Uh-oh.

Having temporarily mislaid my knowledge of the existence of telephones, I walked to reception to see if anyone had heard a local forecast.

'Good morning, Mr Ritchie. How's the hangover?' The chap at reception looked unfeasibly healthy.

'Good morning. Not great. Here, how do you know I've got a hangover?'

'You predicted you'd have one.'

'Did I?'

'When we had a drink at the bar after you got in last night.'

'Oh. Yes. Of course.'

'You're all set then? You're a brave man, I'll give you that.'

'How do you mean?'

'You're flying out' – he started to tick off his fingers – 'in a hurricane. On the thirteenth day of the month. A Friday. Through the Bermuda Triangle. Well, I'd best leave you to get ready. Spill some salt, crack a mirror, walk under a few ladders.'

'Wait. What about this hurricane?'

'According to the forecast, the eye should stay at least two hundred miles away, but you never know. Most likely we'll just get a few flicks from its tail.'

Before I could ask what a hurricane's tail-flicks might be like, there was a shout for help from the direction of the bar. We both hurried over and saw the barman scampering about outside, pulling down the umbrellas of the poolside tables. Seeing us, he pointed first to a stack of chairs and then out to sea. As the healthy chap from reception ran across to carry the stack of chairs indoors, I stared open-mouthed at what was happening to the sea. Darkness was advancing over it and heading straight for us. I picked up a couple of loose chairs and ran inside, where the barman and the healthy receptionist were frantically shutting all the windows and doors they could find. I looked out. The darkness was about to reach the shore.

'Here she comes!' yelled the barman. The shore disappeared in the darkness. The palm trees below us were suddenly bent by an awesome weight. And boomf! The darkness hit us.

From the precarious safety of a sturdy, thick-walled, stone-built hotel, I looked out at the storm's shocking blasts of horizontal rain. Then, after ten minutes of natural mayhem, the sky suddenly cleared and the wind vanished. The palm trees dusted themselves down and stood up straight again.

'That was incredible,' I remarked. 'You pair might be used to this, but I've never been in a hurricane before.'

The barman exchanged a quick frown with the healthy receptionist and shook his head. 'That was a hurricane, you'd know 'bout it. What we just had was a squall.'

'Not a hurricane?'

'Nothing like a hurricane.'

'So how much stronger than that is a hurricane?'

The barman pursed his lips to make his rough calculation. ' 'Bout four times. Minimum.'

I spent most of the five hours I had left in Bermuda, or, let's be realistic, my life, at the bar, nodding glumly while listening to fiercer and fiercer gusts of wind and a succession of locals discussing their favourite hurricane stories.

'Yeah, that was a bad one, but I still say Emily was the worst.'

'Emily, yeah, she was small but she was a fighter.'

'Did for Club Med, that's for sure.'

'Moved the top storey nine inches out of kilter.'

'Never reopened.'

'She was s'posed to miss us but she took a sharp turn and headed straight for us.'

'Those ladies are fickle.'

'But I guess we're due another one. Last was Emily back in '87.'

At this point, I looked up from my dark 'n' stormy – it seemed the obvious drink to choose and it was bloody strong – and made my sole contribution to the discussion. The locals laughed.

' 'Course you had a breeze going in Britain in '87. That was Emily.'

'But Emily after she had made it three thousand, five hundred miles 'cross the Atlantic. Poor old girl was on her last legs by the time she got to you.'

'You should have seen her when she was in her prime. I tell you, Emily mowed my lawn.'

'Lifted buses up and off the road.'

'Yes sir, she was so strong she lifted the top of my grass clean off.'

'See that beach down there? When Emily hit us, that beach disappeared. Ran off and came back with the tide after Emily said goodbye.'

'Wall of my house was green. And that grass could not be scraped off. No sir. Took a rainstorm to clean that wall.'

'Emily, she was compact and she packed a punch.'

Nobody with my portfolio of phobias has any right to be super-stitious, so I wasn't bothered by this being Friday the 13th. Nor by the Bermuda Triangle, whose paranormal ability to vacuum up boats and planes has been variously ascribed to extraterrestrial kidnappings, the triangle being the entrance to hell (the area was officially exorcised in 1978), the presence in the region of a temporal warp or anti-matter, and the lingering damage wreaked by the sunken generators of Atlantis. Sadly, the mysterious power of the Bermuda Triangle dates back not to the dawn of time but to February 1964, when it was invented by a writer called Vincent Gaddis in an article for *Argosy* magazine.

But who needs ghosts when you've got a serial killer skulking in the garden? Biffed by the wind, I staggered out to the taxi and clambered in just before the wind walloped the door shut. Progress to the airport was, perforce, slow, so the cabby had plenty of time to tell me his own hurricane anecdotes. Meanwhile, the wind seemed to be gaining even more strength. As we drew up outside the terminal, I watched a bulky businessman, who was carrying two large suitcases, head for the entrance and miss because a blast frogmarched him ten yards down the pavement. It was obviously high time I called a hotel, for there was no way any plane was going to take off in this.

I told the taxi-driver so. 'There is no way any plane is going to take off in this,' I said.

'What you flying?' asked the cabby. 'American Airlines or British Airways?'

'BA.'

'Then you'll take off. American Airlines'll most likely turn tail and head back to the States, but those BA guys, they can fly through anything. Have a good trip now.'

With no sense of triumph, I realised that I had finally found one devastating flaw in Bermudian society. There is simply no law against BA pilots showing off in a gale.

Chapter Two

Flying to Mars: Ascension Island

There were just three of us on the night coach from Swindon – the driver, the man whose job it was to chat to the driver, and me. As we lurched through the Cotswolds, the driver and his assistant exchanged their views about the state of the road – not a topic, curiously enough, that they had exhausted in the fourteen years they had been employed to take this route six times daily – and I distracted myself by savouring the local signposts.

Broad Blunsden. Broughton Poggs. Filkins . . . Like most English villages south of, well, to my ears, south of the Tweed, the placenames smacked of places whose pub-cum-post office is home to wall-eyed folk who will nudge you in the chest with their shotguns as they slowly confide their great news: 'Oim gawn marry moi thithter.' It was before we could reach somewhere allegedly called Charterville Allotments that the coach turned off the A40 to weave down a little road slap bang in the middle of sister-marrying country, though I had yet to see any signpost to our destination, the RAF base at Brize Norton.

As would anyone who has seen *Deliverance*, I was beginning to get just a little edgy when I finally spotted a road sign so small it managed to announce only 'Brize Ntn'. The coach did some more weaving until I caught sight of another sign behind a hedge: 'Br n'. And this in a part of the world where the track to each and every hamlet was indicated with the typesize of those blue motorway signs to 'The North'.

Now I knew why I had failed to find any reference to Brize

Norton in my gazetteer and two atlases, and only the tiniest mention on my road map. I was about to travel 8,000 miles on an RAF plane which would take off from what was obviously not an airport at all but a field equipped with a lean-to shed and a tattered windsock.

The coach lumbered past a few more cottages, negotiated a few more tight bends and suddenly arrived at one of the ugliest towns I have ever seen. If anyone you know ever feels tempted by an initiative-challenging, ski-improving career in the services, tell him or her to head off the A40 and visit Carterton, the military's very own town in the Cotswolds. After passing through estates whose inhabitants still ate dried egg and voted for Clement Attlee, the coach finally reached the airport.

Which is what Brize Norton is – very much so. Tucked away in the heart of Oxfordshire, hardly signposted, an establishment so deftly concealed that you might just glimpse the odd tail fin as you drive along the A40, is the military equivalent of Gatwick. It reminded me of the lion in the Tom and Jerry cartoon, who flees from the circus and successfully hides underneath a lampshade.

The coach was greeted at the airport entrance by three adolescent soldiers carrying very big guns and by a variety of warning signs. Most of the latter were written in Servicespeak ('No Parking Near Airport BLG UTFN') but no translation was required for my favourite – a 'Highly Flammable' announcement beside a group of nursery trees. We pulled up outside the airport blg, which closely resembled a bad community centre and was teeming with battalions? squadrons? of crop-haired youths sitting on kitbags.

Resisting a sudden urge to mince, I made my way to the colonel-major or whatever he was at the check-in desk. Thence to a waiting room which might have been considered quite swish in Minsk. It was large and it was jam-packed, but I saw only two women and one non-white man. Mind you, it was difficult to see much through the fog created by squaddies topping up their nicotine levels before the cigaretteless flights, to Hanover, Cyprus and, finally, my destination, Ascension/Mount Pleasant.

It was ten in the evening by the time we were called through, in alphabetical order, to the departures lounge, a mere 105 minutes before the plane was due to take off. The closely typed, three-page instruction leaflet provided by the RAF had been very strict about the check-in time, as well as about every other conceivably relevant issue, and now, as the tannoy shouted out the information that our seat numbers would be on our boarding passes, I understood why. We were infants. I settled down beside a group of soldiers who were watching a *Blackadder* video at the back of the class, but the dragon in charge soon put a stop to that. She marched over, switched off the TV, glared at us and marched back to the microphone on her desk to announce that *someone* had left a blue, V-necked jersey at the security check. A crop-haired youth rose shame-faced to be escorted off in silence.

Since the alternative was to examine my shoes for the next 103 minutes, I rummaged in my bag for my paperback of *Middlemarch*. It was a cunning choice for the trip, I reckoned, since it stretched to 908 pages, if you counted the notes about the Reform Bill and so on, and weighed only fifteen ounces. Dorothea had just offered to help Casaubon by reading to him in Latin and Greek when the flight was called, an announcement which was swiftly followed by a reminder that we should take our handbaggage with us and once on the plane occupy the seat designated on the boarding card.

I had been half expecting to spend a huge portion of the next eighteen hours sitting on a parachute with my back to the fuselage, so picture my delight at discovering that the plane was a normal plane, with seats and everything. Or just about normal . . . The RAF does its best to imitate a civilian flight, but a couple of things do give the game away. One was that the pilot welcomed us aboard the Tristar on behalf of 216 Squadron and that he did this with the piping tone of a head boy congratulating our 1st XV on the victory over Harrow. Another was that the in-flight magazine carried lots of ads for lesser boarding schools, the British Legion and a DIY appliance called, in all seriousness, the Leatherman Super Tool – a single entendre bested to my knowledge only by the title of the *Sunday Post*'s twee column about plucky pensioners and puppies with a limp, 'Seven Days Hard' by Francis Gay. But that was not an observation I would be sharing with the cabin crew, who wouldn't stand a chance at auditions for a Singapore Airlines commercial but who looked as if they could prove very useful in the scrum.

The flight attendant who served me with a drink soon after take-off did so with a forearm the colour and girth of a chimney pot. A

short while later, the same prop forward passed over my meal –
supplied courtesy of the NAAFI, so it arrived not on a pre-packed
tray but in a cardboard box, which contained a plum, a pastry, a
cheese roll and a packet of beef-flavoured Hula-Hoops.

I checked my watch. Half-past midnight. For something to do, I
spent some time working out that we had 96 and a bit per cent of the
flight to go. I think. Envious of the squaddie who had fallen fast
asleep next to me, I hauled out *Middlemarch* again and settled down
to finding out why Mr Casaubon was not fond of piano recitals.

Six hours later, we were given a cup of orange squash and then
breakfast, which was a bit of a disappointment because it didn't
include a Wagon Wheel. By this time, Rosamond had fallen in love
with Lydgate, Fred Vincy had lost the money he'd borrowed from
Caleb Garth, Dorothea and Casaubon had returned from their
honeymoon, and I had become increasingly bothered by the way
I had once defaced this paperback. 'Harry Ritchie, 7th Jan. 1974',
announced the Biro scrawl which managed to occupy a quarter of
the title page. Therefore, I had, as I thought, first read *Middlemarch*
in the days when I was so obsessed by Carol Stevenson that I
sacrificed two periods of football a week to sit in on her Maths class.
But, although I tried to convince myself otherwise, all the underlinings and marginalia dated from a good five years later when I was
obsessed by Sandra Wilson, and not reading but doing *Middlemarch*,
that is, studying it for an English Literature degree.

God alone knows what I wrote about the book in my exams, but
my comments to myself were not encouraging. 'V imp!!' and 'NB!!!!'
I had scribbled in the margin beside paragraphs adorned with double
underlinings. And those paragraphs would describe such matters as
Fred Vincy still being in debt. Even worse were the marginal graffiti
that required no guesswork. A comparison of Mr Casaubon to 'any
ruminant animal' had inspired the remark, 'NB! Implicitly debasing'
– thus proving that the person who wrote that was, implicitly, a
twerp. Equally damning evidence was provided by the comments
that accompanied my image-spotting: 'thread and web ref.', 'VVV
IMP – WEB IMAGE AGAIN!!'

I was busy reflecting on the benefits that would accrue to our
literary culture from the closure of every English department in every
university in the country, the pulping of every book of academic

literary criticism, the scrapping of every supposedly learned Eng. Lit. journal, when the chap next to me, having polished off his orange squash and Penguin biscuit, abruptly launched into a eulogy of Ascension Island.

'Fucking magic place. Best fucking posting I've had. Apart from Cyprus, of course.'

'So how long were you on Ascension for?'

'Six months. Lovely fucking jubbly. Fucking great climate, fucking great beaches, a good little fucking Yank base with a fucking burger bar, nightclub, the fucking lot. And it was fucking cushy. All we had to do was refuel a few fucking Tristars a week.'

'When was this?'

'Fucking . . . eight years ago.'

At that time Ascension had had six years to recover from being, for a short while, the busiest airport in the world, before the Task Force headed south to battle in the Falklands. Although Ascension Island is British property, the airstrip at Wideawake airfield, where we would soon be landing, was then operated, under the Lend–Lease agreement, by the United States, so Britain had to request permission to use it. And the island is still used by the American military or, more specifically, by American spies toiling away, under the aegis of the National Security Agency, at electronic surveillance of such a top-secret nature that even the Americans refuse to admit that the spies and surveillance exist. Anyway, the whole arrangement just goes to show, does it not, that the UK and the US still enjoy a special relationship – in the same way that an eighty-five-year-old widow in a decaying high-rise enjoys a special relationship with the sixteen-stone skinhead who visits her to help spend her pension and tidy up her flat by carrying off her TV.

But just to show that Britain really is a globally important power and not at all an insignificant country on the edge of Europe with a fast-declining economy that's now rated below Taiwan, with lethal livestock and with international teams whose purpose is to boost morale in the unlikeliest nations by losing heavily to their makeshift sides at sports we invented, we have our own spies on Ascension as well. So there. Now, if the Americans are cagey about their espionage activities on the island, it goes without saying that the British government has to have the electrodes placed on its testicles before confessing that Ascension itself exists. As a result, there are the customary rumours that the British spies here are engaged in employment so hi-tech and ultra-ultra-secret that they have evolved into Morlocks who live and work in a massive underground facility, where they break all known codes and zoom in on satellite-transmitted images of Saddam Hussein's cornflakes. By mundane contrast, officials do acknowledge the presence here of British personnel employed by the Composite Signals Organisation to monitor satellites and stuff, and of British personnel employed by the BBC to run its Atlantic Relay Station, which transmits the World Service to Africa and South America. All I can say is that, judging by the local flora I could now glimpse coming into view down below – abnormally tall aerials and those vast golf balls the military go in for – Ascension may well be home to some heavy, scary shit.

The competition is extremely strong, but politically, militarily and in every other way the place where we were about to touch down, just south of the equator and in the middle of the Atlantic, is my contender for the title of Strangest Last Pink Bit. I suppose Ascension Island isn't even a colony but a dependency of a dependency, since it comes under the governorship of St Helena, 700 miles to the south. Because it is very small indeed (thirty-five square miles), has no indigenous or permanent population and remains significant only for unknowable espionage activity, Ascension's entry in the *Dictionary of the British Empire and Common-wealth* is padded out to twelve lines – one less than that for Catchpole, Margaret, the well-known, nineteenth-century Australian letter-writer.

Those thirty-five square miles, the tip of a massive sub-aqueous volcano, rose to the surface only two million years ago. It was discovered shortly afterwards, in 1501, by a Portuguese person, possibly moonlighting from his hairdressing business, called Alphonse d'Albuquerque. Fortunately, he decided not to name the island after himself and noticed that he had bumped into it on Ascension Day. For the next 314 years, this barren spot of volcanic debris was used by sailors only as a place to leave letters which would be picked up by homeward-bound ships. Then Britain decided to dump Napoleon on St Helena and this mid-Atlantic mailbox, along with Tristan da Cunha, far, far to the south, was taken over by the

Admiralty lest the French miraculously summon up the resolve and courage to mount a bid to rescue the little fellow. For the next hundred years or so, the Admiralty pretended the island was a boat, calling it HMS Ascension, until 1922, when it came under the jurisdiction of the old Colonial Office. By then, Ascension, for all its tininess, had established itself as one of the British Empire's most important cable stations.

Apart from the news that sea-turtles come here to lay their eggs, that just about covers all the information I could glean about Ascension from the *Dictionary of the British Empire and Commonwealth* and assorted history books. Another useful source was a wildlife documentary about the island, which I braced myself to watch with the aid of a stiff whisky and a cushion to hide behind. Both came in useful because, like all wildlife documentaries, it featured a marvellous variety of things bright and beautiful, creatures great and small, whose task it was to find a mate, breed and nurture their beautiful, fluffy young, and to avoid the attentions of greater or less small creatures who wished to turn them into raw, living, one-gulp snacks. (It always strikes me as very clever of Tennyson to have composed his line about nature being red in tooth and claw without the benefit of BBC-2.) Toe-curling, cushion-gripping footage included, for the sake of mere example, a sequence showing a baby sooty tern being snatched from its house and mum by a frigate bird, who flew off with the baby in its beak, tried three times to swallow it, brought it up three times, and then discarded it, whereupon it was caught in mid-air by another frigate bird who had no problem in popping it down its gullet. How great is God Almighty, who has made all things well.

According to the documentary, many of the glowing colours and tiny wings on Ascension Island arrived courtesy of human beings: waxbills and mynahs imported to brighten the place up; house mice that stowed away and emigrated here; a few donkeys and sheep that were shipped over by the first garrison and then allowed to run wild; cats which promptly went feral and destroyed a colony of two million birds that used to nest on the island, and just about every form of Ascension's present plant life. The plants took to the place (but only high above sea level) with such enthusiasm that one of the landmarks was soon christened Green Mountain. Up there can be found the island's nineteenth-century farm, a forest of bamboo (transported from Kew Gardens to increase the humidity and rainfall), and a pond constructed by members of the Navy at a time when it still ruled the seas, and which they populated with lilies and goldfish.

Or so I gather. My own experience of Ascension, like that of every other passenger on the Tristar, was to be, and I think I should be candid about this, limited. I do certainly have experience of landing at Wideawake airfield, which turned out to be a runway surrounded by steep volcanic hills the colour of rust or chocolate. A harsh description of the view outside my porthole might be that it consisted of nature's slagheaps. A less harsh, and oddly more convincing, interpretation is that this was what it could be like arriving at a holiday destination far into the future; although NASA astronauts practised their moon landings here (since Ascension possesses the nearest this planet can offer to a lunar surface), the landscape I was peering at in astonishment reminded me of some other extraterrestrial adventure. Yes. That was it. *Total Recall.* I was gazing at the countryside of Mars.

We disembarked into a warm, sticky, equatorial morning and were greeted by a handful of bronzed soldierly types in khaki shirts and shorts, as well as a firecrew kitted out, appropriately, in futuristic space suits, possibly made of kitchenfoil. Hastily tugging off jackets and jumpers, we stumbled through the military gauntlet to the airport. Well, I say airport . . . We were herded into a pen furnished with picnic tables whose creosoted slats (inadvertently, I suspect) exactly matched the colour of the nearby Martian hills. Beyond the pen was an upmarket shack with a corrugated-iron roof and a little sign sporting a six-year-old's painting of a rock in the sea and the slogan, 'Welcome to RAF Ascension'.

I wandered inside to the shunkie, where lots of squaddies had stripped off their shirts, the better to throw water over themselves and to contribute to the dramatic sour stench of stale male sweat. I escaped to the queue at the little kiosk which was stocked with a few postcards, some sweets, a cursory selection of the kind of porn wherein wives and mothers are captured in close-up tugging apart their labia, and a cabinet of chilled drinks. Having bought only an early-morning can of Sprite, I forsook the chance to watch yet another episode of *Blackadder* on the video, and made my way over to a small information display.

This informed me that Ascension is visited every summer by giant green turtles who swim over from South America to lay their eggs under the sand, that Boatswain Bird Island to the east was a nature reserve favoured by lots of birds, that three miles to the north lay the capital, Georgetown, where there were a few shops and bars, that safe bathing could be had at English Beach, that basic emergency accommodation was provided at the foot of Green Mountain at a place called Travellers Hill, a.k.a. Bunk Bed City, and that the American base had a burger bar and nightclub.

I just had time to scribble that lot down in my notebook and swig the dregs of my can before joining the rest of the flock as we were shepherded back to the Tristar through the same gauntlet of khaki soldiers and kitchenfoiled firecrew. For all I or anyone else below the rank of Home Secretary know, Ascension Island could be the headquarters of Thunderbirds, but my own experience of this imperial outpost, a dependency of a dependency, top-secret communications base, summer destination of giant green turtles, permanent home of sooty terns, feral cats and wild sheep, is that the airport has a few picnic tables and a shack where you can buy lemonade and Rustlers. And that it looks like Mars.

Chapter Three

That Little Ice-Cold Bunch of Land Down There: The Falkland Islands

MECHANICS' INSTITUTE LIBRARY
57 Post Street
San Francisco, CA 94104
(415) 393-0101

Ascension Island was two hours to the north, I'd finished my latest cup of squash and bag of crisps, and Lydgate had been unable to resist the temptation of kissing away Rosamond's tears, when, shifting from one ossified buttock to the other, with another eight hours or more of this flight to look forward to and, at the end of that, in all probability a week of shrieking tedium punctuated by welcome moments of screaming boredom, I reminded myself that I only had myself to blame, because, given that the circumstances had made me cheat a teensy bit with Ascension Island, I really should have done the same with this chapter and paid a visit to the rather charming village in Fife called Falkland or taken the number 19 bus down to Bloomsbury and spent a day in the Falkland Arms. If only I'd been smarter, I could have created a post-modernist pastiche, an innovative indictment not only of post-imperial delusions but of the very constructs of the travel genre itself. And my bottom wouldn't be aching.

But no. I was stuck on a Tristar somewhere above the South Atlantic and heading to Mount Pleasant on the Falkland bloody Islands. It was at this low moment that George Eliot came to my aid. Twelve pages after Lydgate's tear-kissing, at the end of chapter 32, *Middlemarch* fell to the floor and I fell fast asleep.

When I was wakened by the offer of yet another cup of squash, the ossification process had spread throughout my body and we were still somewhere above the South Atlantic. But very soon – after a mere three hours or so – the head boy fluted the news that he was about to begin our descent. And then there was a commotion among the soldiers across the aisle. They had spotted land.

My stomach felt queasy and my pulse was racing – not with excitement but with anxiety, just as a tribe of hunter-gatherers, assembled under an ancient African sky, must have felt twinges of panic when one of their brethren first demonstrated his new magic with two bits of flint to produce fire. For, as that tribe had surely also intuited at the fearful moment when the stones sparked to ignite the grass pyre beneath, I suddenly realised that my whole way of life, one that I had known since time immemorial – of sitting and gazing out at blue sky above and blue sea below – was about to be transformed.

I peered out of the rain-streaked window. Nothing yet but murky, violent sea. And then the sea abruptly stopped in a thin white line as it met the shore. So there it was – land. Nothing else, mind you, just rocks and hills and beige, sodden land. No sign whatsoever of any civilisation. Ah . . . I fear I may have yelped at this point because an aeroplane had appeared alongside us – a small aeroplane but one furnished with missiles. It was, the squaddy behind informed me, a Tornado fighter, and it was now so close that its left wing was, I guessed, six inches from the Tristar's right. So close that we could see the two chaps inside the cockpit waving to us. So close that I could see the chap behind the pilot laughing. Amalgam fillings. It took a couple of seconds for the fighter to dip underneath us and reappear on the other side. With a waggle of its wings, it disappeared once more and emerged at its original position to escort us in. The Tornado veered away for only a moment as the Tristar dropped its undercarriage, but the Tornado readjusted then promptly lowered its own undercarriage. 'Taking the piss,' as the squaddy behind observed. What I later learned was a routine escort service, a bit of a giggle for bored fighter pilots, ended as suddenly as it had begun. The two chaps in the cockpit waved bye-bye, the Tornado went into warp drive, its jets turning into cones of orange, and two seconds later it had blasted up and away and out of sight.

The Tristar touched down at Mount Pleasant, the Falklands' fancifully named military base which, like everywhere else in the islands, is in the middle of nowhere. That is no accident. Had the garrison been stationed near the Falklands' only town, Port Stanley would have been transformed into the South Atlantic equivalent of

Aldershot. Commendable though it is, the siting of Mount Pleasant hasn't helped endear the islands to the troops, who rate this posting second only to Northern Ireland in dismalness. And the lack of contact between civilians and soldiers means that the soldiers retain an off-handed disdain for the civilians, whom they call Bennies, since they think Falkland islanders dress with the same woolly-hatted panache as Benny in *Crossroads*. (When officers banned the nickname, the troops started to call the islanders Stills. Because they were still Bennies.)

The dreariness of life in Mount Pleasant was immediately obvious because quite a few soldiers were hanging around outside the arrivals area, seizing the chance to watch us disembark from the Tristar as an exciting alternative to the 978th rerun of the *Blackadder* videos. A buffeting wind drove us inside, where we were greeted by two more soldiers who jumped the moat of the carousel and took possession of the island in the middle. The first soldier bawled for our attention and the second soldier began to yell his advice on 'ordnance recognition' – that is, how to identify and where to report unexploded Argentinian landmines.

The condition-red security level was maintained by the immigration official, who made us fill in all over again the form we'd all had to complete back in Britain. After that, he examined every passport as though it were a pirate's treasure map. Then he quizzed each one of us about the purpose of our visit, our proposed length of stay, and our opinion on the sinking of the *Belgrano*. Okay, I made that last bit up, but I really had been taken aback by my first impressions of the Falklands, which were what I would have expected had I come here a month, rather than fourteen years, after the war ended.

And now that I'd passed my security exam and been allowed outside the airport building, to be freshened up by an icy shower, I found that I had walked on to the set of a war movie. Quite as unconvincingly as those extras in *Jason King* who would sip cocktails and exchange silent repartee in the background while Jason was being smooth to the dollybird suspect, two officers with sticks tucked under their armpits marched by. Right on cue, a jeep drove past and then, from stage right, appeared a column of jogging infantry. I wished I'd been the star of this film because in that case a laconic major would have already whisked me off to a warm debriefing room. Sadly, I had been condemned to play the role of unnoticed extra who is waiting in the icy rain for his mini-bus – a mini-bus which, though I had now spent an hour and a half in the Falklands, would be my first sign of civilian life here.

Controversy rages in the Falklands about the road from Mount Pleasant airport to Port Stanley. Indeed, even as the mini-bus trundled out of MPA, as we old Falkland hands call it, the local media – i.e., the Falkland Islands Broadcasting Service (unfortunate acronym) – were preparing a report which would be preceded in that evening's radio news only by coverage of a diplomatic row with Argentina over fishing rights in the waters round South Georgia, a report which would exclusively reveal a British surveyor's analysis that the clay composition of the surface was far too high. Or something. Anyway, why the fuss? Well, the road we were now on was just that – the road. As it would later pain me to discover, there are in the islands other surfaces marked on the map and that skilled drivers can negotiate – just – but none resembles a road as the term has conventionally been understood elsewhere for the past century.

So it isn't surprising that the locals get excited by the road. Not that it has a supporters' club or receives fan mail accompanied by saucy Polaroids. The excitement manifests itself in the giddy abandon of shifting up beyond second gear, a unique opportunity for drivers in the Falklands and one that can produce such carefree glee that the road has become something of a death trap – six people, a fair fraction of the local population of 2,000, have died on it in the decade since it was constructed.

Fortunately, the mini-bus was content to trundle, so we made stately and reassuring progress through drenched countryside that could have belonged to the more desolate parts of Ross and Cromarty before the Picts arrived. Barren heath gave way to barren moorland which climbed to barren hillock or barren mountainside. The two noteworthy features were the many 'stone runs' which my bumf said were unique to the Falklands – freeze-framed avalanches and rivers and lakes of jagged boulders of grey quartz – and the many fences sporting signs that carried a skull and crossbones and the warning, 'DANGER UNEXPLODED MINES'. There were a few other clues that this place might at some point have been inhabited – a telltale group of diggers abandoned at the roadside, a couple of prefabricated buildings abandoned in the distance, and, on one occasion that reminded me strongly of the kind of inexplicable eyesore you sometimes come across in the Scottish Highlands, a turquoise Commer van on a hill beside a ruined black cab. Both abandoned.

Conversation in the mini-bus was desultory at best, since the ruddy-cheeked woman driving it was either very shy or in a bad mood, and my four fellow-passengers consisted of one chap who managed to tell me he was a sub-contractor from Arbroath before he fell asleep and three Koreans shivering in shiny suits and tassled loafers, who, like me, didn't talk much because we were too busy staring at the treeless tundra outside to clamp our mouths shut.

An hour later, the mini-bus trundled round a corner to reveal several bungalows and then a school, a hospital and a few rows of bright red or green roofs glistening in the sunlight. Port Stanley. Home to three-quarters of the Falklands' population yet still one of the world's smallest capital cities and certainly the most southerly. And clearly a centre of telepathy, for even as I recited the address of my b & b to the driver, she pulled up the handbrake and nodded to her left. We had pulled up outside a little whitewashed cottage with a green corrugated-iron roof, a tiny porch and an adjoining garden full of flowers and swarming with gnomes.

I was welcomed by my landlady for the week, Kay McCallum, a slim, trim woman in her late fifties or early sixties, who ushered me past her little scullery and through to her little dining room, where she plied me with cups of tea and large wedges of home-made cake. I told her about my flight and Kay told me about the recent weather (windy and not very warm at all). Then Kay's granddaughter Tania burst in to tell us both about her recent pony trek across the islands with her friends, her day at school and her preparations for tomorrow's flower show.

Kay took Tania outside to the garden. My mouth hamstery with sponge, I looked around the room – at the flowery sofa, the shelves adorned with knick-knacks, the calendar of picturesque Scottish sunsets. I had travelled 8,000 miles south and forty years back in time. The wireless was carrying the early-evening news bulletin about the row over the road surface. It sounded as though the government back home was in a bit of a pickle, too, with more protests about Eden sending the troops into Egypt.

Still replete with sponge, I sat down to dinner (a succulent hotpot and home-grown veg) with Kay's two other lodgers, a young couple who were on the last leg of their six-month trek through South America. Heather was an Irishwoman who now lived with Stephan in Munich, a city, I informed them, that I had recently visited for a second-round UEFA Cup tie, the most important football match in my team's history. Luckily, Stephan was a big Bayern fan so he knew what I was wittering on about: 'So naturally you are a follower of Raith Rovers, yes? Your Danny Lennon scored with a free-kick. My father was telling me this in a phone call I made to him in Bolivia.'

They were an eminently friendly couple, so I concentrated on providing Stephan with a full and unbiased match report, paying due attention to Raith's complete dominance of the game, instead of telling him what I thought about his home town, for Munich had brought back feelings I thought I'd discarded after I stopped reading war comics and skulking around shrubbery with a stick for a rifle. Raith lost 2–1, by the way.

But let's return to the Falklands, where Heather had recommended that I look in on the Victory Bar later and I was about to take her advice. It turned out to be just along the road from Kay's house. (Well, everywhere in Port Stanley is just along, up or down the road from everywhere else.) Thirty minutes in the Victory Bar was long enough for me to appreciate the continuing popularity here of the feather cut. And of darts; one of the men playing in the pub had earned a place of honour above the gantry, which displayed a photograph of him with former champ John Lowe. Having naffly ordered a scotch on the rocks and been asked if I wanted ice with that, I then appreciated another crucial fact about life on the Falklands: okay, beer came in cans and not on draught but whisky was 75p a nip. After as many drams as I had doomed attempts to strike up conversation with regulars at the bar, I celebrated this big Friday night out by toddling up to the edge of the town where I listened to the wind and gazed up at the most wonderful star-spangled display I have ever seen. There was the rivery cloud of the Milky Way, and Orion, and what had to be the Southern Cross, and God alone knew what constellations in this alien, southern sky.

I drifted gently awake to find that my little attic bedroom was flooded by light. Outside, a child laughed and a cock crowed and then there was silence. Eight-thirty. I jumped out of bed, pulled on some clothes, tumbled downstairs, bade Heather and Stephan a hearty good morning and tucked into breakfast. I should add that all five of these events were shockingly uncharacteristic for one who doesn't normally recover the power of speech or the will to live by lunchtime.

By lunchtime on this particular Saturday, I was trampolining around in the back of a Land Rover. It had been a trial of self-control hanging on to any available bit of protruding metal while the Land Rover zipped along the road to Mount Pleasant – damn, MPA – and the rutted track after the turn-off had meant an instant deterioration in passenger comfort. However, now that the rutted track had dwindled away to no track at all, I had been left with no option but to retaliate, by regularly nutting the roof while sorting out the bodywork with lots of hefty blows from my kidneys. Opposite me bounced Stephan and making infrequent contact with the pew in front were Heather and a couple of young islanders, Lois and Keith, who had rashly promised to chauffeur us to Volunteer Point in a remote corner well north of Port Stanley. We were now passing Estancia, a place which merited a mark on the map as well as an honourable mention in histories of the Falklands War (British troops established a forward logistics base there), and which turned out to consist of a couple of farmhouses and a few outbuildings.

The next landmark, a good thirty minutes' scrapping with the Land Rover later, was Port Louis, the Falklands' first settlement. What had been a fortified hamlet built and occupied by the French and then the Spanish in the 1760s was eventually abandoned in 1806. These days, Port Louis consists of a couple of farmhouses and a few outbuildings.

As does Johnson's Harbour, where we stopped to slip the farmer a few quid for the privilege of driving over his land. I have never parted with money with such joy, since doing so involved escaping from the Land Rover. I staggered out, feeling much as I would after turning up at an Orange Lodge fancy dress party disguised as the Pope. Rubbing and massaging as many sore bits as I could identify, I limped through with the others to the farmhouse kitchen, where a sturdy couple were sitting by a Raeburn for which my more pretentious acquaintances would have assassinated their partners.

What with the heat from the stove, the fug of cigarette smoke and the occasional crackle from a massive radio-telephone transmitter in the corner, the scene reminded me forcibly of all the times I have sat in a mini-cab office in London and hoped against hope for a driver who would not be (a) a Nazi, (b) on parole or (c) a recent arrival from Lagos with no A–Z or change. Quite in keeping with the ambience, our conversation turned into a protracted exchange of views on our best route henceforward. There was a lot of talk about a container to our right, a fence, and a boggy patch, plus some chat between Keith and the farmer about the quality and width of Keith's tyres. I was baffled but Keith apparently understood it all.

The key word being 'apparently'. We set off again across terrain that was, though I would have considered it impossible ten minutes before, much rougher than anything we had encountered so far. How Keith kept the Land Rover moving or even upright I will never know. His face was pressed up against the windscreen. His hands whirred round the steering wheel as he instantly reacted to each obstacle-littered yard ahead. With a top speed now of 8 miles an hour, the Land Rover slithered up a hill, pogoed down the other side, lurched, slewed, pitched, hurdled, plunged and jolted its way through this rocky, heathery, watery moorland.

After a long, long while, we stopped. Abruptly. With the left side of the Land Rover slithering in a large hole filled with peaty mud. The engine screamed as Keith tried to reverse up and away, but the wheels only churned further into the mud. He climbed out to inspect our plight. His being the only door that we could open, we followed him out. Only Keith spoke, and only one word.

'Bogged.'

With that, he returned to his seat to put out an appeal for help on the radio-telephone, a piece of equipment whose importance I now appreciated. Someone responded immediately. The nearest jeep was on its way.

We ate our sandwiches, picked diddle-dee berries (indigenous to the Falklands and the raw material for diddle-dee jelly, which is said to be a delicious speciality), examined the left wheels, and admired the view.

It was a magnificently clear day with high wisps of cloud drifting across a sky that seemed twice the size of the regulation British model. I remembered reading unlikely claims in the few available tourist brochures about the purity of the Falklands air, and now I really could see what they meant. Simply by standing on a boulder, I could take in a view that went on and on and on. Moorland stretched to the horizon, where, far to the east, I could just make out the coastline. To our right there was an inexplicable metal container, the landmark mentioned back at the farmhouse. Beyond that was a dishevelled fence. And that was it. There was certainly no speck on the horizon that might have been a jeep. I dug out from my bag the binoculars I'd recently bought for just such an occasion. They afforded me a shaky view of even more moorland stretching to the horizon and, far to the east, a now clearly visible coastline. Still no speck that might have been a distant jeep. I took the chance to wander off on my own and, after ten minutes, with the Land Rover and the fence and the container out of sight, I had reached a place where, for the first time in my life, I could see far and wide and spot no sign of human or any other mammal's existence. All I could hear was an occasional birdcall and the wind.

The jeep that answered Keith's appeal for help – the jeep that was nearest to us, mind – turned up two hours later. Granted, our rescuers – two farmers and a little boy – had slightly misunderstood our position at first, but even so . . . Two hours . . . As the jeep tacked its way towards us, the pair of turkey vultures that had been circling hopefully high above us flapped off.

A nerve-racking rigmarole followed, involving the farmers' jeep itself getting stuck for a while in a neighbouring bog, several failed attempts to haul the Land Rover up and out, a good deal of work with two corrugated-iron planks placed under the Land Rover's wheels, and very little conversation. Here is the unabridged dialogue for the last five minutes of the rescue:

Keith: 'That tow rope okay?'

Farmer in jeep: 'Reckon so.'

(Pause while jeep manoeuvres to gain purchase. Longer pause. Much longer pause.)

Second farmer, monitoring rope: 'Steady.'

(Jeep takes strain and revs. Very long pause. With a violent lurch, the Land Rover jumps free.)

Second farmer: 'She was deep in.'
Keith: 'Yeah.'
Second farmer: 'Bye then.'
Keith: 'Cheers.'

It took only another half an hour of lurching and jolting for us to reach Volunteer Point – a coastline patch of grassland tended by a few sheep which mingled with several dozen perky gentoo penguins. And then we could see them – hundreds of king penguins, the kind with the patches of yellow on their faces and necks that you see on the wrappers of the eponymous biscuit. They were standing in a huge circle. They looked as though they were attending a get-to-know-you party at a convention of small, well-fed butlers. We walked up next to them. I had planned to make some kind of chipper reference here to my disappointment that the penguins weren't singing and tap-dancing as they do in the beer adverts, but that would be to cheat on the sense of wonder we all felt as we walked round the colony and peered into its centre, where there huddled a group of large, brown, fluffy young.

Through stupidity rather than apathy, I am hopeless at ornithology, and every other branch of nature study. I still get mixed up between freesia and fuchsia; my two rather suave mentions so far of Orion fail to add that it and the Plough are the only constellations I can identify (with the Southern Cross having recently provided a third, but it's as easy to spot as a six-footer in Glasgow), and by the end of my week in the Falklands I could recognise and name, among the hundreds of species and millions of birds on the islands, gentoo and king penguins, turkey vultures, the ubiquitous Upland Geese, and – I'm proud of this one – the meadowlark, a blackbird-sized creature with a bright red breast, unique to the islands. My apologies, then, for being able to convey only a few facts about king penguins – they do nothing much but stand in a huge circle, they make a lot of noise when they throw their heads back and let rip with a long, low squawk, and they stink.

Because they were camping out at Volunteer Point for a couple of days, Stephan and Heather could stay on to do some more marvelling at the king penguins. Keith, Lois and I could afford to indulge in all of fifteen minutes' sightseeing here, since it was now five o'clock and two hours of daylight remained. Wearily, we got back into the Land Rover and began lurching and jolting back to Port Stanley.

I limped into Kay's parlour just as dusk was falling. I was about to launch into an extended apology for my late arrival, but Kay beat me to it.

'Got bogged, then?'

'. . . Yes, we did, but how—?'

'Oh, word gets around,' she explained and served up not the burned, cold supper I had expected but a massive, freshly made pie and a steaming cloud of mashed potato.

This being Saturday night, after I had eaten and recovered from eating, I wandered down the hill to the waterfront and the Upland Goose Hotel, an establishment made famous as the base for the journalists who were covering the Falklands War – until, that is, the owner banned them, describing the hacks as 'worse than the Argies'. Perhaps he was influenced by the incident in the hotel's lounge bar, retold by Robert Harris in *Gotcha!*, his cracking book about the media's coverage of the war. Harris describes how the *Glasgow Herald*'s correspondent, outraged that another journalist had used his old-boy military contacts in order to be the first person to walk into Port Stanley after the Argentinian surrender and had then sent back his personal scoop while somehow mislaying the pooled dispatch written by his colleagues, had threatened that journalist with an Argentinian bayonet. He had to be pulled off the man who was to become the editor of the *Daily Telegraph*, with the advice, 'This is neither the time nor the place to murder Max Hastings.'

Fourteen years later, the hotel's lounge bar was a far jollier place. With its swirly carpets, brushed pink and blue upholstery and smattering of middle-class, middle-aged customers, it looked like any lounge bar in any Royal, Station or George Hotel. Apart, that is, from the three nautical-looking Chileans who were gathering, with great glee and gusto, empty cans, for what I trust is an unrivalled collection. My tin of McEwan's Export was a real hit.

Having been exhausted and pummelled by the Land Rover, I was content to sit back and eavesdrop on the conversation at the adjoining table, occupied by two elderly couples. Unlike the rest of us in the lounge bar, this foursome were Falkland islanders born and bred. If they hadn't exchanged a word, I think I'd have guessed this, for they all had what I could already recognise as Falkland faces – slightly podgy, with weatherbeaten cheeks and, the biggest give-away of all, very large noses. But it was their conversation that stood out even more, for the most noticeable characteristic of islanders is that, when they do manage a few words, they talk funny.

I was surprised by this, daftly assuming that the population just wasn't big enough to have nurtured a distinctive pronunciation. But it is easy to see why one has evolved – it would be hard to find a more isolated linguistic community and many people here are fourth- or fifth-generation islanders, so there has been plenty of time for an accent to develop. (Or possibly accents, for some locals claim to be able to discern differences between the speech of West and East Falklanders.)

What neither I nor anyone I asked could explain was why the descendants of settlers who came from all over Britain, with, if anything, a disproportionate number of Scots (doubtless attracted to the islands by the relatively luxurious lifestyle and balmy climate), should come up with an accent that combines the upward, laconic lilt of Australia with the vowels of the West Country. So, for your first lesson in the *Let's Speak Falklands!* course book, practise the following dialogue, remembering to mumble the words and not to use any movement of the lips or jaw, while noting that every sentence must rise at the end and that every other sentence must be the local catchphrase to show how unimpressed you are.

> *Howard*: Oi loik caawfee in the maarnin'?
> *Stanley*: Aw yeah?

The second lesson introduces the crucial elements of the local vocabulary. I had read that the local lexicon had been influenced by the gauchos who worked here in the nineteenth century, but that influence was restricted to a few terms concerning saddles and the like. The gauchos lacking words for mudguards or four-wheel drive, the one Spanish-derived word that remains in common usage is 'Camp' – Falklandese for everywhere on the islands not in Port Stanley, and descended from *campo*, the Spanish for countryside. However, there is one astonishing feature of Falklandese vocabulary, apart from its consisting mainly of pauses and silences, which is that, uniquely among varieties of English, it contains no superlatives or any dramatic expressions. Note the following examples from the phrase book:

> *English*: That's the most extraordinary thing I've heard in my entire life!
> *Falklands*: Aw yeah?

> *English*: I have had an accident, doctor. With my chainsaw. Here is my leg. Please sew it back on.
> *Falklands*: Aw yeah, doc? Reckon oiv stubbed me toe?

I didn't have a white terrier called Scamp or a black comma of a kiss-curl, I wasn't wearing shorts and I wasn't spending the summer hols with my aunt on the Cornish coast, but in every other respect I felt like a boy hero in a vintage *Hotspur* as I bounded down the stairs at seven the following morning. I tucked into another hearty breakfast and gulped down lashings of tea, ready for another day of adventures. Would Scamp lead me to a secret cave filled with bullion? Maybe we'd unmask a Jerry spy . . .

No! Today I was off on a plane trip round the islands! But first I had to take in Kay's news about the dramas I'd missed from the night before. While I'd been savouring my two cans of McEwan's in the Upland Goose, the rest of Port Stanley had witnessed all manner of Saturday-night mayhem. A Land Rover had been stolen – by young soldiers on the piss, folk reckoned. Kay was confident it'd turn up abandoned outside MPA as usual. She'd also heard about a fight in the town. Well, a brawl. Sort of. It had taken place under the aegis of a well-refreshed local who, having already been bound over to keep the peace, encouraged a pal to have a pop at a foreign fisherman. I hoped the victim wasn't one of the shivering Koreans in the mini-bus. Last and far from least, Kay had had ructions of her own to contend with: youths had kicked in several slats of her garden fence. She'd phoned the police, who had taken twenty minutes to arrive, a remarkable delay even by British standards. The cop who'd eventually turned up explained that he'd got lost – an excuse every bit as convincing as a pupil's faked note from his mother claiming he can't do jim because he's got the phloo.

My inspection of the damaged slats was cut short by the arrival of the taxi which was to whisk me off on the bypass – that is to say, road at the top of the town – past the miniature industrial estate and the hydroponic nursery to Port Stanley's airport. I vaguely recalled the airport starring in triumphant MoD briefings at the start of the Falklands War, when we were assured that RAF planes had destroyed the Argentinian-held runway. However, the craters which appeared on British surveillance photographs were actually piles of earth which the Argentinians removed at night to allow planes to land and take off. But these were only transport planes and light aircraft and definitely not the hi-tech Super-Etendard jets, because, as the Argentinians soon learned to their dismay, this was the main runway for a run-down British colony. So it was small and crap.

These days, all the big planes use the big runway (the one that successive governments announced they could never afford to build for the Falklands and then was suddenly built after the war) at MPA, so Port Stanley's airport has remained a very modest affair. I walked across the tiny reception area to what looked like a lost-luggage office but was really the departures bit. It was here that I began to get a little wary of my forthcoming tour, because it was here that I had to step on to scales. Just how small did a plane have to be before it required its passengers to pass a weight test?

And the answer is 'very small indeed'. A young pilot with an unsettling crewcut led four of us out and into what was not so much a plane as a hatchback with wings. Once we were buckled in, the pilot stopped fiddling with the switches on his dashboard and murmured the forecast that the flight ahead might be 'a bit bumpy'. A bit bumpy. I had heard islanders describe a two-day hike as 'a good stroll' and a gale which had me walking at an angle of 45 degrees to the ground as being 'breezy', so 'a bit bumpy' is how locals might describe the effect of white-water rafting down the Niagara Falls. The engines having roared into life – much as a hairdryer on a low setting roars into life – the hatchback zoomed down the runway at, oh, a full 20 miles an hour before staggering into the air.

I was so busy tightly crossing my fingers and fidgeting with the sick bag that it was a while before I had to acknowledge that the flight wasn't too bad at all – a bit bumpy in fact. I risked looking out of the window and saw MPA ahead of us. It would only be fair to say that the hatchback looked out of place on the Mount Pleasant runway – like a three-year-old in a nightclub – but the other six airstrips we visited on this tour were constructed to the same scale as the hatchback, being, at best, fields equipped with a lean-to shed and a tattered windsock.

The next stop for this airborne taxi/post van lacked the lean-to shed. Sea Lion Island, four miles long and barely one mile across, once had a population consisting of Terry and Doreen Clifton. That was until 1990, when the Cliftons sold the island to the Falkland Islands Development Corporation, which built a five-bedroom Tourist Lodge, run by the Gray family, who fled here from Middlesbrough. Sea Lion Island was a fifteen-minute hop from MPA, but although it is only four or five miles south of the mainland and is now visited most days in the summer by flights such as this, it used to be the most isolated spot in the Falklands, where ships would call once or twice a year. It's still unspoilt, still home to lots of birds, including, so I am told, a very rare bird of prey which goes by the name of the striated caracara. We swooped down over hundreds of penguins and elephant seals on the beach, then over large clumps of tussac grass, before bumping down on to the bit of pasture that served as the runway.

While the two women who'd been sitting next to me clambered out to spend a few days here birdwatching, I looked back towards the mainland and realised that, since Sea Lion is the most southerly part of the Falklands, I had reached a landmark. Not counting a couple of villages in Tierra del Fuego and some research stations down in the Antarctic, every inhabited place that was south for the rest of the planet was north. So by the law which states that south equals soft, Sea Lion Island was the poofiest place in the world. Ah, but since everything was upside-down in this odd hemisphere, wouldn't this mean that it'd be a northward journey that'd lead you to the increasingly girly – so that, for example, inhabitants of Hobart must all have tattoos on their teeth while residents of Darwin or Cairns are, by comparison, cissies? Interesting.

The subsequent stopovers, all (obviously) north of Sea Lion, suggested that the amended theory needed a bit of fine tuning. They included three of the main settlements in Camp – North Arm in the south-west of East Falkland and Fox Bay and Port Howard over in West Falkland. Each has a tiny school and a shop, and each has a population hovering around the forty mark. Even at North Arm, which after all does have a community centre for darts matches, whist drives and all manner of cosmopolitan frivolity, our arrival was evidently a cherished highlight. At each field we'd be greeted by a huddle of burly farmers wearing wellies and wondrously low-slung jeans. They'd collect and hand over parcels, mumble brief, halting pleasantries with the pilot, and wave us goodbye. The excitement over for another day, they'd wander back to the settlement – perhaps half a dozen Nissen huts, a handful of cottages and outbuildings and a pair of larger whitewashed houses.

From North Arm, the plane swept low over the surprisingly green and flat pasture of Lafonia, then, as it crossed Falkland Sound to West Falkland, climbed to 3,000 feet. At that height, the two contradictory responses I always have to flying (apart from te-dium) became overwhelming. One moment I'd be seized by terror, because all that was keeping us up here were two engines that sounded too weak to give a decent blow-wave, and what about those stories of rescue crews coming across bits of crash victims, here shards of leg, there a mushed head, and over there a severed hand with the fingers tightly crossed? And the next moment I'd be filled with joy at travelling like this through the high air, exulting in this god's-eye view of the calm sea and the cliffs of West Falkland ahead.

Joy was the outright winner once we'd crossed the water to Fox Bay on West Falkland, which was noticeably more mountainous and even more deserted than East Falkland. I now began to appreciate the significance of some key facts about the Falklands – the two main islands are roughly the same size, and combined they are slightly larger than Wales, and fewer than 200 people live on West Falkland – for the landscape below was nigh-on empty of human life. And it was beautifully empty, particularly from the air, where jeep-eating bogs and sodden heath shrank into insignificance. (Like idealistic politics, sightseeing in the Falklands benefits greatly from taking a grand overview.) On such a clear day, it was easy to spot the few tracks and the individual farms marked on my little map. That was bound to be Sulivan House below. And there, over the pilot's crewcut, was Goring House. That had to be Mount Robinson to the north and those bluish hills to the east would be – ach, was there no getting away from the man? – the Hornby Mountains.

We passed over what was presumably Shallow Bay House on the north coast and crossed another stretch of water so pure that I could admire the detail of rock formations on the seabed and the swathes of brown kelp rinsed by the tide. Westward lay a good fraction of the Falklands' 200 or so smaller islands. Checking my map, I was pleased to see that the British Empire includes specks of land called Annie, Fanny, Blind, Triste, Motley, Beaver, Shag and the Jasons. The two we landed on to the north of West Falkland were Saunders Island and Pebble Island. With a population of 14,000 sheep, 240 cattle and 14 humans, Pebble Island is an unlikely spot to have acquired great significance in British military history, but a sign that it had done just that was awaiting us beside the grassy strip with the lean-to shed and tattered windsock – the wreckage of an Argentinian plane, one of eleven destroyed by an SAS raid early in the war. Most of the planes were put out of action by grenades dropped into the cockpit, but some of the SAS were so fired up by adrenalin they managed to rip instrument panels out by hand.

Having picked up an elderly gent who'd been holidaying at Pebble Island's miniature hotel, the plane headed back down to Port Howard, over Goose Green and Darwin and back to Stanley, where we landed at noon. The whole trip had taken three hours and, save for a total of perhaps thirty minutes of undiluted fear, had been wonderful. I was in such a good mood that I no longer harboured the slightest grudge against the fellow who'd hogged the seat beside the pilot.

Fair play to him, the seat-hogger offered me a lift back to the town in his Land Rover. He confessed that he often did the round trip because he just loved flying, despite having witnessed a Harrier crash at Port San Carlos when he was a kid and living in his wartime home – a foxhole he and others shared with paratroopers. He lived in Stanley these days, and still loved the Falklands – the scenery, the flying, the fact that his own kids were safe from harm – despite the obvious disadvantages.

'What obvious disadvantages?'

'It's a small town. Everyone knows your business. And say if you have a row with someone, or you think someone's a prat – there's no avoiding them.'

'Have you ever thought about moving away for a while, to Britain maybe?'

'Sure. Matter of fact, I have been to the UK. I stayed in Doncaster.'

'And what did you make of it?'

'Very strange. I was sure I'd meet at least one person I knew. My first day there, I walked up and down all those streets, and you know what?'

'Let me guess.'

He laughed. 'Yeah. Not one familiar face. I couldn't believe it.'

He dropped me off on the harbourfront outside Port Stanley's main shop, the West Store. I wandered through the touristy bit, bought some postcards but none of the toy penguins, and meandered across to the supermarket and the clothes shop. So this was where the locals came to snap up their chunky sweaters and low-slung jeans at comically high prices? Small wonder that most Falkland islanders shop by catalogues. I stocked up with a packet of chewing gum at the supermarket and joined the check-out queue. There was one woman in front of me, which I assumed was something of a result until I saw her trolley, which would raise eyebrows even in a Sainsbury's on a Saturday. She hauled out sacks of flour and sugar, breeze-blocks of biscuits and crisps, litres of ketchup, cooking-oil cans the size of a weightlifter's torso . . .

Some time later, clutching my gum like a ticket, I handed over my twenty pence and asked the lady at the till if she sold stamps.

She shook her head. 'Post office,' she explained.

'I see. Then could you tell me where the post office is, please?'

'Be closed today.'

'Yes, but I'll—'

'You know where the old bank used to be?'

'No, I'm sorry, I don't.'

'Well, it's just past there.'

Ah-hah. The thing is, the lady at the till was neither stupid nor rude. It was just that it was clearly inconceivable to her that anyone could not know where the old bank used to be. I thought back to Kay being able to tell me at seven this morning about a late-night scrap she'd already heard about, and delaying my supper because she knew, via the radio-telephone and the Port Stanley bush telegraph, that I'd been stuck in a bog in the middle of desolate moorland. That chap who'd visited Doncaster was spot on – this was a very small town, and, for all its wide open spaces and deserted landscapes, the Falklands was an intimate country, where everyone knew everyone else and most of everyone else's business, and where everyone certainly knew such famous sites in Port Stanley as that of the old bank.

Walking along the harbourfront, admiring yet again the brick-work on Christ Church Cathedral and its whalebone arch, I realised that, on my third day here, I was able to recognise 50 per cent of the people I passed. And this was the teeming capital which many people in Camp regarded as a cross between Tokyo and Sodom. There was a couple in Port Howard who came here only for holidays and medicals, a Pebble Islander who'd refused to take work in Port Stanley even when she had been young and single, a shepherd who had left West Falkland only when he was ninety and dying. Those settlements I'd visited today – I'd got them hopelessly wrong. People didn't necessarily feel isolated or lonely out there. Living in far-flung communities of forty, or fourteen or four, they faced the opposite problem: of never knowing, and in fact of fearing, the freedom of anonymity.

I'd lived in towns all my life and I'd been living in London for eight years, so I relished this chance to make the new quickly familiar. I enjoyed already knowing that that was Davis Street just up the hill, that the 'Stop Whaling' posters around Stanley were the work of the chap who kept sheep and whale skulls in his garden, that Snake Hill on the edge of the town earned its name because the road wiggled a bit. Back home, a forensic team would have to be ducking under a cordon of yellow tape round the house opposite before I roused myself to look out the window, but here I could enthuse about the gossip and the news. A horse had just bolted into the cabbage patch next to Kay's garden? Never! Go away! And how had Tania fared at the flower show? Oh, good for her! Still no word on the fence-kicking investigation?

There is just no getting away from the fact that it is pretty cold in the Falklands. Nonetheless, the Falkland Islands' representative in

London had gamely attempted to convince me otherwise.

'What most people don't appreciate', she said, 'is that Port Stanley has more sunshine hours per year than Torquay.'

'Yeah, but—'

'And much less rainfall than the UK average.'

'Even so—'

'And farmers in Camp are often afflicted by drought.'

'I see. So if I'm going in March, which is their late summer—'

'Oh yes, it'll definitely still be summer.'

'—then what should I pack? Shorts? T-shirts? Swimming trunks?'

'Perhaps something a little warmer as well.'

'What, so I go out there with sun-factor 10 and an Arran jersey?'

'Sort of thing.'

I assumed at the time that she was being polite or had failed to decipher my accent. Her advice, however, was spot on. Having been brought up on the coast of Fife, I had always reckoned that I was at home with changeable weather – on the few days a year when my family could risk a trip to the beach, we'd always pack, along with the sandwich spread and the towels, our anoraks, gloves and scarves – but the Falklands had me stumped. A typical afternoon stroll around Port Stanley would see me kitted out in a pair of jeans, a shirt, jersey and a more than fetching bomber jacket. Five yards down the road, I'd have stripped off the bomber jacket and the jersey, only for the wind to pick up, so it'd be back to being fully dressed for a few sticky minutes, the wind having abruptly died down again, then I'd whip off my top two layers once more just in time for the sun to disappear behind a cloud and the wind to begin a wintry assault. A walk here always had me performing as many costume changes as a third-rate impressionist.

But it was when the wind came in from the west that the weather really showed who was boss. Late summer it might theoretically have been but the sudden appearance of a gale-force westerly (and I don't think the Falklands has any other kind of westerly) aimed horizontally at the face would transform the balmiest of moments into a battle with the elements, the latter destined to win every time. With their fondness for euphemism, locals called this sort of weather 'fresh' or even 'bracing'. And I suppose it was, in the sense that it might be considered fresh or bracing to snort a metre of quality cocaine while being drenched by a bucket of iced water. One particular episode, when I was heading towards Government House and a west wind abruptly had me striding on the spot – the only occasion when I have managed to perform Michael Jackson's Moonwalk – qualifies as one of the coldest experiences of my life, and I speak as one who was forced as a child to take off my clothes, from duffel-coat to socks, sprint down the beach at St Andrews and swim in the sea. The North Sea. In April.

Port Stanley lies on a latitude equivalent to that of Milton Keynes, but there is an obvious reason for the fact that, taking due account of all the blethers about sunshine hours and rainfall figures, it is a lot colder. And the obvious reason is the Antarctic. As the Falklands' London representative would no doubt anxiously add, the Antarctic is a fair distance away; using an atlas, a school ruler, my thumb and much curling of my tongue over my top lip, I estimated that the South Pole is about 1,800 miles from Stanley (although the continent does jut out a bit, so its nearest tip is only 500 miles to the south). But the relative proximity of a frozen landmass that big does mean that the earth's atmosphere will have to be polluted by a lot more CFCs before the Falklands can play host to its first Club Med.

It gave me a shameful thrill to gaze to the south and tell myself that the Antarctic was a mere ninety-minute flight away. Shameful because I couldn't help thinking about the Antarctic as the site of a long-lost civilisation, having made the mistake of reading a recent bestseller called *Fingerprints of the Gods*, which, among many other claims, proposes that a culture as sophisticated as ours flourished in Antarctica until a global shift of the earth's crust shoved the continent 2,000 miles south, and that descendants of the few remaining survivors wandered the planet, teaching the ancient Egyptians how to build the pyramids and so forth. An unkind critic might point out that this thesis is rather fanciful and the evidence somewhat scanty, but, however much I acknowledge such objections, I am enough of a sucker for that sort of caper to have spent a fair amount of time wondering what may lie beneath the ice a thousand miles to the south. I even found myself looking at the Falklands heathland and wondering if, far underground, there might languish traces of a 20,000-year-old tourist resort.

Of course, I knew this was less than likely and told myself so. Alas, mere reason didn't stop my imagination from jigging about and pulling funny faces. Nor has it deterred others who have increasingly latched on to the Antarctic just as their intellectual forebears used to latch on to Martian canals or ley lines or cave paintings allegedly of astronauts. Antarctica has been confidently identified as Atlantis, or the crash site of a frozen intergalactic spacecraft, or a massively advanced underground society of supermen, or . . .

Let's face it: Santa and all his sodding elves could have their toy factory nestling at the foot of the Transantarctic Mountains and us normal folk would be none the wiser. Granted, Santa, visitors from the planet Bong and the superrace with powers we cannot even guess at would have to survive temperatures as low as –70 degrees Celsius (so far the record lowest score stands at –89.2), wind speeds of 200 m.p.h., white-out blizzards that can last for months, ice that's 6,000 feet thick on average, and the complete absence of food sources, save for a few tiny clumps of lichen, ice and 100 million penguins. But an unexplored wilderness this large (the Antarctic landmass is far greater than that of the United States, and, what with the sea freezing, can effectively double its size in winter; its largest slab iceberg seen so far was bigger than Belgium) is simply too tempting for loons to resist populating the continent with their weird or wonderful creations.

The other factor that has inspired some conspiracy concoctionists is the Antarctic Treaty of 1959. A mundane mind such as my own is foolish enough to take heart from this unique achievement of international legislation, which stipulated that the continent be used for peaceful purposes and urged scientific co-operation, but more incisive thinkers have seen through this and cited the Treaty as proof that something is definitely up down there. In reality, governments signed the Treaty not because they had discovered an intergalactic star cruiser beneath the ice but because they understandably regarded the Antarctic as an unexploitable wasteland.

Under the Treaty, the various claims to territory in Antarctica are not recognised, so all the bother that Britain and Norway went to in carving up the continent at the turn of the century has proved just as futile as the later flag-spearing by China, Australia, New Zealand and France, not forgetting the continuing sneakiness of Chile and Argentina as they build up their 'scientific' bases – which are not military outposts at all, oh no. (So there must be some other explanation for the statistic that Chile and Argentina currently produce less than 3 per cent of the research findings about the place.) A slice of the Antarctic is, technically, disputed between Britain and Argentina, but the South Orkney Islands, the South Shetland Islands and the Antarctic Peninsula are officially part of the British Empire. They rate only a mention in this book for two reasons. One, they have no permanent population. Two, I'd pounce on any excuse not to go there.

My cowardice was clearly not shared by the half-dozen burly young men I bumped into one night at the bar of the Upland Goose. I assumed they were soldiers but then I noticed that their hair was cut too well and they were just too laid-back and unoppressed to be military. With the benefit of some highly skilled eavesdropping, I established that they were homeward-bound members of several teams working for the British Antarctic Survey and now bonding with beer and gossip.

'Was Steve with your lot?'

'Not this time. He's back in Cambridge. Actually, I heard he's near to finishing his thesis.'

'That's bloody quick.'

'Galvanised by marriage.'

'Steve? Married? Not to Sue?'

'Christ no. They split up a year back.'

'So who's the victim?'

'Maggie. From Bristol?'

'Not Maggie in Astronomy? Blonde. Friend of Becky's.'

'That's her. You know Becky?'

'Sure. Through Ben.'

'Ben the guy from Somerset?'

'That's the one. Was he with your lot?'

'Not this time.'

'How's his thesis coming along?'

'All done and dusted.'

'Hell's bells. You'll be telling me Simon's finished his next.'

'Simon from Oxford? Tried to go out with Becky?'

'Yeah, Simon. Got drunk at the department party in first year, had a snog with Becky and was sick in her mouth.'

'That's the man. Simple Simon.'
'Well?'
'Well what?'
'How's his thesis coming along?'
'Finished.'
'Shit. Been examined yet?'
'Ah. You haven't heard then?'
'Uh-oh. Don't tell me. He's had to rewrite the whole thing.'
'He walked into that room and the examiners stood up and applauded.'
'Fuck.'

Port Stanley struck me as such a peaceful wee place that I found it impossible to imagine the town under Argentinian occupation. It was like trying to picture Nazis goosestepping through Camberwick Green. And since my arrival, when my first impressions had been of an army-run country under siege, there had been only occasional reminders that a war really had been fought here fourteen years before – the bomb-disposal unit on the harbourfront, the plane wreck on Pebble Island, the odd green jeep full of soldiers.

So it was high time that I hunted down some more legacies of the conflict. Struggling against the wind, I trekked over to the museum on the outskirts of the town. The route took me on an inadvertent sightseeing tour of military landmarks, starting just down the road, where I came across a ramshackle building adorned with a small sign that announced 'Falkland Islands Defence Force Headquarters'. It looked like a Scout hut. So this was the HQ for the few dozen volunteers who, along with sixty Royal Marines and nine sailors from HMS *Endurance*, comprised the garrison that had to face the Argentinian army. (Such was the mismatch that there was confusion in the first hours of the invasion, early in the morning of 2 April 1982, as Argentinian troops failed to find any Marines to fight.)

It wasn't long before I passed by the site of the first proper engagement of the conflict. With its large conservatory, neat green roofs and various annexes, Government House looks more like a links clubhouse than the residence of His Excellency the Governor. But it was this house which had been a key target for Argentinian commandos; a couple of hours into the invasion and they had the place surrounded. Six members of an Argentinian special-forces unit then tried to capture Governor Rex Hunt. In the skirmish that followed, the thirty-odd British sailors, administrators and soldiers inside the building claimed the first fatality of the war, Captain Giachino, wounded two others and captured the other three.

If any one death can highlight the waste of life incurred by warfare, I'd say it was Captain Giachino's, because of course resistance could only be token. The Argentinians hauled up some heavy artillery and pointed it at Government House. Rex Hunt, after announcing, 'This is British property. You are not invited. We don't want you here,' sort of surrendered. Then, in a touchingly absurd attempt to perform a dignified exit, he kitted himself out in his full imperial uniform, braid, plumed hat and all, but was ordered to change back into a normal person's suit before boarding the plane out to Montevideo. By the next morning, road signs had been replaced, islanders were being commanded to drive on the right, teachers were being informed that the curriculum would henceforth include compulsory Spanish, and Port Stanley had been rechristened Puerto Argentino.

The route also took me past the war memorial outside the headquarters of the Falkland Islands Government, which stands on a road called, I saw to my dismay, Thatcher Drive. I psyched myself up to cope with a museum that a Tory PR could seize upon as a backdrop for the party conference.

But when I stepped inside I was mightily relieved to see a room full of domestic and maritime bygones. I was inspecting a symphonium – evidently a Victorian prototype of the juke-box – that had once belonged to a hotel in Stanley when the assistant asked if I was looking for anything in particular. Uneasy that she might mark me down as a pathetic ghoul, I mentioned that I might be quite interested in any exhibits the museum had from the war.

The assistant nodded slowly. 'We do have one room for that,' she said. 'There on your left. You won't find a lot, though – the curator doesn't want to make too much of something that's still painful to so many of us.'

I adopted my most sincere, sympathetic expression and ambled casually leftwards, idling by an ancient mobile dentistry. So this was what certain gentlemen endured as they browsed in newsagents –

Good Housekeeping, Marie Claire, Club International, Hot Asian Babes . . . I slipped into the small room on the left.

Most of the British memorabilia was conventional stuff – regimental knick-knacks, photos, paintings of battle scenes, the table where General Menendez signed the surrender. The Argentinian exhibits, however, were a surprise. The anti-riot equipment, for example. A recipe in Spanish, found at Goose Green, for napalm. There was also a cabinet displaying two Argentinian ration packs. The parcel for an officer's twenty-four-hour ration featured four tins of corned beef and the like, cocoa, sweets and a pack of Chesterfield cigarettes. According to the little bundle for other ranks, they were supposed to survive on a daily allowance of two tins, a few sweets and – what a morale-booster – some cream crackers.

This accounted for another exhibit, a note passed to a local woman by Argentinian conscripts in Port Stanley:

> We're sorry but we're hungry.
> Please buy only for me, Micky and Juan.
> When you see a man with stars or red lines you can't speak
>   with us.
> Please if you can, buy us these things.
> 2 Tootbrash
> 3 Wafer Cadbury's
> 4 Mars
> 3 Regal Cadbury's
> 3 Orange Sandwich o L'orange Cadbury's
> 8 Whole Nut Cadbury's
> A Piece of Ham
> And if you can buy other things for eating. Thank you.

Several islanders confessed to me that compassion had driven them to smuggle food to such starving, barely teenage boys. They also reported rumours of hundreds of soldiers in Stanley dying of starvation and, in strict accordance with the traditions of the Argentinian dictatorship, their corpses being shoved into planes and thrown out over the sea.

There were only a few items about the wartime experiences of the islanders themselves, but these did include another letter which I scribbled down in my notebook. It was a front-line dispatch from Port Stanley the morning after the Argentinian invasion:

> Dear Nan and Grandad,
> . . . I think it was about 5 am when Gran wolk me up and warned me not to get scared if I heard some shooting . . . There were just about 1000 Argentinian troops and they were fighting with the marines and the Fidf . . . At about 5 or 6 Gran and I got up because we couldn't get to sleep with all the shooting . . .
> A General Somebody with a long name is coming and he is going to be the chief . . . I hope the british ships come soon. We are not allowed out of our houses untill the top feller gets an order to let us carry on normally . . . If you need food or help you have to put a white flag in your window. Sorry this isn't a very nice letter but I wanted to tell someone about it.
> Lots of love
> Lisa

That evening I had a drink with John Fowler, the editor of the Falklands' weekly, the *Penguin News*. He was a chap in his mid-forties whose obvious affability was at odds with the sadness of his eyes and his rueful smile, a contrast which gave him the appearance of someone who has suffered a recent bereavement but is much too considerate not to persevere with small talk.

We chatted for a while about the MPA road surface and other matters of state before I risked asking him the one question about his newspaper that puzzled me.

'People here appear to know everything about everything as soon as it happens.'

'The grapevine is very efficient, yes.'

'So isn't this one country in the world which doesn't need a newspaper?'

'It's true that every story I print will already be known to the readership, but, you see, the paper validates events. And don't forget that we have many readers overseas – subscribers plus people who are sent copies by relatives or friends here. And it's a journal of record. You can even read the *Penguin News* in the New York Central Library.'

'What's your print-run then?'

'Twelve hundred.'

I did some hasty mental arithmetic. To achieve the proportion-
ately equivalent circulation, the *News of the World* would have to sell
thirty-three million copies. John's success with the paper and his
knowledge of local politics became even more impressive when he
mentioned that he had returned to the Falklands only three years
before and had originally trained to be a teacher.

'Yes, I first came here in '71 and taught in Darwin. Then I left in
'84.'

'Why was that?'

He laughed. 'Well, I had no idea that the money was about to flow
in . . .'

'. . . and?'

His laugh faded away. We sat in silence for a moment while my
heart sank and he gazed at whatever horror it was that, I realised
only now, was constantly re-enacted in his middle distance. When
he did speak again it was with quiet deliberation, as if he was giving
evidence to a hushed court. 'Looking back, I think my wife and I
both suffered from post-traumatic stress disorder. For ages, the
most mawkish things on TV would reduce us to tears . . . The
house we used to have in Stanley was a bit unusual because it was
built of stone. We'd have maybe ten or eleven people sheltering
with us each night . . . A shell landed outside. One of ours. There
was a computer failure in the guidance systems . . . This is a real
advance.'

'Sorry?'

'See – I can talk about it without crying.'

'Please. I didn't . . . You don't have to.'

He gave a slight nod of his head. 'I was in the room I'd prepared
with tea-chests full of peat dust and old clothes. I knew with absolute
certainty that I was going to die. I was lying over my three-year-old
daughter, covering her. She woke up and said, "Hello, Daddy. Is this
a bad day?" ' He managed a grim laugh. 'I knew my wife was alive
because I could hear her shouting. Then I looked around, with the
pipes burst and the electricity fizzing. And three very dead bodies
there.'

I remembered that there had been a separate list on the war

memorial, with the names of three women, the only civilians to die in the war.

'We moved after it was all over to John Street, a house that had large double-glazed windows. I had a nightmare, the most vivid I've ever had, where we were shelled all over again and I knew we hadn't sandbagged all the windows . . .' He paused. 'I had an Argentinian boss – nobody wanted to be part of their administration but we had to keep things going. He saw me just afterwards and he said, "I am so very sorry."'

'And did you know what was going on? I mean generally?'

'We were all so confined. But we did become aware of the misery of the young lads who didn't want to be here.'

I mentioned the pleading note in the museum.

'Oh yes. And it was to some people's credit that they did help some mother's son begging for food.'

Naively trying to encourage a happier recollection, I asked John what it had been like here after the war was over. He sighed in wonder.

'What a mess this town was in. At the bottom of Philomel Street they'd just dumped their kit. You were crunching over ammunition like gravel. And the enormous number of human turds around. It was the compo rations – they're meant to keep soldiers constipated. Apparently, you can tell within half an hour when they've ended. Huge turds they were. Quite incredible some of them.'

We finished our drinks and wandered out into the pristine street.

After I left John, I strolled up to the edge of Stanley and found a boulder to perch on in the dusk. There was still a glimmer of light silhouetting Mount Tumbledown, the hill where British troops had finally looked down on Stanley after their eight-day yomp, lugging full battle kit, across the moors and bogs of East Falkland at the beginning of winter.

I sat on the boulder and tried to arrange my thoughts about the war into some kind of order, but it was impossible – mainly because I suspected my own motives. Wasn't the crass purpose of the orderly arrangement to create a ledger of good and bad, and to tot up the score to see if the war was justified? On the credit side: the fulfilment of colonial responsibilities, the assertion of a widely accepted claim in international law, the protection of British interests and possible petrodollars, the freeing of British citizens – actually, at that time, British-owned citizens – against a hostile incursion by a totalitarian regime. And on the debit side: the deaths of those three women in John's house, 255 British men, 746 Argentinian men and boys (officially) and Lord alone knows how many (unofficially), plus the thousands on both sides who were maimed and burned. The question of whether or not the Falklands War was justified couldn't be answered by double-entry bookkeeping. The only feelings I was sure of were two gut reactions which coming here had made stronger – that the war was as morally justifiable as any war could be, and that, like most wars, it was very avoidable.

Although Margaret Thatcher claimed responsibility for the victory won by the British military, she was ultimately responsible for the calamity of a war that should not have happened. Her government had continued the policy of its predecessors in giving the Argentinians the – correct – impression that the Falkland Islands were nothing more than a nuisance, which, in an ideal world, could be somehow quietly coloured in light-blue and white stripes and suffixed on the map with an '(Arg.)'. Before 1982, Thatcher's government gave every sign that it cared about the Falklands as little as most British citizens, who, if pressed, might have had a wild guess that the country lay south of Iceland. Eager though she was to wrap herself in the Union Jack afterwards, until the invasion happened Thatcher had not given a shit about the Falklands or any other British colony; like an impartial civil service, the NHS and the BBC, the empire was seen as just another expendable, unprofitable institution, overstaffed by dodgy traditionalists.

Thatcher's government reinforced this impression by announcing that Britain's entire naval presence in the area – the ice-patrol ship HMS *Endurance* – was to be scrapped because of the public-expenditure cutbacks to which that government was so devoted. Thatcher's government remained culpably oblivious of this penny-pinching measure's appalling timing – just when the Argentinian junta was preparing to meet public expectations that the Falklands should become the Malvinas by January 1983, the 150th anniversary of the date when the Malvinas became the Falklands again. Why did this escape the attention of Thatcher's government? Because Thatcher's government had introduced cutbacks so that British intelligence operations in the whole of Latin America amounted to a bloke called Mark Heathcote. Britain also had various defence attachés in the region, but they had been instructed by Thatcher's government to concentrate on selling arms as well as gathering information. Even so, one defence attaché had visited the Falklands in January 1982 – a trip he had to pay for himself – and warned Whitehall about the threat of an Argentinian invasion. The warning was ignored.

The result was an invasion three months later, and then hostilities so anachronistic that initially the rest of the world regarded the conflict as almost comic. When Anthony Parsons, Britain's Ambassador to the United Nations, informed the Security Council on 1 April that a war was imminent, he was greeted with disbelief and the sneaking suspicion that this was an elaborate prank to celebrate the date. Four days later, when the United States' National Security Council tried to discuss the matter, it did so without many key members and without President Ronald Reagan, for they had all flown off for a holiday in the Caribbean with the President's ex-Hollywood pal, Claudette Colbert. For once, Reagan really can't be blamed for not being able to comprehend what was happening. He pronounced himself utterly bemused by this war over 'that little ice-cold bunch of land down there' and continued with his spring break, leaving his energetic Secretary of State Alexander Haig to engage in frantic shuttle diplomacy, though Haig himself couldn't believe that war would really be engaged over 'a thousand Scottish shepherds'.

Haig's bid to gain a million air miles in record time was utterly futile because Thatcher made only a half-hearted effort, then a token effort, then no effort at all to achieve a peaceful solution. While Haig and the UN's Pérez de Cuéllar and the soon-to-be-sacked Foreign Secretary Francis Pym tried to avoid war, the order was given to sink the *Belgrano* as it headed away from the British-imposed total exclusion zone. Just as the sinking of the *Belgrano* made war inevitable, the very presence of another vessel in the South Atlantic ensured that, for all the talk about Thatcher's great gamble and courage in staking her political career – though not her life – on the outcome of the war, it was a gamble played with a hand of five aces. For, lurking off the South American coast was a Polaris submarine, which, in case the Task Force operation went awry, was primed to nuke.

The gung-ho bungling which was the real hallmark of Thatcher's government during the war inspired the needless diversion of the raid on the Argentinian garrison at Goose Green. We have the testimony of the officer in charge of establishing a bridgehead on East Falkland, Brigadier Julian Thompson, that he was under irresistible political pressure to get a move on and kill some Argies. The paratroopers who were sent on this mission to satisfy politicians' bloodlust had a little surprise awaiting them as they huddled for warmth in a farmhouse just north of Argentinian positions; they tuned in to the early-morning news to hear the BBC World Service cite 'unnamed sources' claiming that the battle the paratroopers were preparing to fight was already under triumphant and glorious progress, thus helpfully alerting the Argentinians to their existence, purpose and probable position.

Finally, when the British military overcame the conditions, the enemy and the politicians back home, and were negotiating surrender terms, Thatcher demanded that those terms be an unconditional – and unacceptably humiliating – surrender. We owe it only to the decency and common sense of the Task Force commander, Admiral Fieldhouse, who chose to ignore that demand and offer General Menendez an honourable surrender, that one last devastating battle for Port Stanley was avoided and that the Argentinians were allowed to go home to boot out their dictatorship.

Argentinian democrats were one of the beneficiaries of the conflict. The British military command also had a good war, gaining renewed status and the sort of useful work-out not available in the streets of Belfast. The islanders won a sense of worth and security they had always been denied before, plus the injection of cash and facilities as the garrison was established at Mount Pleasant, plus full British citizenship (well, it seemed churlish not to, and there were only 2,000 of them, and they were all white).

But it was Margaret Thatcher who had the best war of all. At the trifling cost of one thousand and four lives, the person who was presiding over the destruction of British industry, with record levels of bankruptcies (two hundred each week by the time of the war), and record numbers of people chucked into unemployment (by then, officially over three million, but add at least another million to that), thereby fully earning her rating in the opinion polls as the most hated prime minister in the history of British democracy, ordered her subjects to rejoice in her victory. Swept along by the patriotic fervour unleashed by the Task Force, Thatcher was re-elected and re-elected, but allowing her credit for winning that war is like hailing as a heroine someone who has left her house with the front door open, spotted robbers inside on her return, dialled 999, egged on the police as they battled with the robbers, then run around the garden in a lap of honour.

It hadn't taken me long to realise that my comparison of the Argentinian invasion to Nazis stomping through Camberwick Green was insulting to the islanders, who were well equipped to cope with the conflict. Still, in these relatively pampered post-war days, even office-workers in Stanley were used to dealing with dire weather, rough terrain and occasional shortages. As for those who lived in Camp – few non-mountaineering civilians in Britain not resident in the Shetlands would be as prepared as the farmers and shepherds in the Falklands to withstand a war spent in enemy-occupied settlements or isolated houses or foxholes. And, as I now knew, it wasn't only hardship but often real danger that locals had to contend with. Not from the Argentinians, who kept the riot gear in reserve and were under strict instructions not to harm civilians (one slapped face carrying disastrous diplomatic implications), but from the British: besides those fatalities in Stanley, there were near-catastrophes when an RAF Harrier dropped a thousand-pound bomb close to a farm in Port Howard, and when paratroopers bombarded a house outside Goose Green, to discover that it held not the Argentinian outpost the SAS had told them was based there but four locals prone on the floor and one sheepdog with a cheek full of shrapnel.

Indeed, islanders were able to provide significant help to the Task Force. Many of those 800 locals who left after the invasion (allowed to do so by the Argentinians to show that these were free people who now lived under an unjustly maligned and really very nice regime) could give detailed reports on ground conditions, troop movements, equipment and patrols, which proved very useful to the SAS and SBS.

Demanding though conditions in the islands seemed to me – you got about by spleen-denting jeep or terrifyingly small plane, the weather could be atrocious, there were minefields and you couldn't find an espresso for love nor money – life here had become much cushier since the war. Older islanders couldn't believe their luck and revelled in telling stories – no, these were Falkland islanders: revelled in letting slip little bits of muttered information – about the bad old days. I kept on harassing Kay for autobiographical details, because each snippet was astonishing. She fondly remembered a happy childhood in West Falkland where her father worked as a shepherd and then as the doctor's guide. The only method of transport was by foot or on horseback, and when her family moved house they did so by putting all their possessions on a horse-drawn sledge. Her dolls were made by her mother and on one occasion her father managed to mend the wireless by replacing knackered tubing with dried-out sheepgut. Direct contact with the rest of the world was restricted to sending urgent messages to the next settlement by lighting fires, with diddle-dee twigs if there was no wood; two fires announced the arrival of mail, three fires the need for a doctor.

Wages have always been low in the Falklands (the doctor summoned by fire would have received a third of the salary of his British colleagues), but to illustrate just how low they had been in the past Kay dug out the accounts book of her husband's grandfather. These dated back to the 1920s when, as a worker in San Carlos, he received £24 a quarter. In theory. Until well after the Falklands War, many workers in Camp were not used to handling money at all, for their outgoings consisted of quarterly payments to the doctor and bills totted up at the settlement store (open only on Saturdays), with the all-powerful farm manager checking each worker's books.

Delving further into the past, Kay then unearthed the journal she'd inherited of a farm manager, detailing each working day on Saunders Island in the late nineteenth century. Being a record of chores completed, it was no thriller, but a storyline did emerge from between the lines of spidery copperplate in the autumn of 1885:

> *Saturday 25th April 1885.* Hood Maguire McCaskill doing odd jobs. Bad weather. Mercer & Grierson repairing white dinghy. McKenzie cooking. Maguire McCaskill carted 3 loads of peat to the cookhouse.

Sunday 26th April 1885. Rest day. There was a fire lit on the other side. Mercer & Grierson went over in the dinghy and brought W McCaskill over.

Monday 27th April 1885. Grierson & Mercer working at the white dinghy. Maguire part day digging potatoes. McCaskill gathering up horses brought home 3 loads of peat. McKenzie cooking. Hood not at work. Refused to work.

Tuesday 28th April 1885. Grierson after breakfast went for sheep and killing 7 for consumption. Mercer working at the white dinghy afternoon. Myself Mercer Maguire went around in the black boat to drag for the moorings blowing too hard. McCaskill away in the camp looking up stray horses. McKenzie cooking . . .

Monday 4th May 1885. Grierson away for sheep and killing for consumption. Mercer Maguire McCaskill over to the other side landed Hood *for good.*

As I lay in the bath that night, I wondered what became of Hood. That final mention of him in the journal saw him stranded at the northern coast of West Falkland, at the start of winter, without companions, job or job reference. Perhaps that was the day he ventured forth, a spring in his step, to other farms, Port Stanley, a ship to New Zealand, a flourishing career and a beautiful wife, a street named after him in Auckland . . . Perhaps not. And what had pushed him to the point of bluntly refusing to work? Maybe he was just a surly, selfish, work-shy git, maybe he was lovelorn for Maguire or allergic to W. McCaskill. I preferred to think that he'd cracked, that he'd simply had enough of wet, windswept drudgery, of cutting peat, mending fences, killing sheep, of being able to look forward only to yet another ghastly meal cooked by McKenzie. Because that's what I would have done if I'd been him. Born here and a hundred years earlier, by the age I'd reached (thirty-eight) I'd have been a ragged alcoholic. No – I'd have been long dead.

Pink and clean and warm, I stepped out of the bath, wrapped a thick, soft towel around myself and absent-mindedly watched the steaming water spiral down the plughole the wrong way.

When Hood got the push, the Falklands had been in British hands for just fifty-two years, and it would be seven years before the islands became officially part of the empire as a crown colony. British and then Dutch sailors had sighted the islands long before, at the end of the sixteenth century, and the honour of being the first person to set foot on the last islands of any size to have remained virgin territory (save for Antarctica) probably belongs to Captain John Strong in 1690. Ownership of the place was disputed – motivated only by simple, knee-jerk territorialism – for the next century and a half by the French, the British and the Spanish, who all tried to establish settlements and kick out the others. Argentina's dodgy claim to the Malvinas is based on its having had a settlement and a penal colony here (although Britain still claimed the islands) for over a decade after 1820, until the United States Navy kicked the Argentinians out, accusing them, flamboyantly, of piracy. (The Argentinians also claim rightful ownership of the islands because they inherited the possessions of the old Spanish Viceroyalty of the River Plate – a claim which would then logically allow Argentina to repossess Uruguay, Paraguay, Chile and Bolivia.)

The British returned to colonise the islands in 1833, the year when Charles Darwin dropped by on the *Beagle*. The first governor was appointed in 1841, and four years later the British shoved up a turf hut and a wooden cottage beside a promising harbour, claimed the pair formed the islands' capital and christened this metropolis Port Stanley, after an obscure peer who happened to be UnderSecretary for the Colonies at the time.

Several of Port Stanley's earliest timber-framed buildings still stand, and, courtesy of the purity of the air, are in remarkably good condition, as I found out during a guided tour of the town's Victoriana. My guide was Jane Cameron, who works as the islands' archivist, heritage expert and, curiously, lighthouse officer. We met at her office on the harbourfront in a small and undistinguishedlooking bungalow which, she told me, was actually a construction of tremendous historical import, having been built in the 1840s and used as temporary accommodation for new settlers, then as a school, then as a hospital and then as a Theatre Royal.

She led me around Port Stanley, pointing out the astonishingly well-preserved Central Stores, the police station (originally a Victorian prison and with the antique cells to prove it), the town's first cottages, shipped out in kit form, and the bright blue Tabernacle – a church that was also shipped out in kit form and, since the kit had to conform to nineteenth-century colonial specifications, containing corrugated-iron walls that reached six feet underground to prevent hostile, pagan natives tunnelling inside.

I struggled to keep up with Jane as she trotted ahead, flinging her arms around to express joy at the sight of an original chimney, despair as some cladding hoved into view. Hers was a one-woman campaign to preserve the islands' heritage – the brightly painted roofs, the weatherboarding, the Victorian police station, the homes fashioned from Second World War Nissen huts . . . She knew she was up against it because many islanders weren't used to thinking that what they had was worth preserving, and now that people had more money they were, understandably enough, doing up their old cottages.

But she had her enormous and infectious enthusiasm going for her, and real hope. As I admired the disused Central Stores building and tried to imagine it renovated according to Jane's vision, she whirled around, her arms spread wide. 'The great advantage of a small place is that you *can* change things, you *can* make a difference.' She glowed with excitement. 'A lot of people here, their sense of the past is linked to Britain. But we have to have our own sense of identity if we are going to go down the route of independence.'

She'd said it – the 'I' word. Rumours that islanders had begun to hanker after independence, in so far as they had registered in Britain at all, had been met with spluttering disbelief. The reaction back home to any mention of a Falklands free state can be summarised, approximately, as follows: 'After we saved you from the Argies? After hundreds of our boys died? And now you Bennies have cottoned on to the possibility of oil and you think you might get rich on your own? Get. To. Fuck.'

The reality is much more encouraging than it seems. Yes, many islanders are thinking about independence; however, that is a symptom not of criminal ingratitude but of a new self-confidence. (On the contrary, when they do bring themselves to talk about the conflict in '82, islanders show that they are often still badly affected by it, and even those who weren't as traumatised as John Fowler are afflicted by guilt that men died for them.) In addition,

Falkland islanders think of independence as a comfortingly theoretical prospect, something to hope might be achieved far in the future – fifty years' time was the usual airy estimate. And the independence they mean would sensibly involve the Falklands graduating from an imperial possession to become a grown-up member of the Commonwealth. Or, more accurately, a late-teenage member of the Commonwealth, since the Falklands would still rely on the mother country to provide protection in an emergency.

Not at all surprisingly, islanders remain sternly pro-British: portraits of the royal family (and of course HRH Margaret Thatcher) adorn walls; one patriot has even painted a Union Jack on the roof of his house in Stanley, and when President Menem recently offered islanders cash (figures vary from £100,000 to £1 million a head) in exchange for Argentinian sovereignty, the overwhelming response was to tell him to put the money where the sun don't shine. (Interestingly, the scheme was the stunted brainchild of Professor Sir Alan Walters, who had become an adviser to Menem after having been Thatcher's favourite economic and political guru.)

Independence would also offer a much more feasible solution to the issue of sovereignty. Officially, that issue ceased to exist in '82, certainly as far as the British are concerned. When I pressed him on the question of what Britain would do if the Argentinians attempted another invasion, the newly installed Governor of the Falklands, Richard Ralph, bullishly assured me that it wouldn't happen and if it did the Argies would get another bloody nose. But, although the war sets a discouraging precedent for Buenos Aires, the Malvinas malarkey is still part of Argentinian political folklore. Plus, whereas the Argentinians' invasion of '82 was inspired by the need to distract public attention from the wreckage that was the domestic economy and get patriotic crowds back in the streets waving flags and chanting acclaim for General Galtieri, now there is a far more tempting incentive to claim ownership of the islands. Because now the islands are quite prosperous. And likely to get a lot more prosperous. Maybe even more prosperous than Kuwait. Following scientific analyses of the seabed, seismic surveys and whathaveyous, the gloomiest pessimists in the industry have now conceded that the Falklands is surrounded by huge oil fields which could well make this the country with by far the highest per-capita GNP in the world.

The prospect of oil doesn't have any islanders browsing through catalogues of racehorses. Some would much rather that the results of the seismic surveys had been a resounding zilch. They fear another invasion – from Shell, Mobil & co. this time – and, anyway, they're doing rather nicely, thank you, without any rigs or refineries seeing to the peace and quiet.

The current prosperity of the Falklands was unimaginable before the war, when the islands were still suffering a near-feudal economy, one dominated by the Falkland Islands Company – an absentee landlord that owned the West Store (just about the entire retail market), most of the land and most of the farmworkers, whose economic status was a millimetre above that of serfs.

As a traditional, neglected and abused colony, of interest only to shareholders of the Falkland Islands Company, stamp collectors and the mad axemen of the Argentinian military junta, the Falklands had a matching political structure, in which the governor, appointed by Whitehall, figured prominently. Thanks to the new constitution drawn up in 1985, the islanders now have a fully functioning democracy. The eight elected councillors nominate three of their number to the Executive Council, where they join the non-elected chief executive and the financial secretary. The governor (still unelected of course) presides over the Executive Council and can, in theory, overrule it, but that would happen only if it decided to do something like make it an offence punishable by death to have curly hair. His role is confined to chairing committees, getting his photo in the *Penguin News* as he tries out a new tractor or meets a dignitary at MPA, and liaising with Whitehall over the two areas still run from Britain – defence and foreign policy.

Very soon, the rookie politicians had a windfall to cope with. In 1986 a 150-mile fishery protection zone was established round the islands and the Spanish, Korean and Polish ships which trawled Falkland waters for squid now had to pay a licence to do so. Within two years, the gross national product, previously made up of a few million pounds from sheep-shearing and a couple of bob from stamps, trebled to £20 million a year. In 1995 the Falklands' GNP was £35 million.

The chap who oversees this boom economy as well as the civil service which employs about half the Falklands' workforce, is

Andrew Gurr, the chief executive. He was previously employed running a Training and Enterprise Council in Cheshire and got this job – roughly equivalent to that of prime minister – by replying to an advert in the appointments pages of *The Times*. A dapper figure sporting a grey moustache, blazer and slacks, he looked like the kind of middle-aged, upper-middle manager who is proud of his Audi and his still-sprightly serve–volley game. He also looked as though he was thoroughly enjoying this extraordinary career opportunity. He was halfway through a three-year contract and not sure about what to do after his time was up: 'you run a country – what do you do next?'

When I met him in his office, I was busy thinking of probing questions to ask about the Falklands' probable oil bonanza, but he seemed much less concerned about the issue. 'The oil companies tell us we can make as much or as little as we like,' he said in an offhand sort of way before asking if I'd like a coffee.

I was not to be put off in my relentless pursuit of the story. 'What are we talking timescale-wise?' I probed.

'Drilling might start in the summer of '97.'

'How many rigs?'

He shrugged contentedly. 'Maybe one for four or five years. If it discovers oil, there may be other rigs . . .'

'And what about the danger to the environment?'

'We're very aware of that. Actually, you could hide an oil refinery in the Falklands, but I don't think it will come to that.'

'No?'

'No.'

'Oh.'

He smiled. 'I really doubt very much that we'll emerge as the Aberdeen of the South Atlantic.'

I was attacked by a fleeting image of Port Stanley awash with Texans and incomprehensible natives with a fondness for deep-fried Mars Bars. 'That's very good news,' I said and let him move on to the evidently much more pressing topic of land reform. Which for your sake and mine, I shall deal with very briefly.

Pre-'82: sheep ranching on land owned by Falkland Islands Company. Two reports by Lord Shackleton recommend sub-division and diversification but bugger all done about it, despite fact that wool price falling. Seven hundred thousand sheep, sounds a lot, but isn't because spread over three million acres. Grass not nutritious.

Since '82: Falkland Islands Company monopoly gone. Most land now owned by individual farmers and government-owned company, Falkland Landholdings Limited, but still almost entirely sheep ranching, except on smaller and therefore less profitable scale. Only chance of long-term development comes from government – that is, Falkland Landholdings Limited, which wants to see daring innovations. For example, build more fences, plant trees, improve quality of primeval soil (lacks some kinds of bacteria to break it down), raise sheep for mutton as well as wool, raise cattle (at present, MPA garrison gets beef from Chile, shipped to Britain and flown back down here), establish dairy farming.

These sound like pretty good ideas and – a sign of these more enlightened times – the plans take due account of environmental stuff. But, according to one prominent islander (who has to remain nameless since he wants to stay on good terms with the Chief Executive), 'the jury's still out on Gurr' because locals are conservatively sceptical about his proposals and they mistrust his (relatively) slick style. I think Gurr also made a tactical error by including in one of his reports alternative visions of the Falklands in 2050. In Gurr's pessimistic scenario, two intrepid Chilean historians are making an expensive and laborious visit to the almost deserted hamlet of North Arm, to study the settlement's decline – a result of the collapse of squid-fishing, the discovery that oil extraction was unfeasible, and the fierce competition in the wool market after Australian genetic engineers came up with a new superfleece. The happy-smiley scenario sees North Arm in 2050 having increased its present population tenfold to 450 – not only farmers of sheep, pigs and cattle but the artists, poets and philosophers who are obliged to turn up in all utopian visions. There's a primary school, a road, a hotel for the thriving tourist trade, a branch of Sainsbury's International selling tropical fruit grown in Stanley, a market garden, a forest, a sawmill and a furniture factory. Five farm owners are sitting in the village's pub, sipping locally brewed ale and chatting to a wool agent in Bradford via a satellite video link. I found all this rather sweet and even a bit daring and inspirational, but for a lot of islanders Gurr's flights of fancy went down like a rat sandwich.

Uninspirable locals are not the only obstacle Gurr faces as he struggles to boldly go into a glorious future. The Falklands' private sector is laughably weak, the population's simply too small to support specialised services, tourism has limited potential (because, as he said, here especially, 'tourism destroys tourism' – the current boom has 250 tourists a year, and Gurr envisaged a ceiling of 400), and it is very difficult to act on necessary but controversial decisions in such a small community. He mentioned a recent case when a couple on West Falkland applied to the government for help when their house burned down. That help was refused but only after great debate, because, although it was their problem and their fault that they were uninsured, the instinct was to help two well-known and well-liked people.

That this couple expected to be bailed out by the government is also significant, for a racist but convincing summary of the Falkland islanders is that, after decades of being bossed about and patted on the head by farm managers and governors, they lack oomph, gumption and get-up-and-go. How else to explain the fact that, when islanders used to emigrate, they almost all ended up in either Auckland or Southampton? Or, more pertinently, that shoving up some fences and introducing some cows are seen as bold, dangerous measures? Or that they are happy to collect money for fishing licences but it's the Spanish and Koreans who are collecting the big money by actually doing the fishing which only a couple of islanders have dared have a go at? Or that the casualty rate for new businesses, such as the bedevilled venture of setting up a wool mill in Fox Bay, is very high? And that no one knows how high because the Falkland Islands Development Corporation hasn't kept proper records?

Perhaps I'm being harsh, but it did strike me as depressing that one of the newest ventures here was a knitwear firm (I mean, really, how come a country with an annual wool clip of 2.7 million kilos didn't have even a very small knitwear industry?) and that this was set up only on the initiative of Jeff Banks after he had visited the islands for his telly programme, *The Clothes Show*.

Banks' idea was to establish an operation whereby people all over the islands would knit individual and initialled squares, using the wonderfully soft and strong local wool (spun at the revitalised mill in Fox Bay), which would then be stitched together. I visited the headquarters of the resulting enterprise, The Falklander, in the converted church of the convent school, just behind Jane Cameron's favourite Victorian police station. The place was a jumble of half-finished sweaters and boxes of squares. I was greeted by three cheery though harassed women. Margaret, a friendly soul who seemed to be in charge of the place, gave me a short guided tour. She explained that she and Dot and Marilyn over there were the three full-time workers and that she had over sixty islanders, such as Bessie Murphy, Biffo Evans and Sister Bridie Farrelly, knitting in their spare time.

Though very much a fan of the plain, self-coloured jersey, I asked if I could buy a multifariously patterned Falklander as a souvenir but decided to stick to the postcards when Margaret told me the 'factory' price was £197. In reply to my look of horror, she assured me that the sweaters had passed the test of the knit-pickers at the *Clothes Show*'s exhibition in Birmingham, that nearly 700 a year were now being produced and that they were beginning to think about getting a UK agent. Maybe even some kind of mail-order thing . . . I really liked Margaret and Dot and Marilyn, and it was good to see something happen here, but even so I came away thinking that I wouldn't lay any bets on The Falklander managing to prosper or perhaps survive at all with such restricted resources and that fatal absence of entrepreneurial cunning.

Dodgy though its long-term future looked to me, The Falklander is one of several encouraging developments. Others include the growing number of immigrants from Britain, drawn here by the quality of life and the chance to escape fear for their kids. (Treats which incomers confess to missing include getting their hair done, Radio 1 and being able to go shopping.) Then there was the radio-telephone link being complemented by a normal telephone system which started in 1989, so that callers can now gossip in secret and chat to the doctor about their prostate trouble without fearing that dozens of compatriots are listening in. Another sign of growing affluence has increased by 1,000 per cent since the war – crime.

But the most dramatic development of all has been in schooling. So, following my amicable and completely scoopless interview with Andrew Gurr, I fought against the wind to walk to the Education Department. I'd passed it many times before since it was next door to the Upland Goose, but I'd assumed it was someone's house. Nice conservatory.

The Director of Education's office is in what must once have been the sitting room. Phyl Rendell was a handsome woman in her mid-forties who radiated enthusiasm as if she was trying to sell it. The next feature I noticed was that she didn't have a Falklands accent. She explained that, although she was born and bred here, her family had been fairly well-to-do (her father had been a farm manager), so she'd been sent off to boarding school in Derbyshire, returning on holiday only once every three years. (She was very homesick at first, and desperately missed the sea and the farm animals.) Unlike many of her friends, she'd come back for good when she was twenty-four, and was now doing her best to make sure that children under her charge would have a much better time of it than her generation did.

She oversees forty teachers, six of these being hardy types who travel from farm to farm, teaching younger children in Camp. When they reach secondary-school age, Camp kids board in Stanley. A-level students then have to be packed off to a sixth-form college in Winchester. There were currently thirty-seven students studying abroad for A-levels and degrees – a far healthier number than before '82, when there were only two scholarships a year for children wanting anything more than the odd O-level. 'The war changed people's attitudes,' Phyl Rendell explained. 'There was a tremendous increase in confidence. And we owe it to those who died – on both sides – to make this place a success. Parents here value education now. Last year the school-leaving age was raised from fifteen to sixteen, without any parental opposition.'

Compulsory schooling until sixteen? It wasn't much to shout about – after all, this became the leaving age in Britain back in 1972. I think my ho-hum reaction was betrayed by my expression – one supercilious eyebrow raised in the manner of Roger Moore, a slight sneer twitching at my mouth – because Phyl Rendell promptly told me to get lost. Not in so many words, for what she actually did was smile nicely and ask, 'Have you visited the new school?'

I hadn't and it was clearly something I ought to do, so off I trudged again, back the way I had come but still unaccountably fighting against the wind, in the direction of Government House. I tramped past a playing field, where, despite the gale, a dozen Chilean fishermen were playing fancy but inept football and one younger Chilean fisherman had forsaken the game to chat up a neatly uniformed girl. Looking down on the playing field was the school – a butterscotch-coloured building that had cost the islanders £15 million to build. Stepping inside the foyer, I asked a helpful-looking woman if she could tell me where to find the head teacher.

'Of course I can,' she said. 'She's standing in front of you. Judith Crowe,' she said, shaking my hand.

She set off to show me round her school, with the kind of excited pride I had until then thought the preserve of new homeowners. This time my reaction was just what she'd been hoping for, because I could only stammer with disbelief. Here was the school and community library with its art exhibition and 16,000 volumes. Here were the glistening science classrooms. And through this door the main computer room – thirty-four terminals for the 150 pupils. Over here we had the super swimming-pool, and down there were some adults using the gym. Yes, that was Andrew Gurr playing tennis.

'How does this compare to the old school?'

'I don't honestly know. This school opened in 1992 and I arrived here a year later.'

'Where did you used to teach?'

'A small school in rural Lincolnshire.'

'It's a bit of an upheaval, isn't it?'

'Yes it is.'

'So why did you come here?'

She took a deep breath. 'You won't write this down, will you?'

'Trust me.'

'I applied for this job after the Tories won the last election. I just got fed up making teachers redundant. We used to have to hire equipment and even that service was about to be stopped. But here – well, take a look.'

She opened another door to show off a domestic-science classroom. It wouldn't have looked out of place in one of Terence Conran's restaurants.

'And how different is it teaching here? Apart from the resources.'

'The pupils were shyer. To begin with, at least. But there was no us-and-them divide between the children and the staff. That's terrific. And there's no difference in the curriculum because we teach GCSEs. Usually adapted a little bit – we do some local history, for example, and although they have to learn Castilian Spanish, we have a Chilean teacher who also does South American Spanish. But there are only little things that seem out of place here.'

'Such as?'

'Well, the Business Studies exam had a question about health and safety legislation, which didn't mean much here. And we had another tricky one in Geography.'

'What was the topic?'

'Roundabouts.'

I found myself wishing Judith good luck when I left. I might as well have wished Paul McCartney to get lucky on the Lottery. I made my way down some steps to the car park and stopped for a moment to take some notes. It was while I was leaning on a Land Rover to scribble that it occurred to me that there was something odd about my surroundings. There was not a scrap of litter and not a line of graffiti. I flipped my notebook shut and performed a hammy double-take. The Land Rover's front seat was strewn with cassettes, sweets and two packs of cigarettes. And the window was completely wound down.

I arrived back at Kay's, where Heather and Stephan had just turned up. Having survived several days out at Volunteer Point and the yomp back to Stanley, they were devouring head-sized wedges of home-made sponge. They waxed lyrical about the joys of camping – what a ludicrous noun to use in any discussion of camping, far less in the plural – and vied with each other to tell me all about the starlit nights, the penguins and . . . no, that was about it. To celebrate their return and to commemorate what was my last evening in the Falklands, we had promised each other to paint the town red this evening, or at least splash some emulsion around. But the fresh air and the exercise the three of us had experienced in the day – okay, they had walked the best part of fifty miles and I had pottered to and fro around the town, but they were younger – had done for us all. After Kay's last meal (a weightwatcher's nightmare of cauliflower cheese, pyramid of vegetables, apple tart and cream), I lacked the energy even to roll down to the Upland Goose, so I focused instead on shattering the pain barrier to climb upstairs to pack. Last to be crammed in the holdall was the defiled copy of *Middlemarch*. How odd to think that I'd been worried about finishing it too quickly. During my week here, when I'd turned into a somniac, the bookmark had moved on all of ten pages (one of which featured a whole page underlined in red and, in the margin, the inexplicable query, 'Spinozan?'). Still, I would make up good ground with two pointless hours in the departure lounge tomorrow and then eighteen more stuck in a plane next to some pubescent private.

I set the alarm for 6.30. The flight was at eleven, but to conform to regulations the mini-bus would be picking me up at seven. Cursing the defrocked primary-school teachers who evidently ran the RAF, I lay down for a moment to have a think about the Falklands and the next thing I knew I was in a classroom full of gleaming cookers, naked but for a beanbag, and trying to hide from Jeff Banks.

The scene at MPA the next morning was a pretty good replica of the scene at Brize Norton the week before. This time, though, some passengers provided glaring exceptions to the rule of crop-haired uniformity – a middle-aged mum and dad with two small children were conspicuously different, as was a small crowd of scientists returning from polar exile with the British Antarctic Survey. Almost all of the scientists were in their early twenties but, like the group I had eavesdropped on in the Upland Goose, it wasn't so much their rugby shirts as their jovial confidence which made it only too easy to tell them apart from their near-contemporaries in the services.

It may come as a shock to those non-scientists who assume that anyone who knows the meaning of H_2SO_4 will be condemned to nurturing a chinstrap beard and buying their jeans from Littlewoods that only one of the scientists looked odd. Actually, he didn't look odd so much as insane, since he had celebrated his move towards the equator by kitting himself out in T-shirt and shorts, and his bare toes were wiggling in flip-flops.

He was some two decades older than his colleagues and Australian. I offer this as incidental biographical background rather than by way of an explanation for his dress code, and I can do so because, in strict accordance with the loony-on-the-bus syndrome, he chose me to stand next to in the long, long queue for the security check.

'Going far?' he said.

'. . .'

'Pom?'

'Scottish.'

'Hey – you don't know any of the guys at the Royal Observatory in Edinburgh?'

'That's correct.' I found myself staring down at the face of this little beach bum, whose eyes were smiling back up and whose lips were stretched in an eager, infectious grin, and I struggled for something to say. 'But I have got a new pair of binoculars,' I said.

'Hey – grite! Do they hev a diagonalised hemiltonium?'

I opted for the kind of all-purpose response – minuscule head-shake, raised eyebrows and glottal grunt – you have to make when, having stuffed clamps and cotton-wool in your mouth, the dentist asks what you make of the rumours about Prince Andrew.

'Course I didn't hev room for too much of me own gear. But I'm gled I took the cemcorder. It came in useful, specially when I god fed up with the younger guys larking around at the research station. You know whad I did?'

He grinned excitedly at me, like a little boy showing his chums one of his big brother's bare-lady magazines.

'No, what was that?'

'Rigged up a liddle saddelite dish, god on the internet, e-mailed me girlfriend, she's up in the Arctic, rigged up a programme, sent her the stuff I filmed for her down the line.'

My father used to be a physics teacher, so from hard-won childhood experience I knew which of the many questions I didn't know the answer to I should now ask. 'What's your girlfriend doing in the Arctic?'

'Same as me.' He grinned. 'Estrophysics.'

'So what were you doing down in the Antarctic?'

'Sedding up a telescope at the South Pole.'

What do you say to that? I'll tell you what you don't say and that's what I said next to show that I was a Renaissance man.

'But is that kind of thing needed any more now that we've got the Hubble telescope?'

'Ah!' His grin stretched even further. 'You know about scions! Well, with a terrestrial insdrumint . . .'

Some time later, my hand baggage, jacket, wallet, keys, loose change and gum having passed muster at the security check, I discovered a free seat in the departure lounge and settled down for the two-hour wait before we all boarded the plane. I whiled away the time examining the senile football results in the *People*, reading about Mr Featherstone's funeral, watching the *Blackadder* video and regularly glancing across at the most glaring exception of all to the squaddy rule. She was very pretty, about thirty I guessed, had long, blonde, demi-permed hair, and had perched on her lap a stuffed panda large enough for her to be able to rest her chin on its head. She looked, not surprisingly in this high-testosterone context, slightly nervous. An NCO's wife. Hairdresser. Lived in Aldershot.

Mr Featherstone's mysterious heir had caused all manner of ructions and Mr Casaubon was coping with Lydgate's diagnosis of his heart condition by the time the flight was called. We trooped out to be buffeted by the wind. At the top of the steps to the Tristar I stopped for a moment to savour a last gust from a westerly, then remembered just in time not to give one of my devastatingly charming smiles to the member of the cabin crew who checked my boarding pass.

I must have mistranslated his grunt. I consulted my boarding pass again and peered at the seat number above me. 8E, right enough.

'Excuse me, I think that's my seat.'

'Oh, I'm sorry.' She picked up the large stuffed panda sitting beside her and manoeuvred across to cram the creature into the overhead locker, while I pretended to read the safety instruction sheet. An eighteen-hour flight ahead. With any luck, though, the weather would be really bad at Ascension, and we'd have to turn back and try all over again.

'I did have a laugh with the man at the airport.'

What man? Who? Why?

'He was saying he'd have to give Panda a boarding pass of his own.'

'Hah!'

'I got this little chap as a souvenir as well.'

'Oh. He's, er, very sweet.'

'Isn't he?' She put the toy penguin back between her feet and pulled the seat-belt tight. 'Clunk click.'

'Every trip.'

We taxied to the end of the runway, where we loitered for some time because, as the same head boy/pilot told us, we'd be given a send-off by Albert the Hercules, who would soon do a flypast. Eventually there was a brief growling roar above us and we prepared for take-off.

'I'm always scared at this bit.'

'Really, there's nothing to be frightened of,' I said, discreetly wiping my palms on my legs.

The Falklands flashed past us for a few seconds before we hurtled into thick cloud. Lydgate was discussing his plans for the hospital with Dorothea when I secured a drink.

'Whisky,' observed my travelling companion. 'Makes you frisky.'

Damn. I should have chosen a lager. 'So,' I said, 'were you down here for long?'

'Three weeks.'

'And when is your husband's time up here?'

'Husband? Oh, I see . . . No, I was visiting my mum.'

'Your mum?'

'Yes, she still loves the place. First time I've been back though for ten years. But it was good – seeing Mum, catching up on some old friends. And I visited my dad's grave.' She nodded her head reflectively. 'No, it was good.'

Time to kill off the NCO and incinerate the Heads We Do salon in Aldershot. 'So you're really an islander?'

'Well, yes, but I haven't lived here for years.' She smiled shyly and sipped at her mineral water. 'I live in Kent now. I'm a kind of secretary for this millionaire who's got this big estate, and I live in a cottage on it, so I'm right in the country. It's lovely. And the best thing is, I've lots of room for my sanctuary.'

'Sanctuary.'

She began to tick off her fingers. 'I've got five cats, four kittens, two dogs, guinea pigs, rabbits, a chipmunk, and an albino chinchilla. Everyone around knows about it, so if they find a hedgehog that's been knocked down or something, they bring him to me.'

'And, um, where was home in the Falklands?'

'Port San Carlos.'

'Oh, I met a guy from there. He said he spent the whole of the war in a foxhole.'

'That's right.'

'You know him?'

'Well, you haven't told me his name, but that's not what I meant.'

'Wait a minute. You mean that you were there during the war and that you—'

'Yes. We all did.'

'Fucking hell.'

'Language! Yes, I'd just started work in '82. I was only seventeen and I was terrified.'

'Anyone would be.'

'Well, no, I was going to say that I was terrified because I'd just started work as a teacher in Camp. And there was me, not much older than the children, and I was having to go from farm to farm, and some of the parents just thought it was a waste of time when the kids could be out working. And if you didn't like the food they gave you, well, tough. And I was always having to swot up on the lessons in the evening . . .'

'But what was it like in the war?'

'Well, you know . . .'

'That's just it. I don't. So what was the war like?'

She looked away and then down at the penguin. 'Well . . . Really, I was worried a lot of the time about my rabbit.'

'Did the Argies want to eat it?'

'No, no, no. The Argentinian soldiers used to give me food for it. And after they went, the paratroopers did the same.'

'Your rabbit survived then?'

'Yes! But the awful thing was, he died four months after the war.'

'I'm sorry to hear that.'

'He ate a plastic bag. Poor little thing.'

'But the war,' I said. 'Port San Carlos. That was Bomb Alley. That was . . . there was a landing at Port San Carlos.'

'Yes.'

'And were you there?'

'Yes.'

'In your foxhole.'

'. . . Yes.'

'While it happened.'

'. . . Yes.'

'I'm sorry . . . I realise . . . But would you mind telling me a bit about what it was like?'

She sipped at her water. I sipped at my Bell's. She sipped at her water again. She carefully adjusted the position of the penguin with her feet. She fiddled with her watchstrap.

'The Argentinians were on the hill above us,' she said eventually. 'And the beach was down in front of us.' She tried to take another sip of water but the glass was empty. 'There was one time when they were shooting at the helicopters. Excuse me. Could I have some more water, please?'

'Certainly, madam,' replied a nearby second-row forward.

'When! Thank you.'

'They were shooting at the helicopters . . .'

'Yes.' She drank some water and wiped her mouth and paused yet again. 'One of them crashed. I could see soldiers swimming for the shore. The Argentinians just kept on shooting at them. Then I could see that the pilot was really struggling on to the beach. They were shooting at him too, though anyone could tell he was wounded. My friend and I, we were watching it all from the foxhole. Then we ran down to the beach. It's funny, I didn't think about it at the time. There were bullets hitting the sand all around us. We got to the pilot and gave him the kiss of life. I'd done first-aid training, you see . . . We carried him off to one of the nearby houses . . . I got a really nice letter from his wife after the war.'

'Of course. You saved his life.'

She shook her head. 'He had terrible stomach injuries. All I could do was hold him.'

'I'm . . .'

She stared at her mineral water. 'Yes. Yes, it was a really nice letter.'

'Meal? Sir, madam?'

Yet another man whose forearm was the colour and girth of a chimney pot handed us our shoeboxes. Tuna roll, Blue Riband, apple, slice of cherry cake. Suzanne and I chatted away – about her animal sanctuary, my expedition to see the penguins, her millionaire boss, the UEFA Cup campaign of Raith Rovers. After a while, it did occur to me that maybe she was expressing only polite interest in my fairly comprehensive analysis of Danny Lennon's midfield play, so I managed to mumble an apology before nodding off, having bored myself to sleep.

Normally, I hate waking on public transport. It used to be okay, in the days when I didn't snore or dribble, and before that time on the train when my pal Brian fell asleep and we had to shake him violently after he yelled out, 'Please not again, Daddy!' Now, though, after the usual fearful start, I managed to reflect that it was actually quite nice to wake with my head lolling on Suzanne's shoulder. We'd already begun our descent towards Ascension Island, where we were again herded into the airport pen for an hour while the plane was refuelled and we gulped Coke and lager in the sticky evening heat. With my jersey and padded jacket now bundled on an airport picnic table, I began to appreciate the foresight of the astrophysicist, who flip-flopped over and excitedly pointed out a gleaming Venus and then Orion, sparkling and turned on its side.

That stopover seemed even more surreal by the morning when we finally stepped out at Brize Norton and into a raw, windless, dirty cold. I pecked Suzanne goodbye. Suitcase in one hand, panda in the other, she made her way off to the arms of a waiting man. The astrophysicist and I exchanged addresses which, we admitted, we'd probably never write to or call on but which, we admitted, it was heartening to exchange. I milled around, groggy and shivering, idly watching a soundless TV. A breakfast weatherwoman seemed to be apologising for the temperatures she was sticking on the map. And it looked freezing on the outside broadcast that followed from some-where I couldn't quite recognise in Scotland.

After a long while, the coach condescended to arrive. It took us through a landscape of houses and farms and villages and industrial estates and trees and fields and cows and horses and people – God, there was so much of everything – to the railway station at Swindon, where jet-lag and a week in the Falklands made me agitated at having to join a short queue to buy a ticket.

The whole place was so shabby and odd. And the newspapers were very strange. I stared at them stupidly. Why did they all look like that?

Only much later did I realise that the comparison was glib and wrong-headed. But for now I had to think back to Tania and her parentless pony trek with her pals, and all those islanders who revelled in letting their kids disappear on their own over the horizon. Because now, looking at the newsagent's array of papers with all the front pages carrying that classroom photograph of beautiful, eager, delighted faces, I was slowly beginning to realise why breakfast television had been showing an outside broadcast from Dunblane.

Chapter Four

The World's Biggest Pebble: Gibraltar

The one grand feature of La Linea de la Concepción is its name. La Linea, as it is usually called, lies at the southern tip of Spain but it could easily pass muster as one of the less favoured towns in Mexico. I stumbled over cracked pavements, past grim blocks of flats and squalid cottages and on to the beach, where murky wavelets flopped over litter and died. I kicked a can towards one of the many broken boats marooned on the beach and wondered if a geographer might argue that, technically, La Linea marks the southern boundary of the Costa del Sol. But the world of difference between La Linea and the clipped lawns and holiday haciendas of Sotogrande ten miles up the road is that between the third world and the first.

I kept stumbling in the direction of the mountain which rises preposterously at this peninsula's end to cast its shadow over La Linea, and the rest of Spain. From this angle, the sudden grey and white cliffs of the Rock of Gibraltar looked like a vast, stone sail, an elegant shock of nature that made La Linea look even meaner and shabbier.

I bypassed La Linea's small and crumbling sports stadium, where, the previous week, the son of a local cocaine-dealer had been shot in a drugs dispute. The next landmark was a legacy of General Franco – a couple of massive, rotting gun emplacements directed at the Rock. Beyond them was wasteland.

Although it was December, the midday sun was bright and warm, and I was beginning to sweat by the time I had picked my way over broken glass and bricks to reach the next landmark, the border between Spain and the British crown colony of Gibraltar. The rest of the European Community may regard borders as *passé*, but anyone nostalgic for the good old days, when moving from one country into another carried with it a sense of occasion, not to say menace, can find a real, proper territorial boundary at the edge of La Linea's wasteland, where it comes to a sudden stop at a tall fence.

Having sized up the fence, I threw a stick at it. It fell to the ground – the stick, that is, because it was a fairly gentle throw and quite a small stick and the fence was sturdily embedded in concrete. And, I feared, possibly even electrified. Hence the experiment with the stick. Just to make doubly sure, I checked my shoes, which did indeed have rubber soles, and saw that the bit of Spanish wasteland I'd been standing in was, more precisely, a bit of Spanish dogshit. The stick proved useful again. Eventually, I grasped the fence with one hand, narrowly avoiding a big roll of barbed wire decorated with bits of razor, and with the other gave a cheery wave at the surveillance camera which was pointing down at me. Interestingly, the cameras and razory barbed wire were on the Gibraltarian side of the fence. As were the warning signs. I'm not sure how effective a deterrent these signs might be to any marauding Spaniard since they were in English and upside down –

In truth, I had my doubts about the whole security operation because it was unfortunately compromised by the fact that, ten yards to my left, Spanish wasteland became what was probably, beneath the muck and rubbish, Spanish beach, and, very soon after that, Spanish sea. The fence and barbed wire extended rustily out into the water but even I could have doggy-paddled round and smuggled myself into Gibraltar. Only a very strong swimmer could have made it to the Rock itself, for that was about half a mile across the flat isthmus that serves as the runway for Gibraltar's airport.

The plane on the plain at the moment was a British Airways number revving for take-off, its engines frothing up the Mediterranean immediately behind it. The jet shot off behind a clutch of sheds to reappear moments later as it took to the air. I peered through the fence to watch its progress, because planes taking off from Gibraltar have a unique entertainment value. This jet, doubtless bound for London, started off heading due west, then, as it continued its climb, made an abrupt turn to head due south, then another turn to head due east. Only then would it be allowed to enter Spanish airspace and head north.

The plane's rectangular flight path as well as the ferocity of the fence augured ill for the border crossing I was about to make. Inspecting the ground carefully this time, I made my way along the edge of Spain and, this being the world's shortest border, soon arrived at the frontier gates. A long queue of cars and lorries stretched some distance back into La Linea but progress on foot proved to be disarmingly quick. Brandishing my passport like a referee handing out a red card, I was waved through Spain and then waved through into Gibraltar. I seemed to have been teleported from Mexico to King's Lynn. A smart and cheery customs chap bade me a good afternoon as I walked past a poster urging caution with fireworks and out into a clean, neat street where a billboard announced the opening of a new branch of Safeways.

What fun. I decided to have another go. I crossed the road, left Gibraltar, strolled through Spanish customs, entered Spain, left Spain, and went back into Gibraltar. I had passed through six customs posts in the time it takes to cook a very runny boiled egg.

I spent much longer, a hundred yards into Gibraltar, sitting in a taxi and waiting for a set of traffic lights to change from red. It was a long wait because the one road into town crosses the airport runway, and that was about to be used by another jet. After the plane had screamed past us and up – and turned very sharp left – the lights changed to green and the taxi continued its progress over the runway and into the colony. So far, the place seemed to consist of petrol stations. I pointed this out to the driver, who had noticed this phenomenon for himself. He explained that, since everything in Gibraltar was duty-free, shoppers flooded in from Spain, to return with carrier bags bulging with booze and fags and in cars swilling with petrol.

Gibraltar occupies less than three square miles of the Iberian peninsula (it is Britain's smallest remaining colony), so the journey to my hotel on the other side of the town took all of five minutes. Nevertheless, this proved long enough for the taxi-driver to give me many of his opinions on the condition of what is the last colony on the European mainland. His short tutorial began when I asked him casually if Spanish officials still caused queues at the border.

'Fwah. They make people wait two, three hours in a car. Just to annoy us.'

'I see.'

'Six hours sometimes. All that does is prove that they are still our enemies.' He thumped the steering wheel with resolution. 'And they will never win.'

'You want to stay British, then?'

'Fwah. Better than Spanish. But the military's moving out of Hibraltar.' (It was an odd accent, occasional Cockney touches mixed in with a Hispanic sound.) 'You see these dockyards on the right? Used to employ seventy per cent of the people. Now, seven per cent.'

As he negotiated a series of crowded streets and tight bends, he kept up his litany of information. About the Treaty of Utrecht which ceded the colony to Britain in 1713, the colony's paradoxical status in the EC as a member without official representation in Brussels or Strasbourg, the expansion of the offshore financial centre (so that the 30,000 inhabitants are outnumbered by the companies registered here), his loathing of the previous Chief Minister, Sir Joshua Hassan, and devotion to Sir Joshua's successor, Joe Bossano, Bossano's magnificent speeches to the UN Committee on Decolonisation . . .

As we swung round another bend and passed a bar advertising itself as the local branch of the FC Barcelona Supporters' Club, he was scoffing at General Franco's stupidity at closing the border in 1969. 'You know what he side? "Hibraltar will fall like an overripe plum." Fwah! All that happened, the Spanish who worked here had to leave and La Linea had even bigger dole queues.'

He slapped down a couple of gears as the taxi struggled up a steep curve to the hotel, while he explained that recent reports in the British papers about Gibraltar being a money-laundering centre had to be part of a smear campaign orchestrated by the Foreign Office to discredit Bossano, who was a great man. The taxi came to a halt. 'I grew up on the sime street as Joe. He was a little kid but he always had this.' He pointed to his head. 'You here on business?'

'Sort of.'

'Lot of business here.' He winked. 'Enjoy your sty.'

'Thank you.'

After I'd checked in, unpacked and wondered if my room had been used by any of the celebrity guests trumpeted by the hotel brochure (Winston Churchill and Frankie Howerd were two patrons mentioned), I sat out on the balcony and admired the view. A girl was jogging round the Botanic Gardens below. Further down were several blocks of cream-coloured and distinctly Spanish-looking blocks of flats and then the dockyards, empty but for one frigate guarding the colony from attack by the trawlers and tankers parked in the Bay of Algeciras. The *Marie Celeste* was towed in to Gibraltar in 1872. Now it was the waterfront itself that looked deserted.

While I was mooching about back in the room, doing the kind of things you do when you've just arrived in a hotel room – prodding the bed, fingering the stationery inside the big leather folder on the TV, trying to operate the mirrors inside the wardrobe so that I could see my back – something caught my eye. A telephone directory. Not large enough to serve as a lethal weapon, like Birmingham's, but it would definitely deliver a smart blow.

I would like to stress that this is not one of my hobbies or interests, but I did on this one occasion enjoy a browse through the directory. Thirty-six Smiths, thirteen Joneses, seventeen Bossanos, twenty-seven Mifsuds plus Mifsud Electrofreeze and the Mifsud Cumberland Garage, one hundred and one Garcias. I flicked through to see if it listed the number of Sir Joshua Hassan. Indeed it did. The entry for JA Hassan & Partners had ten lines and a fax. His private address was listed twice, once normally, the second in bold: **HASSAN THE HON SIR JOSHUA GBE KCMG QC JP**. I assume he won't mind my revealing the number – 77295.

Sir Joshua's contribution certainly helped, but the local phone company had found other cunning ploys to pad out a directory, serving a smallish town, to metropolitan bulk. One section listed all the numbers in numerical order. (Why?) Another contained Gibraltar's Yellow Pages, where most of the adverts advertised the Yellow Pages. There was a section providing key information about the colony, its history, key attractions, chamber of commerce, etcetera. Over fifty pages offered explanations of how to react to 'service announcements': such as what to do when you heard the phone say, 'Please replace the handset and try again' – the answer being, 'Replace the handset and try again.' Now would you find that degree of public service and consideration just over the border? I think not.

Looking out of the window, I realised that Gibraltar now had something else Spain lacked. Rain. I could see the sun still shining warmly down on La Linea to the north and the countryside beyond the Bay of Algeciras to the west, but this British colony was now cocooned in an authentically British downpour. It's the fault of the Rock, which is so large that it generates its own climate, attracting whistling winds and swirling, sodden clouds that suddenly turn fine days like this into bank-holiday depressions.

While the Spanish continued to frolic about in shirt sleeves and light frocks, I hauled on a jersey and coat for a tour of the town. I trotted damply down the hill, past the local cinema, now showing *Braveheart*, past an arrowed road sign that announced simply 'Spain', and turned into what I reckoned had to be the main street, judging by its busyness and its overhead Christmas decorations. Plus the fact that it was called Main Street. Backing up the taxi-driver's point about Gibraltar's attraction as a massive duty-free centre, most of the shops were selling cartons of cigarettes, litres of spirits and a variety of competitively priced electrical appliances. Far from looking like an airport terminal, though, the place reminded me of a British provincial high street of the early 1960s, before every British provincial high street was pedestrianised and precincted and chainstored into clones of each other. Even the local Marks and Sparks had an old-fashioned frontage. The nearby gents' outfitters was a real period piece, featuring a properly dull window display of mud-coloured sports jackets and, inside, lots of staff and no customers, so that when I walked in, drawn there by nostalgia's magnet, I was immediately pounced on by two salesmen and had to buy a ghastly checked shirt that, a few weeks later, I would wrap in Christmas paper and hand over to my unpleasantly surprised father.

The time travel continued when I escaped the rain by popping into a local café for a late lunch. I hadn't seen a menu like this since childhood. I chose the most exotic dish, a dish so exotic that the menu surrounded it with inverted commas and suffixed an explanation. It was Chicken 'Kiev'. A couple of miles down the road, amid the desolation of La Linea, there had been a host of restaurants where I could have savoured sardines, patatas bravas, garlic mushrooms . . . Ah, well. I took a bite of the chicken and was singed by an explosion of hot mush.

The pain had more or less abated by the evening. This time I played safe and treated myself to dinner in the hotel's restaurant, which looked, by Gibraltarian standards, rather sophisticated. Mind you, so would a mobile burger bar.

First impressions were very favourable – (1) there was no sign of the advertised resident pianist or, indeed, any piano, and (2) two waiters took it upon themselves to guide me to a choice table by the window. But, as is the way with first impressions, they did not last. As soon as I sat down, I realised that these two waiters and their four colleagues outnumbered the diners, and this in a restaurant large enough to accommodate the annual dinner-dance of a major opera company, plus orchestra and back-room staff. As it was, there was one old chap of military aspect sitting behind me and a middle-aged couple in a mutual huff in front of me, and I really couldn't see why one of the many, many other tables was garnished with a Reserved sign.

Having whispered my order (leek and potato soup, swordfish with anchovy butter, half-bottle of white) to the waiter who had given me the menu and then stood resolutely by my side for something to do, I broke open a bread roll, which unfortunately was not equipped with a silencer. A second or two later, the soup arrived. Normally, I eat with the carefree gusto of a hungry hod-carrier, but now I found that, in an effort not to shatter the silence, I was trying to eat the soup by kissing each spoonful.

The old chap of military aspect had no such qualms.

'WHAT WINE DID I HAVE YESTERDAY?' he enquired of one of his waiters.

'The house red, sir.'

'DID I LIKE IT?'

'Very much, sir.'

'SAME AGAIN THEN. AND THE SOUP AND THE SWORDFISH. I LIKE ANCHOVIES.'

'Very good, sir.'

The moment I finished kissing the soup, a hovering waiter whisked away the plate and spoon, with the flourish of a conjuror removing the cloth from his magic table. At the same time, one of his colleagues materialised at my side to serve me with the swordfish and ladle on attendant vegetables. I began to wonder if I had walked into a competition. If so, my lead was being threatened by the old chap of military aspect.

'THANK YOU. VERY GOO— AH . . . YOU, COME BACK. WHERE'S MIH ANCHOVIES?'

'You ordered the swordfish, sir. With anchovy butter.'

'I THOUGHT I ASKED FOR ANCHOVIES.'

'No, sir.'

'GOOD LORD. AND WHAT'S THIS YOU SAY?'

'Swordfish, sir.'

'GOOD LORD.'

Now that he was lagging behind, I could afford to toy with this main course. I tried five, then a dozen chews per fish morsel, and, always wary of clinking, performed a little topiary with the spinach. There – a scale model of the Rock. And, hey presto!, a penis. Even so, when I placed my knife and fork to attention on the empty plate, and a waiter sped in to remove it, my watch told me that it was now sixteen minutes past eight. When I had left my room, my digital alarm clock had read 7:59.

A sweet trolley screeched to a halt and double-parked beside me. Yet another waiter was hastily pointing out a fortress of gateau, gun emplacements of crème caramel . . . I declined and asked for a coffee to accompany my still four-fifths-full half-bottle of white. Just when things seemed to have calmed down, there was a flurry of excitement as three waiters rushed to the door. A very small lady old enough to have been a squeeze of Campbell-Bannerman tottered in and accepted the arm of one of her eager escorts.

'What day is it today?' she asked him in a quivery voice.

'Sunday, madam.'

'Sunday? . . . Sunday?'

'Yes, madam.'

'Do you mean to tell me that yesterday was Saturday?'

'Indeed, madam.'

'And that tomorrow is Monday?'

'Madam.'

'I don't believe a word of it. Now take me to my table.'

This turned out to be, perforce, very near the door. A shame that it wasn't closer to the table occupied by the old chap of military aspect. It would have been nice to see the old lady and the old chap hit it off, have a few drinks, a few laughs. Then forget themselves.

By adopting a regime of ultra-cautious wine-sipping, I managed to extend the restaurant experience until nine o'clock. Then, with the zealous help of several waiters (one to hold my napkin, another to steady the seat as I effected the manoeuvre of rising out of same, a third to guide me to the door), I made my conspicuous exit, uncertain if I felt like a celebrity or the culprit in a Bateman cartoon.

No two doubts about which I felt like a quarter of an hour later when I walked into the Horseshoe Bar. I'd come downtown in search of a bit of nightlife, and the Horseshoe Bar seemed from the outside to be just the kind of lively, happening pub I needed after the restaurant experience. And if those two adjectives evoke a pub that was, on the inside, heaving with tattooed, skinhead, cuboid sailors who were all wearing T-shirts that advertised Guinness or the Devonport Field Gun Crew, and who were all laughing very heartily until they noticed me, then the Horseshoe certainly was both lively and happening. I tried to impersonate someone so afflicted by thirst that he was visiting the pub only as long as it took to admire the naval memorabilia above the gantry, ask and pay for a refreshing pint and then swallow it in three gulps max.

That is actually quite a traditional method of drinking in Gibraltar, because, although it has had the reputation of being a military Butlins, the colony offers the off-duty serviceman little in the way of rest and recreation – that is, there isn't a red-light district – other than hectic sessions on the piss. And that night, because HMS *Illustrious* had docked while I hadn't been looking, there seemed to be a lot of cuboid sailors enjoying very hectic sessions indeed. No pub was quite as terrifying as the Horseshoe (though the Angry Friar came close), but every pub was packed.

Thinking better of spending the rest of the evening trying to chat to drunken sailors, I popped into Safeways (the wee branch on Main Street, the one next to Marks and Sparks, not the new hypermarket), and invested in a litre apiece of Highland spring water and Spanish brandy to make appropriate but not very interesting cocktails back in my hotel room.

Deciding, with no difficulty, to postpone the diluted brandies for a little while, I headed off to the hotel bar, in one last effort at trying out Gibraltar's nightlife. The only other customers were eight chaps who were all grasping tumblers of whisky in that self-conscious way men have when they are playing the parts of relaxed sophisticates by grasping tumblers of whisky. I suspect that they were officers from HMS *Illustrious*, because they were talking utter nonsense.

'So he had the fo'c'sl'e gibleted.'

'What, without spinnakering?'

'Didn't even check the aft.'

'Then how on earth did he boom with the leeward?'

'Well, this is it.'

I was woken the next morning by the sound of rain and helicopters whirring over HMS *Illustrious*. The sun soon came out but the helicopters kept on buzzing fussily overhead, for no reason that I could see other than to spend my tax for the next three years. And yours. It wasn't worth the cost, but I did quite enjoy the bit when they flew a mile north to what must have been the edge of Spanish airspace, and jinked about naughtily before executing a ninety-degree turn to stay within British-owned sky.

While I hauled on my clothes, I gave myself a proper talking-to. I was being ridiculous, I was going to do what I had to do, and I was going to enjoy it whether I liked it or not, was that clear? Right then. Cable car? Cable car! I'd give me cable car.

What could be simpler? I just walked down the road to the station thingy, handed my money over to one man, and he handed back a ticket. I sauntered over to another man, he inspected my ticket, and ushered me in. I was the only customer . . . but that would only make it all the more exciting, wouldn't it?

The two men shouted a few pleasantries at each other in what sounded very much like Spanish before the second man strolled in beside me, pulled the door shut and pressed a button. The cable car lurched off and within moments we had climbed high above the town. Within a few more moments we had come to an abrupt halt and were swinging like a metronome in the suddenly vigorous wind. I stared at my shoes, concentrated on taking very deep breaths and performed an enquiring glance at the cable-car man, in the manner, I hoped, of someone smoothly letting it be known that he was ready to pay the bill. The cable-car man in turn glanced a nod upwards. I followed the direction of his header and gathered that we had stopped because, high above us, the downward-bound cable car had also stopped, to pick up some passengers at a little midway station. Having dared myself to look down on Gibraltar's now-minuscule high-rises, I wondered anew at the widely held assumption that vertigo is a phobia. What in the name is irrational about a fear of heights – about, say, looking out of a first-storey window and knowing that it would take merely a freak accident to have you toppling head-first into terror and death?

Perhaps it was time for some small talk, just to let the cable-car man know I was okay.

'Do you get many accidents?'

'Now.'

'What?'

He shook his head. 'Now. Now acksidence.'

So how did he explain the fact that this side of the Rock was littered with at least three sets of broken, rusty ex-cable-car-hauling pylons? Fortunately, I posed that little puzzle to myself after the cable car had reached the top, without any further scares – not counting the panic attack which had stayed with me for every shoe-inspecting, hyperventilating centimetre of the journey.

Calmly and sensibly and with the merest hint of twitching hysteria, I stepped out and into the terminus at the top of the Rock. The terminus was a jumble of concrete. It was a small jumble but had been constructed according to the 1960s' architectural principles of brutal functionalism, so, inevitably, I got lost. After a third attempt to get out, I turned a corner to discover that I'd reached the shut cafeteria once more. For the third time, my path crossed that of the only other person in the complex, an elderly fellow in a red kagool. We'd given up on mutual greetings long ago, so he trudged by in silence and started to climb wearily down the concrete stairs I had just climbed up. Obviously, the only conventional way out of here was to head back to the cable car. The thought spurred me into action. I heaved myself up and over a crumbling concrete wall and dropped to the ground, a free man.

I looked around. No sign of anyone else up here. No sign either of the tourist route that was supposed to lead to the Barbary apes and so forth. Every sign, though, of a disused military installation. Having passed through a padlocked but meshless rusted gate and then slithered downhill over scrub, I happened on a path. Success – it led to a group of apes sitting on some slabs and picking at old fruit in a plastic basket.

The apes were once thought to be the last group of a species that roamed as far north as the Chilterns until the Ice Age drove them further and further down through Europe to this last, southernmost dead-end . . . The prosaic truth is that they were imported from North Africa by the British in the eighteenth century. Far less prosaically, the state of the tribe invariably foretells that of the colonisers. For example, at the beginning of the twentieth century, the population expanded, but then split into two factions which conducted a bitter and violent feud until, by 1913, there were only a few left. Under the watchful eye of the Army and the Colonial Office, the tribe kept going, surviving a blip that presaged the Depression and a critical decline in numbers just before the Second World War. When only seven remained by 1943, Churchill ordered the introduction of some fit and randy newcomers, which secured the tribe's survival and assured the Allies' eventual victory. The perfectly sensible Spanish legend has it that the Brits will leave the Rock when the apes disappear; the bad news for Madrid is that the ape population on the Rock is almost four times the human population on Pitcairn.

The apes are very unsettling creatures. Not because of their open disdain for humans, or even their appearance, although that is a bit odd (no tail, huge teeth, grey fur on the hindquarters, dirty orange faces and front), but because they relish climbing up and over and round the fence at the edge, a mere 1,200 feet straight up. Gripping that fence as I would a tow-rope when water-skiing, I managed to peek over just far enough to appreciate that on the other side was a cliff-face so sheer that it appeared to cut back inwards until it reached the disfiguring steep slope of water-catchments constructed, presumably by highly trained mountain goats, a hundred years ago.

According to my map and guidebook, there was an old Moorish look-out post to my right. And indeed there it was, precariously perched further along and further up the thin spine of the Rock.

Lord have mercy. I climbed up some decayed steps while holding on to a wobbly railing and shouting encouraging obscenities at myself until I reached the remains of what looked like a grey stone dovecot on the cliff edge. The walls, especially the wall on the cliff edge, did not appear at all safe. They were also far too low. I hugged my knees in a crouch and whimpered.

After a series of little jumps, executed while still in the crouch position, I gathered that, were I forced to stand up – under the threat, for instance, of losing a substantial bet – I would be able to look down on the Costa del Sol, at least as far as Marbella, to the east, the Bay of Algeciras to the west, a vast tract of Andalucía to the north and the mountains of Africa to the south. (The only eyesore was the large refinery in La Linea, built by Franco – not, it is said, to boost employment in the area but to ruin what had been a prospect much enjoyed by the Gibraltarians.) It was a splendid spot for a look-out post and emphasised just why the Rock has been prized as a military aid.

It is all the more curious that this massive hunk of limestone – in the words of a local T-shirt, 'the world's biggest pebble' – which commands the stretch of water between Africa and Europe and between the Mediterranean and the Atlantic, wasn't occupied until the Berber chief Tarik arrived here in 711. Tarik used the Rock to establish a bridgehead for his invasion of Spain and founded a Moorish settlement here that would last for another six centuries. An even more durable legacy was that the place was named after him – Jbel Tarik (the Rock of Tarik). Of course, Gibraltar had been a famous landmark long before this. This is, after all, with Jbel Musa over the water in Morocco, one of the pillars that Hercules was supposed to have rent asunder, thus creating the Strait. (The geological reality is much more spectacular; the Strait opened five million years ago, by which time the landlocked Mediterranean had evaporated, so that the Atlantic poured down in a 10,000-foot waterfall that lasted a hundred years.)

After Tarik had set the precedent of fortifying it, the Rock never again had its troubles to seek. It was eventually captured by the Spanish in 1309 after a siege, recaptured by Muslims in 1333 after another siege, re-recaptured by the Spanish in 1462 after a – go on, have a guess – siege. For the next couple of centuries, the Rock was repeatedly raided, attacked, bombarded and besieged, until an Anglo-Dutch force finally overran the Spanish garrison in 1704. Six thousand civilians were allowed to scamper off into Spain, where they settled on a hill with a view of their erstwhile home; the settlement still exists, the Ciudad de Gibraltar en San Roque to give its full title, the entrance to which is adorned with a statue of a lion roaring at the Rock and bearing an inscription lamenting the loss and injustice of the exiles and the vow that one day they will return.

The Spanish spent the best part of the eighteenth century trying to fulfil the pledge, although Gibraltar did become officially recognised as British territory under the Treaty of Utrecht (which also allotted Minorca to the growing British Empire). A series of Spanish sieges culminated in the Great Siege which started in 1779 and continued for three and a half years. That Gibraltar and the British garrison survived this last onslaught – just – can be attributed to the ingenuity of the defenders and the hapless zeal of the attackers. Two British heroes were Sergeant-Major Ince, who led a team that cut a tunnel into the Rock and who realised that the ventilation shafts he had drilled into the cliff-face would make ideal gun emplacements, and Lieutenant Koehler, who then developed a gun which could fire downwards on to the besiegers. Spanish schemes were to be more eccentric and less effective. Towards the end of the Great Siege, the Spanish tried out the gimmick of cramming lots of guns into old ships, moving them into the Bay of Algeciras and conducting a fierce but tremendously inaccurate bombardment. This came to an abrupt end when British gunners retaliated with furnace-heated cannon-balls. The Spanish ships went up in flames and more than 1,500 sailors were drowned.

There followed a long period of peace, if you somehow discount the Battle of Trafalgar in 1805, when Gibraltar was the British Navy's base and the first port of call for Nelson's corpse (carried here, so legend has it, pickled in a barrel of rum). The Rock's next crisis was the Second World War. In the eighteenth century, the civilian population of Gibraltar had to endure starvation, drought and disease, but their descendants in 1939 were promptly evacuated, to Jamaica, Madeira and, evidently for those who drew the short straws, London.

There has been a spate of scares more recently. During the

Falklands War, when much of the Task Force gathered here *en route* to the South Atlantic, the Argentinians attempted a raid on Gibraltar. The escapade may sound unbelievable but I prefer to think it's true, partly because it was reported by the reliable Simon Winchester and mainly because the raid could have inspired a storyline for *Mission Impossible*. According to Winchester, four Argentinian frogmen came to Spain to swim across to the docks, lay charges under the fleet, then heave themselves on to land and flipper over to lay more charges and blow up the Rock itself. The mission came unstuck when the Spanish, eager to show their credentials to join the EC, arrested the frogmen at the other Gibraltar in San Roque. There were further full alerts in 1988, after the 'death on the Rock' business, when three unarmed members of the IRA were executed by the SAS outside one of the petrol stations just inside the border, and three years later during the Gulf War, when local bobbies were armed for the first time, sniffer dogs were employed at the border, soldiers guarded the airport, the rest of the military ran around sandbagging every stationary object, and all travel to and from North Africa was suspended.

Relics of the Second World War fortifications litter the Rock. The disused area I dropped down on to after being stuck in the terminus is one. Another lies quite near the Moorish look-out – an observation post even higher up the Rock's spine and reached by an even more dangerous path. (My apologies for not being able to describe it; my bottle had gone.) I decided instead to visit another Second World War construction mentioned in my guide, a big gun called O'Hara's Battery. I followed the road south and up to the highest point on the Rock, 1,396 feet above sea-level. The reassuring tarmac, plus the trees and shrubbery that separated me from a fall to my death and, more importantly, from the precipitous view, helped allay vertigo, so I was in fine fettle when I reached a bunker under the gun and handed over my 40p entrance charge.

The very bored attendant pointed me in the direction of a long, low tunnel which led to a cavernous room filled with machinery. This, I guessed, was the Engine Room mentioned in my guide. No doubt the machinery was state-of-the-art in the 1940s but now these vast items of equipment, with their outsize knobs, wheels, clamps and dials, seemed charmingly dated. The room looked like the control tower of a space rocket designed by the young H.G. Wells. I pictured a maverick scientist with a florid moustache and a three-piece tweed suit, scurrying to and fro, checking the ampere readings, fiddling with the huge fuseboxes, heaving on the thick metal wheels to produce more steam for take-off. No blipping computer screens here, no *Star Trek*-style monitors and flashing panels. Just huge Bakelite blocks and cylinders. 'Lawrence Scott Electromotors Ltd,' announced the proud brass panel atop one mighty object: 'Norwich and Manchester.' Those were the days, eh?

I lingered by a bulky box which merited another plaque – 'Do not switch off supply to Governor's cottage' – thought better of it, and stooped down again to pass through a tiny tunnel that led up and out to O'Hara's Battery. Blood in sand. Those who know about such matters will appreciate the gun's size from the information that it is calibrated at 9.2 inches. Those who, like me, haven't a clue what that means will have to take on trust my assurance that it is very big indeed, resembling a gun in the sense that Buckingham Palace looks like a house.

I moved on to the circular platform on which the gun was mounted and inched round under the barrel that was jutting out to threaten some villages in the Atlas Mountains, whose peaks were clearly visible. So too was the ground on both sides and in front of the Rock, 1,396 feet directly below. Now this *was* vertigo. I realised that there was a worse job in the world than that of Partick Thistle goalkeeper or even cable-car operative – O'Hara's Battery main-tenance engineer.

'Private Ritchie?'

'Sah!'

'Blockage at the end of the barrel. Crawl along to the end, sit astride the damned thing, 1,396 feet above the ground, lean forward and give it a good clean. Take this stick.'

'Sah!'

I clambered to safety, yelling with fear, to the surprise of the elderly fellow in the red kagool who was just emerging out of the tunnel.

Back on the road, I consulted my map and plotted my route to the next attraction, St Michael's Cave. I tacked downhill and ended up at a little wooden souvenir shop-cum-restaurant. Terror had made me hungry and I was sorely tempted by a St Michael's Fried Platter or maybe a St Michael's Club Sandwich, but a Santa was playing an electric piano inside, so I had to keep going, past the Gents and into yet another tunnel. This one led into the Rock and opened out into an enormous grotto decorated with stalagmites and stalactites in all manner of shapes – mushrooms, willies, folds, organ pipes, fungus . . . The Greeks and Romans strongly suspected that this petrified gallery was an entrance to the underworld. I could see why. And why this cave had been a significant site a hundred millennia before the Greeks and Romans, for a Neanderthal skull was found here. (Other Neanderthal remains were first found in Gibraltar in 1848, eight years before the discoveries in the Neander Valley in Germany, but since nobody on the Rock recognised that the bones were pre-human, we are stuck with a daft Teutonic name for the species. Gibraltar Man. It may not sound right, but only to someone who hasn't wandered into the Horseshoe Bar by mistake.) To give an indication of just how awesome this cave was, let me just say that I remained agog despite the *son et lumière* display (Christmas carols on the tannoy and shifting green and red spotlights), despite the graffiti ('Monica 1965' and suchlike) scrawled all over any reachable surface, despite the conversion of part of the cave into an auditorium full of red plastic bucket-seats, despite the plaque commemorating the visit here of the Queen in 1954, and despite my rounding a corner and coming face to startled face with an elderly fellow wearing a red kagool.

Whoever coined the phrase 'as safe as the Rock of Gibraltar' not only had never tiptoed along its precarious peak but also stayed ignorant of the fact that the whole edifice is hollow. St Michael's is one of many caves within the soft limestone, and the British Army has done its damnedest to help turn the Rock into a shell. Courtesy of the Army, the tour of St Michael's Cave can take longer now than it did before the Second World War, when the place was excavated to provide space for a subterranean hospital and another cave was found. But the Army has been enthusiastically tunnelling its way through the Rock ever since Sergeant-Major Ince started the craze. There are now over thirty miles of tunnels inside the Rock, containing roads, ammunition dumps, reservoirs, a secret communications centre, a mocked-up Northern Irish village (with pub, church and fish-and-chip shop), and a thermonuclear arsenal.

An untimely reminder that military technology isn't always infallible can be found along the road from St Michael's Cave, where a plaque commemorates 'Healy's Mortar', an eighteenth-century contraption that was cut into the rockface. The device was supposed to hurl 1,000-pound stones on to attackers in the Bay far below, but most of the stones dropped like, er, stones on to Gibraltar itself.

My stomach was growling like an old drunk by this time because I had decided to postpone lunch until I reached sea-level, Santa having been belting out a samba version of 'In the bleak mid-winter' when I left St Michael's Cave. My cunning plan was to save time and reduce misery by boarding the cable car at the nearby midway station. And there was a cable car swaying down now. I jogged over. Perfect timing.

Not so perfect architecture. The midway station consisted of a rickety pylon reached by an even ricketier bridge. Both pointed out at a sharp angle from the Rock and into empty space high, high above the town. There was a warning sign on one of the pylon's feeble struts:

DANGER OF
DEATH
DO NOT CLIMB

As I stood staring, aghast, at this ludicrous construction, the cable-car man beckoned me aboard. Aye. Sure. I patted my jacket pockets to indicate a lost wallet or similar, shrugged ruefully and waved the cable car on. All was not lost. There was another way down, and it wouldn't take long. I hauled out my map, thanking God I am male – therefore blessed with both a sense of direction and a way with maps.

An hour later, I was standing on a promontory on the north side of the Rock, 500 feet up, overlooking the airport, within spitting distance of Spain, and extremely hungry. Only a couple of wrong turnings after that, I marched down into a series of alleyways and stairs that eventually led on to Main Street, spotted a pub sign, and barrelled into the Star, one of several establishments that claim to be Gibraltar's oldest pub.

The place could have been a five-minute-old wine bar called the Vodaphone for all I cared at that moment, but soon, with a pint of Websters and a plate of fish and chips at my side, I was able to appreciate my surroundings. Slade's Christmas anthem was howling out of the juke-box. Mike Atherton was battling for a draw in South Africa on the TV. Below him sat four middle-aged women, sipping tea and jabbering in what sounded like heavily accented Spanish. Outside a couple of aged men wearing jellabas limped round the corner into a street called Irish Town.

Gibraltar has had a markedly cosmopolitan population ever since the Spanish inhabitants were replaced by an eclectic mix of British soldiers, chancers from different parts of Spain, merchants and sailors from Portugal, Malta and Genoa, Jews and Moors – although the latter two groups were supposed to be banned from the colony under the Treaty of Utrecht. Out of the present population of 26,000 (plus 4,000 British expats), there are about 500 Sephardic Jews, 600 Hindus and 2,000 Muslims. Gibraltar makes much of its history of religious tolerance (doctrinal feuds having been ignored under the pressure of regular sieges and of making money), and locals now enjoy citing such phenomena as the town's kosher restaurant employing a Muslim head waiter.

Hmm. It seemed to me that Gibraltar has the kind of ethnic and religious harmony to be found in the departure lounge of a major airport. Those old Moroccans in jellabas wouldn't dream of popping into the Star for an orange juice, just as the regulars at the bar would never stop to have a chat in one of the many Moroccan groceries near by. And there is an ethnic pecking order here. At the bottom of the social heap lie the guest-workers who were shipped over from Morocco in the 1970s, housed in grim hostels, refused citizenship and faced with deportation as soon as they lost their jobs. (A small group of Moroccans keeps up a constant protest outside the Governor's official residence about this treatment. Not once did I see anyone pay them any attention.) Sallow-skinned Spanish-speakers tend to occupy the social middle ground and pale-faced English-speaking colonial types, such as the two ageing amnesiacs in the hotel restaurant, tend to think of themselves as a cut above the rest.

Actually, the Spanish–English distinction is much more complex and murky than that summary allows. Most Gibraltarians would say they are bilingual, with English remaining the language favoured by officialdom, expatriates and descendants of the more recent émigrés from Britain, and Spanish the more popular vernacular choice. Ah, but . . . As I learned to my cost, no Gibraltarian likes to be thought of as Spanish, even if he or she has an olive skin, a surname such as Lopez, and a poster of the Barcelona squad above the mantelpiece. And though it sounded as if they were speaking Spanish to me, those four women in the pub, like most locals, don't have Spanish, or English, as their first language but a peculiar mixture of the two. Snatches of conversation that drifted over to me in the Star sounded very strange: 'Paracarosamente paracarosa Christmas decorations paracaracara teatime paracara cheque book?' They were, in fact, speaking a hybrid mightily despised by the Spanish and known, inevitably, as Gibberish.

The town itself displays the social equivalent of Gibberish. Shops accept sterling or pesetas. Cafés offer eggs on toast or churros for breakfast. The pavements have that Spanish waffle pattern and red pillar boxes carry the insignia ER (not EIIR, because the initials stand for King Edward VII). Swarthy cops wear *Dixon of Dock Green* uniforms. Cars drive on the right (uniquely among British colonies) but stop at pedestrian crossings. Helmetless teenagers zip around on mopeds with yellow British-made numberplates. Pubs sell pints or chicos (half-pints) of bitter but customers pay on leaving.

After I paid up and left the Star, I felt refreshed enough to have a look round the newest part of Gibraltar, the land reclaimed from the Bay of Algeciras, which is now home to a gleaming array of flats and office blocks. That, at any rate, was the notion I'd gained of the new development from my vantage point on the Rock, but, as with all new developments, it was much less impressive at close quarters. Unlike much of London's dockland real estate, Gibraltar's was being used and inhabited, but it still had an unfinished air to it, and of course it completely lacked the charm and bustle of the higgledy-piggledy old quarter. And of course it was designed not for people but for cars.

I trudged along enough anonymous, empty, windswept pavements to be able to tell myself that I had done the new bit and that it was high time for another beer and sit-down. Such was the allure of both that I decided to enter the nearest bar-restaurant, a place called Gatsby's Eating House. As you would expect with a name like that, it was full of American pop and film memorabilia and empty of customers. I withstood the tension of being Gatsby's first client of the evening, or quite possibly the year, for as long as it took to down a bottle of Becks, and stumbled off to find a taxi that would take me back to the hotel. No way was I walking.

After a long and soothing bath and a dinner in the hotel restaurant which was neither of these but once again delivered at breakneck – nay, Olympic – pace, I retired to my room to swig some watery brandy and collect my thoughts. More accurately, thought, for I stared at the map and guides I'd spread out on the bed, fixated by the puzzle of what to do next. Two days here and I appeared to have seen and done the lot. Okay, not quite – under duress I could go back up the Rock to visit the Great Siege Tunnels or the Moorish castle. And the guide did list a few places I could still tick off – the Casino, the lighthouse on the southern tip at Europa Point, the dockyards . . . But, to be quite honest, I would be ticking off these items in the spirit of one who, having spring-cleaned for days, resorts to toothbrushing the bit underneath the kitchen taps and vacuuming the walls.

This admission led to my second thought: how on earth did the locals cope after 1969 when Franco closed the border, thereby condemning the Gibraltarians to the territorial equivalent of house arrest? For thirteen years? Granted, there had been flights out, as well as a ferry service to Tangier, but even so the Rock must have been no place for claustrophobics. Or car enthusiasts. The image of Gibraltarian drivers zipping round and round the same little circuit inspired the Spanish to rename the colony Scalextric. As I would learn many times over, Gibraltarians maintain that their imprisonment by Franco inaugurated a mad social whirl and brought them all together, confirming their anti-Spanish resolve, affirming their sense of their own identity, and so forth. After only two days on the Rock, I found it far easier to sympathise with the chap who, a decade into Franco's siege, somehow leaped over the high border fence and into Spain. He explained to the Spanish police who immediately arrested him that he just couldn't take the tedium any more. His punishment was to be deported, via Tangier, back into Gibraltar.

Anxiety about going a little stir crazy propelled me the following morning down towards the town's library and community centre, the John Mackintosh Hall. Well, I *could* join the Gibraltar Photographic Society. Or the Gibraltar Astronomical Society. Take a class on kick-boxing. Attend the forthcoming seminar on world peace. Find the one true light in Jesus . . .

Oh, I hated doing this but there was only one thing for it.

Down at the Tourist Information Centre, the lady behind the desk was eager to help, handing me a few thin leaflets about the tour of the Rock and asking if I might be interested in this week's meeting of the Gibraltar Astronomical Society. Recognising that we were both up against it, she tapped into her computer and scrolled down a very short list of current events and attractions.

She took a deep breath. 'Oh dear. There is a tea-dance tomorrow at the pensioners' club . . . I'll have one more check.' She picked up the phone to consult a colleague. 'Paracarosa paracara tea-dance? Paracosamente paracasa Astronomical Society. Si? Si? Si!'

She didn't quite slap her forehead after she put the phone down but her mime of stupid-me amazement was otherwise complete. 'Today,' she said, shaking her head with wide-eyed wonder. 'Today we have the arrival of the new Governor.'

'Fantastic. Is there some kind of ceremony or something?'

'Ceremony, oh yes.'

'Where do I go?'

'The House of Assembly.'

'Haha. Sounds like a disco.'

'Discotheque? No, the House of Assembly is our parliament. You know Main Street?'

'Yip.'

'So turn left here, go down Main Street, towards the piazza.'

'When does it all happen?'

She looked at her watch. 'In half an hour.'

'Excellent. Thank you, thank you, thank you.' I shook her hand and was heading for the door with great purpose when I was halted by a sudden reflection. 'How often does this ceremony happen?'

She shrugged. 'The last Governor left early after only two and a half years.'

I marched out, only now fully aware that cops were stopping the traffic and that crowds were lining the streets. (In my shame-faced defence, I'd like to point out that crowds were always lining the streets as shoppers heel-toed their way along the fearfully narrow pavements.) I nudged into the porch of a camera shop opposite what

I hoped was the House of Assembly. Certainly, the building looked important, in a small-town-hall sort of way, and assembling outside it now was a guard of honour. Ah, sweet. There was a rank of bobbies – twelve of them. And a short line-up from the St John's Ambulance Brigade. And the Sea Scouts. And the Cubs. And the Brownies.

Then, drifting over the hubbub of gossip and mothers fretting over the guard of honour's skew-whiff neckerchiefs, came the sound of applause. Lacking in rapture, to be sure – more of a polite and interested ripple – but applause nonetheless. A socking big black Daimler glided slowly towards us and came to an imperceptible stop. The bobbies, Cubs, Brownies and so on snapped to attention as two people disembarked – someone wearing a ceremonial uniform, all braid, sash, badges and sword, and his companion, adorned with the sub-regal kit of a matching dress, cape and large hat. The one in the large hat bent down to talk to selected Brownies while the swordy man made some show of inspecting the bobbies on parade. Then both of them went inside.

Marvellous. Well, that was that for the next three years. Noon. If I returned to the hotel now, I could be on a London plane by two o'clock. However, lest I miss out on some more thrilling pageantry, I followed some people who were drifting down a little street and into a square on the other side of the House of Assembly. Something was up, sure enough, judging by the steadily growing crowd, the office-workers spectating from balconies, and now the entrance of perhaps forty members of the Gibraltar Regiment and a small Dad's Army complement of fatties, speckies and gangling youths that comprised Gibraltar's military band. To much more enthusiastic applause than the new Governor and his wife had received, soldiers and musicians marched and oompahed into the square – where, like the rest of us, they stood and waited.

And waited.

And waited.

Before doing some more waiting.

Three-quarters of a bloody hour later, when many in the crowd had long since sloped off to shop and several members of the band appeared to be in some discomfort, the new Governor and his wife appeared again. The soldiers stamped to attention, the band played the first six bars of 'God Save the Queen', the Governor ran his eye over the troops, and then he was handed the keys to the colony's gates.

Hardly worth the wait – forty-five minutes for a paragraph. But I did get a better look at the new Governor. He was a very thin cove in his fifties, with a bony face stuck in an expression of smooth hauteur. (It was quite easy to impersonate, I discovered, when I stood in front of the bathroom mirror that evening – the secret is to narrow your eyes and suck in your cheeks.) Deck the man out in a urine-stained overcoat with string for a belt and hand him a can of Kestrel – he'd still look posh.

And there was one further boon to his re-emergence being hugely delayed. There had been a moment back there, when the band and soldiers first marched in and the crowd cheered and the sun shone down on this contented scene, when I had felt a twinge of pride in Britain and its empire and the fact that these Gibraltarians were obviously grateful for their luck in being subjects of Her Majesty. Forty-five minutes had been more than enough for it to sink in that these Gibraltarians were cheering the soldiers and the band because they lived next door to them or had known them since primary one, and that it clearly hadn't occurred to the posh VIP with his braid, sash, badges and sword to quit nattering to the dignitaries inside and put in an appearance pdq for the mere public.

Amazingly, some people were still lining Main Street when I followed in the wake of the Daimler ferrying the Governor and his wife the hundred yards to their official residence, the Convent. Here the residual sense of occasion had got to the Moroccan protesters, who had formed their own stiff-backed guard of honour, holding their placards as soldiers extend their rifles when they stand at ease on parade.

> We have served the British Crown
> for More than 25 Years The
> Reward Starvation

> IN SOME
> COUNTRIES
> THERE ARE
> RACIST PE
> OPLE IN GB
> IT IS THE GV

As usual, though, the rest of Gibraltar was passing them by, oblivious.

After milling about, aimlessly window-shopping and wondering what on earth to do next, I took myself off for a walk round the Rock to Europa Point. I'm sure the exercise was good for me. And going there meant I could put another tick on my list. Alas, the trip didn't really help fill up my notebook: 'Pavements v narrow or none. S/west – prefab Army housing – looks like Cowdenbeath. Europa Point = lighthouse, Sunflower Snack Bar, raised platform with telescope – 10p but rip-off couldnt see bastard thing. South of Rock = flat wasteland and crap cricket pitch. Rockface pock-marked cf Emmental.'

For the sake of variety rather than efficiency, I caught the bus back into town and visited an establishment called Truly British Fish n Chips on the grounds that a meal here would be a deal more relaxed and leisurely than another dinner at the hotel. Having toyed with, and rejected, the notion of an Irn-Bru from the soft-drinks cabinet, I settled for the traditional accompaniment of a mug of tea. This turned out to be strong and hot and – how rare but how right – the colour of freshly harvested caramel. As the maîtresse d' was anxious to reassure me, she spurns all locally caught fish, and takes immense care to ensure that all her cod, haddock and plaice are shipped and ferried over from Iceland in freezer containers. To fine effect, I must concede, for my cod was in excellent condition and had been deep-fried to perfection (the batter crispy but yielding), which piscine attraction arrived properly escorted by some terrifically handsome chips. Nor did the bill dismay, for it amounted to a more-than-reasonable £4.70. Drink included.

I waddled back up the hill to the hotel and straight to my room for a prone groan on the carpet. It was all I could do to switch on the television. Astonishingly, there was actually a programme from the local station, GBC. I'd been a fan of late-night GBC when I was on holiday along the coast several years before, because its output consisted of adverts (usually a series of still photographs) and fillers (usually a series of still photographs) that would have been considered amateurish by a Grampian viewer in the 1950s. Alas, GBC had been downsized and now barely coped with a daily quota of an hour. Tonight, though, I could lie on the floor and savour a special edition of its news bulletin. Footage of the Governor's arrival was followed by some excerpts from his speech to the House of Assembly in the afternoon. I now knew that the Governor was Admiral Sir Hugo White and that he had a fondness for bland reassurance – 'lost none of its geostrategic significance to the crown . . . optimum conditions both to retain and attract investment . . . stand solid as the Rock itself . . .'

The programme really picked up, though, with the studio discussion afterwards, which immediately forced me to banish any thoughts I'd had about sneaking back home early. This place was extraordinary. Where else would you find a television pundit cheerfully expound his view that northern Europeans had much higher standards of ethics, behaviour, the lot, than ghastly Mediterranean types? Where else could you watch four political commentators happily discuss their shared opinion that, since their new head honcho was a serving submariner, he was more likely to press the thermonuclear button? It took me a while longer to appreciate that the four panellists almost invariably all agreed with each other, an unlikely feature of TV discussion programmes and one camouflaged by the passion with which they debated such issues as Britain's commitment to Gibraltar, the Governor's role (i/c external affairs, with the House of Assembly responsible for domestic concerns), and the relationship between the Governor and the Foreign Office.

The last, it transpired, was a very touchy issue indeed, for the consensus in the TV studio, as in the rest of Gibraltar, was that the previous Governor, Field Marshal Sir John Chapple, had been recalled months before the end of his first three-year stint because the Foreign Office feared that he had gone native. Those fears had some justification judging by one of the local obituaries for Chapple's truncated term in office; the article fondly described his recent after-dinner speech at a Mediterranean Rowing Club bash during which he attacked Whitehall, urged locals to make sure they had a say in their future, and climaxed by belting out a Gershwin song that mentions Gibraltar, 'Our Love Is Here to Stay'. He received a standing ovation, a hearty chorus of 'For He's a Jolly Good Fellow', and, most worryingly for the Foreign Office, a ringing endorsement from Joe Bossano, the hard-line Chief Minister.

Very reluctantly and, I am sure, in direct contradiction to anything my taxi-driver would have to say on the subject, I have to concede that I can see why the Foreign Office had to act as it did, for both Chapple and Bossano gave every impression of being guilty of sins of omission. Chapple seemed to have done little to encourage Bossano to take more than token measures to curb Gibraltar's booming industries – money-laundering and smuggling. By the summer of 1995, Gibraltar had yet to implement some EC directives on banking (no hindrance, mind you, to its growing reputation as an amenable offshore financial centre) and Gibraltar-based super-fast speedboats were performing sterling work in their import–export drive – ferrying a yearly total of 500 tons (at least) of hashish from Morocco to the Costa del Sol and the small matter of 100 million packets of duty-free cigarettes (at least) from Gibraltar round the airport fence to the beach at La Linea. Bossano was reputed to be less than bothered about the entrepreneurial drive of the local 'Winston Boys', basically because they happened to perform the invaluable service of upsetting the Spanish authorities. Unfortunately, they were also beginning to upset the Americans, who saw the illegal service between Europe and North Africa as offering a potential route for Algerian fundamentalists, evil Libyans and assorted Muslim extremists to skedaddle over into NATO territory with backpacks full of Semtex.

All the Spanish could do was lodge official protests and show how pissed off they were by causing six-hour delays at the Gibraltarian border. (Favourite tactics to ensure the latter went well beyond the obvious measure of examining every bit of vehicle and luggage; the Spanish enjoy checking that each car meets their requirement of being equipped with a warning triangle, first-aid kit and fire extinguisher, and, if the driver wears spectacles, a spare pair.) Obviously, none of this buttered many parsnips in Whitehall, but as soon as the Americans' Drug Enforcement Administration and then the Central Intelligence Agency expressed concern that this British colony was home to a massive and potentially terrorist-friendly smuggling operation, Whitehall's parsnips were drowned in cholesterol.

The result? The Foreign Secretary Douglas Hurd immediately threatened Bossano with direct rule from London unless Gibraltar cleaned up its act. Bossano immediately clamped down on the supply and retail of cigarettes and impounded the smugglers' speedboats. The boat-owners immediately protested by blockading the road to the border and the Winston Boys immediately went mental in Main Street, wrecking and looting off-licences, natch, and, intriguingly, the local branch of Dorothy Perkins. Bossano held firm. He had no other option.

There was much talk among the TV panellists about whether or not these measures and tighter controls on the financial sector really had given Gibraltar a sparkling new squeaky-clean image. Probably because they were all Gibraltarian they couldn't see that there was no need for any discussion of the point. The truth is that it will take much more and far longer to erase Gibraltar's image as not just not squeaky-clean but begrimed by crime. For a start, name me one offshore banking centre (apart from Bermuda) that isn't associated with, at the very least, a hint of iffyness. But Gibraltar's unsavoury reputation stretches back much further than the mid-1980s, when its financial sector began to grow to accommodate such companies as Barlow Clowes International, which was wound up by liquidators in 1988 and whose main man, Peter Clowes, was convicted on charges of theft, conspiracy and false accounting. That reputation stretches as far back, in fact, as 1310 when the Spanish King, Fernando IV, tried to lure compatriots here by offering a welcome to everyone, 'be they bandits or thieves or murderers or any other man no matter what wrong he may have done or any married woman who has left her husband'.

Obviously, naturally, of course, it goes without saying, the vast majority of the present populace are faithfully married and law-abiding. But let's be realistic – this is a frontier town and a port and so temptingly situated, what with Morocco just across the water and lots of secluded coastline spots next door in Spain . . . I think it can reasonably be said that more than a few Gibraltarian families can boast a long and happy tradition of criminal activity – and often very ingenious criminal activity at that; for example, in the nineteenth century, the ancestors of the Winston Boys used dogs rather than speedboats, training the luckless mutts to run away from officials by wearing uniforms while beating them, then sending the police-phobic animals off on their errands with contraband tobacco strapped round their bodies.

I assumed that the present-day smugglers had already exercised their own ingenuity to make sure that the impounding of their speedboats was no more than a temporary and minor setback. Certainly, it looked business as usual at their favourite bar when I paid it a visit. Even my best friends think I look like a policeman and, to make matters worse, I realised too late that I was wearing big shiny black shoes, so I resolved to breeze in and brazen it out. This resolution evaporated as soon as I set a big shiny black-shoed foot inside the joint. No doubt the chap with his arm in a sling was an upstanding citizen and the shell-suited Moroccans thought hash was something you did with corned beef, but as for some of the other types there – the guy with the face as pock-marked as the southside of the Rock, the teenager wearing a gold medallion the size of a barometer, the truly frightening chap in a suit – well, they gave new resonance to the adjective 'dodgy'. I smiled expansively, ordered a beer and some frayed tapas and stood at the bar, telling myself that I felt like the Invisible Man, but knowing deep down that, in grim reality, I was the Visible Prat.

'Excuse me,' I said cheerily, but in a disconcerting falsetto, in the direction of the pock-faced guy who was not exactly next but definitely nearest to me. 'Could you pass over that salt?'

He studied his lager and lit a cigarette. 'No.'

'Oh. Sorry. Er, could you possible lend me one of your cigarettes? I've given up, but you know how it is, sometimes you just really like one, don't you?'

'No.'

'What, you don't know what it's like having given up?'

'No.'

'You mean, no you've not never given up? Or no you'd rather not give me a cigarette?'

'No.'

'No you don't want to give me a cigarette?'

He turned to face me for the first time. Just be cool, I thought. Doesn't matter that I sound like I've inhaled helium. I'm bigger than him. And think of the outside world, with all its *Dixon of Dock Green* bobbies.

I tried as hard as I could to match his expression of withering contempt. No chance. As slowly as I could manage – that is, with ill-concealed haste – I paid the bill and sauntered, loose-bowelled, back out to civilisation. I might have the right face and shoes for it, but I'll never make the CID.

Continuing the trend which had me spending much of my time in Gibraltar in the pub, my next appointment of the day was in the fortunately respectable surroundings of the lounge in White's Hotel, situated in a pretty little square just up the hill from Main Street. Having left the smugglers' bar a tad earlier than I had anticipated, I was, very uncharacteristically, early for the meeting so I wandered round the square and came across an old whitewashed building called the Garrison Library. The guidebook told me that this was founded in the eighteenth century by one Colonel Drinkwater, who, after being bored senseless by his incarceration during the Great Siege in the 1780s, decided that he would never again spend three and a half years here without any books to read.

I could see cases full of leather-bound books in Colonel Drink-water's library but only by peeking in through a window. I'd walked into the place but had swiftly been told I'd have to leave by a smug youth who went on to announce that the building was open only to students such as he who were attending the Bournemouth and Poole International College. I bet that his father gave him a Fiat Campus for Christmas and that he'd spend most of the next academic year talking loudly to gullible girls in the Steve Biko Bar at, oh, I don't know, the University of Solihull. Muttering to myself, I crossed the little square back towards White's Hotel.

There I exorcised my sudden bad mood by nursing a gin and tonic along with my resentment. 'Two lectures a day . . . subsidised bloody bar . . . rag week . . . Gav or Biff or Scooby . . .'

'Mr Ritchie?'

'What? Oh. Yes. Sorry, I was just . . . Dominique? Good to meet you. And thanks for taking the time to, um . . .'

'Quite all right. It's hardly far to come.'

'Oh?'

'That's my office over there.'

'But I thought it was only for students at whatsisname, the Swanage Institute?'

'And us.'

So this bespectacled, bushy-haired fellow was Dominique Searle, highly recommended contact and editor of the local daily paper, the *Gibraltar Chronicle*. Just like the lady in the hotel dining room, the *Chronicle* is very small and very old. Its first issue came out in 1801 and its first and last international scoop arrived in 1805 when it broke the news about Trafalgar and Nelson. These days it looks like the lovechild of the *Daily Telegraph* and the *Hexham Courant*, reflecting the peculiar nature of Gibraltarian concerns by providing a strange mix of national, international and parish-pump stories. (The issue I'd just bought led on Sir Hugo's arrival and featured inside the welcoming speeches in the House of Assembly, a report of heavy snowfalls in East Anglia and a picture story about the jolly reunion at the Cool Blues disco of sixty women from Westside Comprehensive's class of '84. I'd also like to add the quite irrelevant information that one of its adverts was for farming ostriches – 'the meat of the next millennium'.)

Since the topic was vying with that of smug, sponging students to be top of my current agenda, I asked Dominique first about Gibraltar's smuggling problem. He was confident that now there was no smuggling problem. In addition, there were tighter controls on the offshore banks which made it far more difficult for the smugglers to launder their profits here. So Gibraltar's image could only improve, couldn't it? (Not a difficult task, I thought, but let it pass.) Dominique was much more eager to discuss the subjects which have dominated Gibraltarian public life for nearly three centuries – Spain, sovereignty, colonialism, the Spanish . . .

Not for the first time in Gibraltar I was disconcerted to hear a highly intelligent person come out with a – let's be charitable – robust assessment of the Spanish. According to my notes, Dominique did indeed preface one of his remarks with the rider, 'I'm not anti-Spanish but . . .' It was a pretty big but. Spain was a racist country, one that was just getting used to the idea of democracy after 'losing most of this century under Franco'; the Spanish, though not a brutal race of course, demonstrated the politics of extremism when it came to Gibraltar; the Gibraltar question was being used and abused by Spanish politicians to divert and hoodwink their credulous electorate . . .

To be fair to Dominique, his was by far the mildest and most considered view of the Spanish I had yet heard on the Rock. Raise the topic of Spain in any pub here and you are guaranteed to hear a degree of violent abuse of fellow-Europeans rivalled only by the *Sun*. On asking other Gibraltarians their opinions about the Spanish, I found that 'apes', 'fascists' and a spit on the floor were three of the more typical replies. When it comes to having a go at the Spanish, Gibraltarians don't miss a trick; local pensioners celebrated a recent dispute between Spanish and Canadian fishermen by flying the Maple Leaf flag from the pensioners' club (handily situated near the border), and the lark caused an official protest from Madrid to Whitehall. Hostility towards Spain is such that it spices up the conventionally bland business of diplomatic protocol; during the televised speeches at the House of Assembly the night before, Joe Bossano had been at pains to remind the new Governor that Spain 'cannot be trusted to honour anything she agrees to'. Thereafter, Bossano couldn't bring himself to say 'Spain' and skirted the taboo by using the euphemism 'the country next door'.

When the last referendum was held on the issue, in 1967, the number of people voting to remain a British colony was 12,138. Votes for integration with Spain totalled 44. The turnout was 96 per cent. Were a referendum to be repeated now, the result would be the same, assuming that the same number of people got confused and placed their crosses in the pro-Spanish box by mistake. So Spain's dispute with Britain over Gibraltar isn't going to be solved by the Gibraltarians – or by any foreseeable British government. Little as anyone in the mother country cares about Gibraltar, the sight of the Rock and its lamenting, Union Jack-waving inhabitants being handed over to the Spanish would constitute political suicide, and, besides, successive British administrations have properly stuck by the guarantee to respect locals' wishes regarding their sovereignty, a guarantee enshrined in the Preamble to the 1969 Constitution.

Dominique thought that the future of Gibraltar had been put on hold, pending what he described as the 'savage disposal' of Hongkong. Although he was certain Gibraltar wouldn't share Hongkong's fate, he was far less confident that people back in Britain really understood the contemporary politics of colonialism, especially the desire of the colonised to remain colonised. Fair point, but one that conveniently avoided the fact that few people in Gibraltar seemed able to specify what colonial or post-colonial future they wanted, beyond mentioning the attractive and attractively vague catchword 'self-determination'.

After Dominique left to go back to his day-job, I stared at all the notes I had scribbled and was utterly bamboozled by the whole bang-shoot. I left White's Hotel and walked back down to Main Street, feeling as if I had left on a long journey knowing deep down that I had forgotten to pack something crucial. I found myself on Main Street outside the Splendid Bar. Inside, there were tiled walls, tapas, mementoes of Real Madrid on the gantry, which also had Sobrano brandy on an optic – I think I could be forgiven for thinking that the Splendid Bar looked rather, as it were, Spanish. It seemed an appropriate place for me to prop up the bar and sort out for myself some basic facts.

One, it did seem natural to me that the Spanish wanted Gibraltar back. Imagine the continuing outrage in Britain if the French had for the past few centuries owner-occupied a peninsula in Wales . . . Okay, bad example. Penzance, then.

Two, the Gibraltarians want to be Spanish as much as I want to be American.

Three, even if Britain could no longer be bothered about the Rock's strategic value, the dockyards and the thermonuclear arsenal, and even if a British government reneged on its guarantee to respect the wishes of the locals, this wasn't an obscure and distant dependency that could be nastily and quietly disposed of, and almost all the inhabitants were white. So no chance of any British government ridding itself of its responsibility.

Four, the whole problem might be solved by Gibraltar opting for the independence that many Gibraltarians are now mulling over as an option, but the colony is probably too small – and too vulnerable – for that to work. In any case, the much quoted Treaty of Utrecht stipulates that, if Britain does walk out of the Rock, Spain has first option on it.

Five, the Gibraltarians could choose whatever sort of semi-independence would be implied by self-determination or 'free association', but they've already got an elected parliament responsible for domestic affairs, as well as that British guarantee about respecting their wishes on sovereignty, so a cynic might assume that what they mean by self-determination or whatever is that they get to do what they want while Britain protects them and picks up the tab.

Six, further complications arise with the status of the airport on the isthmus, which, the Spanish point out, isn't covered by the Treaty of Utrecht.

Seven, the Spanish have some difficulty occupying the moral high ground on the issue of the Rock, since they have two outposts of their own in Morocco – the city enclaves of Ceuta and Melilla. The Spanish say that these are not colonies but Spanish national territory. Not an argument that convinces, especially in Morocco.

Those have been the variously conflicting factors which have amounted to a political stalemate that has lasted for thirty years. Having studied my list for ten minutes, I couldn't come up with a solution either.

Just to make matters more complicated, there is the Gibraltarian political scene to consider – a scene chock-full of passion and activity, with a plethora of parties, each with their activists, news-letters and acronyms. Bossano's Gibraltar Socialist Labour Party was in power at the House of Assembly, but had been demoted to second place by Peter Caruana's Gibraltar Social Democrats in a recent opinion poll. The newish Gibraltar National Party was running a plucky third, according to the poll, with the AACR limping far behind with only 4 per cent, P. Cumming on 0.5 per cent and Others gaining 2.5 per cent. (Now just how small could an Other party be in Gibraltar and how many of them were there that they collectively ranked lower than P. Cumming?)

Those are about the only hard facts I possessed about the parties. I assumed that Bossano's GSLP was leftish and Caruana's GSD more centre-right, but this assumption was based on no more than the parties' titles and the appearances of the respective leaders. (Bossano is a former trade-union official, and, with his barely kempt air and clumpy black specs, looks very much like one. Caruana is a balding, thirty-nine-year-old, public-school-educated lawyer and thus a smoothie.) Try as I did, I couldn't identify the two main parties' policies on offshore banking, law and order, education, employment, etcetera, because all the newsletters, leaflets and propaganda consisted of puffs and insults and assurances that the puffed party was fighting for Gibraltar and the insulted party wasn't.

On the question of sovereignty, Bossano had always been belliger-ently anti-Spanish, pro-Gibraltarian and not very pro-British. Caruana seemed to take a more conciliatory approach, but was also trying his hardest to slough off his reputation as an appeaser, since he was once associated with a group advocating a policy of being a bit less vile to governments in Madrid. With elections only six months away, neither the GSLP nor the GSD had stated their exact policies on sovereignty. Small wonder, since it was the only policy that mattered.

Call it instinct, call it political insight, call it what you will, but I had a very good feeling about the young and thrusting Gibraltar National Party. So, spurning the old guard, I made an appointment to meet the GNP's leader, Dr Joseph Garcia. I was greeted at his modest office in Irish Town by his secretary and a dapper little youngster who was wearing a double-breasted suit for practice. I was about to ask the little chap if his father was around when a hand shot out from somewhere inside a sleeve and he introduced himself. Dr Garcia, for it was he, ushered me into his own cubbyhole and started to talk.

At speed and at length. I scribbled as fast as I could but, shorthandless, missed a great deal of the oration which he delivered with impressive intelligence as well as pace. Much of what he had to say about sovereignty and suchlike I'd heard many times before, but never with such articulacy. I managed to ask a question eventually when he broke off for a split second to breathe.

'So do you think Gibraltarians still feel at all British or not?'

Off he went again. 'We see ourselves as being British like Scots Welsh or Irish the difficulty is that we're stuck at the other end of Europe most Gibraltarians feel let down by Britain but by that I mean the British government which has been weak on the Gibraltar issue until recently'

'Do—?'

'so much so that we're beginning not to trust Britain but having said that you'll never hear a bad word here against the British people or the royals even now'

'Do you think—?'

'however Spain still thinks of us as renegade Spanish with some British mixed in although we've been here for longer than the

Americans have been in the States and with an ethnic mix as well so we surely have the right to be considered Gibraltarian'

'Do—?'

'but we are still facing the anachronistic actions of Spain which now proposes a toll at the border offering yet another instance that it isn't the politicians in Whitehall who suffer from Spanish intransigence but ordinary Gibraltarians on a daily basis'

'Do you think that the—?'

'and this intransigence can have quite ludicrous results to take one instance the Gibraltarian under-21 hockey team hockey being the most popular sport here was drawn against the Spanish who refused to recognise our existence so the Gibraltarian team won on a bye'

'Do you think that the future lies with—?'

'the GNP is the only party which has set out definite proposals on the future of Gibraltar a future as a self-governing city-state within the European Union with the Queen remaining Queen of Gibraltar the Gibraltarians remaining British and the governor replaced by a Queen's representative perhaps a member of the royal family all these moves demonstrating that we can be pro-Gibraltarian without being anti-British'

I held up my hand in a stop sign, winced at my writer's cramp, and pleaded for a rest. After a glass of water and another sustained bout of highly informed, tremendously fluent and utterly exhausting rhetoric, he paused to hand me some political leaflets. I took the opportunity to ask him about himself.

'Have you ever been to Britain?'

'Absolutely. I went to Hull University.'

'Is that where you got your doctorate?'

'That's right. On Gibraltarian politics, 1940 to 1988.'

'And what did you make of it? Britain, that is.'

'I liked Hull. But I think it made me more Gibraltarian. I realised that culturally I wasn't quite British. One thing that really got to me in England was that in the winter it got dark at three o'clock. And the pubs closed at eleven.'

I'd have thought that the main problem Dr Joseph Garcia had faced when fancying a nighttime drink in Hull wasn't finding a pub with a late licence but one that admitted him at all, for he looked barely eighteen now, though he was in fact – I checked his biographical notes on one of his leaflets – twenty-eight. The notes also proudly listed his academic achievements: not just his doctorate but the Kingsley Prize in History that he won in his second undergraduate year at Hull and the Departmental Prize the year after that. No mention of his A-levels, though.

Despite his academic flummery and his youthful tininess, the impression I left with was of an immensely able fellow who was destined to go far. He was bound to be chief minister one day, and, I was willing to bet, very soon. All he lacked was a gift for soundbites and a pair of platform shoes. Maybe Gibraltar had discovered a politician who might just make some sense of its plight as the last colony in Europe.

That evening, I walked up and down Main Street for the last time. It was drizzling and it was deserted, the *Illustrious* having left port under a fuss of helicopters in the morning. Even the Horseshoe Bar was quiet. The Christmas decorations shifted moistly overhead. The mud-coloured jackets stood guard in the window of the gents' outfitters. An olive-skinned bobby wished me a good night. That bit of waffle-patterned pavement near Marks and Sparks was still sticking up. I'd been in Gibraltar for a week and I felt like I'd lived here since childhood.

Back at the hotel, the old lady and the old chap of military aspect were fast asleep in armchairs at opposite ends of the lounge. I tiptoed past and went up to my room, where I savoured the last of my brandy-and-waters and looked out on the abandoned dockyard and the lights of the tankers in the bay beyond. Acht, well. I went to bed and gaped at the ceiling, waiting for sleep and trying hard not to think about the cable-car journey and the fact that somewhere behind me, inside the Rock, was a fake Irish village and a supply of atomic bombs.

Six months after I left Gibraltar, on a plane that had to turn sharp left as it climbed into the sky, the colony held its general election. Peter Caruana's GSD swept to power with 52.2 per cent of the vote. Joe Bossano's GSLP won 42.2 per cent. Dr Joseph Garcia's GNP came third with 4.6 per cent.

Chapter Five

Where on Earth . . . ?: The Turks and Caicos Islands

MECHANICS' INSTITUTE LIBRARY
57 Post Street
San Francisco, CA 94104
(415) 393-0101

I have made some bad decisions in my life, believe me, but the one about not engaging in extensive, on-the-spot research in all five of Britain's remaining colonies in the Caribbean takes the biscuit. Cursing myself for having nobly stipulated that I would visit just one Caribbean possession, I set about finding the answer to a key question – which one? Anguilla seemed promising, with some lovely beaches and several truly splendid hotels. Montserrat was intriguingly favoured as a hideaway for rock stars. The Cayman Islands were no doubt full of lonely offshore millionairesses who would appreciate my company . . . Finally, after many fraught weeks of arduous work analysing each brochure in a pile as tall as my desk, I plumped for the Turks and Caicos Islands. Why? Well, the Grace Bay Hotel looked like the kind of zillion-dollar-a-night establishment that needed to shell out freebees. And nobody, but nobody, had heard of the Turks and Caicos Islands. In fact, one of the very few things I could find out about the place was that, in a recent United Nations survey, the Turks and Caicos Islands had scored the lowest name recognition of any nation on the planet, far, far below the likes of Bhutan or Vanuatu. So comprehensive was this anonymity that it apparently included even the Turks and Caicos Islands' bureau in London.

'Hello,' said the phone in that annoyingly perky, public-relations sing-song. 'Trinidad Information Office, can I help yew?'

'I'm terribly sorry,' I said. 'Is this 0181–364 5188?'

'Yes it is.'

'My mistake, I thought this was the number for the Turks and Caicos Islands Information Office.'

'That's us.'

'But you said Trinidad Information Office.'

'Did I?'

'Yes.'

'You sure?'

'Yes.'

'Oh.' She paused for a moment, then returned to her annoyingly perky sing-song. 'Hello,' she said, 'Turks and Caicos Islands Information Office, can I help yew?'

According to the information pack that the Information Office sent me, the islands' current slogan is 'Beautiful by Nature', but I much prefer its predecessor, which capitalised on the forehead-furrowing effect of its name – 'Where on Earth Are the Turks and Caicos Islands?'

A touch east of the Bahamas, north of Haiti and an hour and a half by plane from Miami is the answer to that one. Other basic questions about the place elicited much vaguer or completely contradictory replies. What was the population? About twelve thousand, was one response. Ten thousand, fourteen thousand, would that be including or excluding illegal Haitian immigrants? were others. How many islands were there? Well, Providenciales, North Caicos, Middle Caicos, South Caicos, Grand Turk and Salt Cay, they were the six inhabited ones, and then there were twelve others. No, thirty-one others in total. I think I would find there were forty-two islands in all. Actually, strictly speaking, sixty-three.

The only certainty about the place was that nothing much happened there. Which suited me just fine. Then, as I was preparing for a nice, leisurely, eventless time in a sleepy tropical backwater, all hell broke loose. Two or three articles about the Turks and Caicos even appeared in the British press. They were reporting protests in the islands against the Governor, Martin Bourke, a career diplomat who appeared to have completely forgotten about the diplomacy part of his job. He had already irked islanders by having his official residence renovated, at a cost of $900,000, but now he had made them really furious by airing his opinion that drug-trafficking was more popular than ever in the Turks and Caicos. Bourke also accused the local police of 'incompetence, sloth and corruption', sacked the Police Commissioner and alleged that the constable assigned to guard the official residence had burgled it.

Britain's Caribbean colonies have had a way of generating craziness. One of the British Virgin Islands, Anegada, managed to cause a rumpus in Whitehall when an enterprising businessman bought the island, then tried to sell it off in square-foot chunks to any aspiring landowners who read the personal columns of the *New York Times*. Although a British crown colony, Montserrat fondly imagines that it retains strong links with the Irish, who actually abandoned the place in 1667; signs proclaim that this is 'the Emerald Isle', passports are stamped with a shamrock, some locals maintain they have an Irish accent (it's as Irish as Cockney), there's a town called St Patrick's, but the capital is called Plymouth and it has suburbs called Dagenham and Amersham. The Cayman Islands, whose economy used to be based on the turtle catch, now boasts one of the largest offshore financial operations in the world and was once a major launderette for the profits of drugs and porn. In 1969, unrest in Anguilla, whose inhabitants wanted to secede from St Kitts–Nevis and become a separate British colony, provoked Operation Sheepskin, which saw the invasion of the island by 315 British paratroopers and forty bobbies; they landed early one morning to encounter a deadly force of Fleet Street photographers. This British invasion of British territory to prevent a British island becoming a separate British colony having proved useless and highly embarrassing, Anguilla was eventually granted its request and became an independently dependent British territory in 1982.

Fourteen years later, it was once again the Turks and Caicos' turn to kick up a stink. There was a protest outside Bourke's newly renovated official residence. In keeping with the traditions of Britain's remaining Caribbean possessions, the protest consisted of a few people standing around for a while. Nonetheless, Bourke stated that he was concerned for his safety and demanded the protection of two armed officers from Special Branch. Back in Manchester a hundred police were put on standby for what would have been the crowd-control assignment of a lifetime – go to gorgeous, peaceful Caribbean island and do nothing. Meanwhile, the Chief Minister of the Turks and Caicos, Derek Taylor, led a delegation to Whitehall to campaign for Bourke's removal.

Bourke's remarkably undiplomatic claim about local corruption was an awkward one, not least because he seemed to have a point. Our man in the Turks and Caicos was branded 'a buffoon, a moron and a mad dog' by a leading politician on the islands, Norman Saunders, but this was the same Norman Saunders who, while he was Chief Minister ten years before, had been imprisoned for four years in Miami for cocaine-trafficking. Two other members of his government were arrested with him – Stafford Missick, the Minister for Commerce and Development, and a legislator, Alden 'Smokey' Smith. Thus, in 1985, 27 per cent of the government of the Turks and Caicos were in a Florida jail.

As sheer chance would have it, Smokey was one of the accused in the much more recent trial which had spurred Bourke on to contend that the islands were a hotbed of vice. Smokey and three other islanders, known as Duck, Porky and Red Boy, had been arrested in possession of twelve kilos of cocaine and a Miami-bound plane. Allegedly. During the trial, the prosecution brought forward tapes of various phone calls to Smokey wherein there was much talk of a forthcoming delivery of lobsters. Smokey replied that he was a victim of entrapment, that Bourke shouldn't have authorised the tapping of his, Smokey's, phone, and that, anyway, the tapes proved only that he was arranging the delivery of lobsters, as he often did because he was the owner of a highly popular restaurant, Smokey's On Da Beach. Smokey found a sympathetic audience in the jury – many or most of whom knew the accused. (How could it be otherwise in a country with a population less than that of Evesham?) Smokey, Duck, Porky and Red Boy were acquitted, and Bourke was incensed.

When he investigated the previous scandal involving Norman Saunders and the incarceration of over a quarter of the Turks and Caicos government, P.J. O'Rourke was delighted to hear local cocaine-smuggling anecdotes worth their weight in grams. There was the one about the local businessman who sampled too much of his own export drive and walked into a propeller on his plane, leaving on the runway lots of bags of white powder; some islanders didn't sleep for a month. And the story of the pilot who landed here with a planeful of Quaaludes but no cash; the pilot left the drugs as security for the fuel he'd bought on tick, and on his return discovered that the Quaaludes had gone and that many of the island's cars were wrapped around trees or floating in the sea.

Unfortunately for P.J., what he didn't find in the Turks and Caicos was even a line of Vim to snort, because the country has always been only a way-station for drug-smugglers, who are attracted to the islands by several appealing features. There are the many secluded runways for a start. Then there's the helpful combination of a law-abiding populace who wouldn't dream of carrying out a heist on any Class-A cargo, but some of whom could be persuaded for a tidy sum to light the odd fire on deserted airstrips at certain times of the night. (Norman Saunders' role was to have been refuelling planes on South Caicos, for which service the DEA undercover team was tempting him with the salary of $250,000. A week. When poor Norman was nicked at the Ramada Inn in Miami – the Ramada Inn? please – he had just trousered a paltry down-payment of $20,000.) But, first and foremost, drug-traffickers use the Turks and Caicos because of its location – 575 miles south-east of Miami, 600 miles north of Colombia.

Handy though the islands are for the intrepid employees of the Colombian cartels, they are not easily reached from Britain. Significantly, there is no direct flight to the Turks and Caicos from Britain, so I had to fly to Miami, stay there overnight (long enough to have me drastically expand my category of non-obese Americans), then catch another plane from Miami to the island of Providenciales – Provo, for short.

Thirty-three hours after leaving Heathrow, I stepped out on to Provo and into an alfresco sauna. It was immediately clear that this was to be the only feature Provo shared with prosperous, organised, dynamic Bermuda. The airport building was a long, thin, mildly ramshackle affair with a corrugated-iron roof. From the outside, it looked very like a tropical version of the office I used to work in. Inside, the place was a mess with lots of people milling and lounging, so the resemblance to the *Sunday Times* office grew ever stronger.

Having dined the night before on a pizza that had been, by American standards, kiddy-sized, my calorie intake for the day so far amounted to a complimentary baglet of peanuts on the plane, but now that it was late afternoon I felt the slightest twinge of hunger. I was waiting for a plane to take me to the Turks and Caicos capital, on Grand Turk, so I had some time to kill. (An hour? Two hours? A week? Nobody seemed to know.) Knackered, hot, bemused, I headed for Provo airport's restaurant/bar, where I ordered a cheese-burger and a beer from a waitress so militantly surly I worried that I'd suffered some dire short-circuit in my synapses and called her something very nasty.

Eventually, a few people started to congregate at the barren kiosk that served as the office for Turks and Caicos Airways. More out of hope than expectation, and really just for something to do, I joined them. Finally, after the crowd had swollen to half a dozen, a very thin and very bullied gofer piled our luggage on to a 'trolley' and wheeled it off down the tarmac, amid shouts and jeers, to a plane that made the Falklands hatchback look like a stretch limo. We six climbed aboard, in much the same way as we would had we been trying to break a world record by cramming an entire Rotary Club into a Mini. The pilot checked both propellers were working, shut his door and flicked the odd switch. The plane bumped along the runway and into the air, while I tried to buckle my seat-belt – no easy task because I was crouched in such a way that, for the first time in my life, autofellatio seemed feasible. Or obligatory.

We left the brown scrub of Provo behind and flew over turquoise sea. To the north, on our left, we passed by a succession of flat, tropically green islands – North Caicos, Middle Caicos, the unin-habited East Caicos – before beginning the short descent to the runway at South Caicos. Preposterously, two more passengers were waiting to get in. They were both large, white, sweating, middle-aged businessmen. Just as obviously, they both came from Laahndin and were thoroughly racist. They continued bellowing their reflections on last night's drinking bout while they climbed over, around and into their fellow-passengers, who were all, with the exception of myself, black and therefore beneath contempt.

By the time we had taken off again and flown over the Columbus Passage – where the shallow, turquoise water turns deep blue as the water suddenly reaches a mid-Atlantic depth – and come down to land on Grand Turk, I realised that I had worked myself into a stonking bad mood. My first three hours here had made me extremely uncomfortable – it was hot, my shirt was soaking with sweat, my knees had been above my head for forty minutes, many of the locals I had come across so far were sulky or aggressive, and those two businessmen, now bawling about some forthcoming deal, were ghastly beyond endurance.

Somehow we all spilled out of the plane. I collected my bags from the hold (in a wing) and squelched into Grand Turk's airport terminal. Was this (1) an ultra-modern masterpiece of graceful steel pylons, smoked-glass windows and Italian marble finishings, or (2) a not very big shed? No conferring. Demonstrating great cunning for someone in her dreadful state, a woman, made bone-thin and desperate by drugs or disease, spurned the six locals and the two white businessmen and chose me to claw as she wailed at me: 'Dollah, jess a dollah.' I fidgeted in my pockets to find some change and forced myself to acknowledge what I was thinking. And what I was thinking was, what a fucking awful country.

'Welcome to Grand Turk. Where are you wanting to go, sir?' A large woman was shooing the desperate beggar away and smiling at me.

'The Turks Head Inn. Is it far?'

'A little ways along the road. Just you wait here a moment in the shade.'

She marched off and returned in her taxi. I piled in and she set off at a leisurely pace down a narrow, sandy lane, past a couple of shacks, some recently built bungalows and a few scrubby fields where horses were trying to graze. She turned into an even narrower lane and I leaned back. It was clearly going to be a little while before we reached the Turks Head Inn because that was on Grand Turk's principal road, Front Street. 'Here you are,' she said after another two seconds. 'Turks Head.' We had rolled to a halt, in the middle of the narrower lane, outside a truly charming, old, colonial-style house. Wooden pillars supported a verandah that ran the length of the upper floor and looked out on a front garden splashed with red blooms and shaded by several lovely old trees. After my saviour had driven off at the same leisurely pace, I plonked my bags in the middle of the lane and listened to a tranquillity broken only by an occasional chirruping of birdsong and the shushing of gentle waves. Waves? I took a couple of steps to the left and saw that immediately beyond the fading, shuttered house on the other side of the road lay an empty beach where there lapped an unbelievably tame Atlantic Ocean. I turned slowly round, gazing in disbelief at the sun-kissed beach, the venerable colonial-style house, the peaceful lane that meandered off round a corner . . . where there appeared two boys, eight or nine years old, leading a donkey. As the boys passed by, they gave me a surreptitious once-over and smiled shyly before returning to the evidently serious task of leading the donkey further up the lane. As I followed their progress, I thought to myself, what a truly miraculous, wonderful country.

I changed my opinion yet again the following day, which I spent mooching round Grand Turk, or, to be pedantic, Grand Turk's and the Turks and Caicos' capital, Cockburn Town, but since the Town spreads in a higgledy-piggledy manner all over the island and the island is itself so small, Cockburn Town exists in name only and on specialised maps. Anyway, as I was saying, I spent the following day mooching around Grand Turk and thinking that this was the kind of place which could be thought unmitigatedly miraculous and wonderful by a socially myopic day-tripper.

It was a restful part of the Caribbean, I'd give it that, for nothing was happening, and it looked as though nothing had been what was happening since the death of Queen Victoria. Fair's fair – there was some action at the back of the hotel, where pelicans were happily dive-bombing the salt-ponds in what might be supposed to be the centre of town. I walked dreamily back to the front of the hotel and round the corner whence the two boys and their donkey had appeared. In this way I discovered that the peaceful lane kept on being peaceful, although it now contained Grand Turk's commercial and administrative centre. One side of this Front Street was waterfront, but there any resemblance to Bermuda's Front Street ended. Opposite the lazily lapping Atlantic there slumped a succession of old and world-weary buildings. Some were no more than shacks, others wouldn't have made the grade as gang-huts (they housed illegal Haitian immigrants), and even the clapboard and corrugated-iron constructions that had once had the energy to grow larger than a single storey looked as if they would crash creakily to the ground on being subjected to a casual, one-handed lean on a flimsy wooden pillar. There were a couple of buildings which looked capable of surviving a gentle breeze – the Victoria Public Library, shaped like a chapel and painted pink, a miniature complex of government offices, and an ugly modern block with a sign announcing, 'ARCLAYS BANK', where I tried to get some money, but there was no ashpoint.

Front Street's best-kept building was the museum. It actually looked spruce. It was sprucer inside and even had a video. The video and much of the ground floor showed the wreckage of a ship that had been found in excellent nick at the bottom of Turks and Caicos waters. Marine archaeologists had become very excited by the wreck because it dated back to the turn of the sixteenth century and was probably the oldest of the 112 ships lost in the Americas between Columbus' arrival in 1492 and 1530. Just where Columbus arrived in 1492 is a matter of fierce debate, but the consensus on Grand Turk was that this was the first island he discovered in the New World. Everything fits, I was to be told again and again – the other islands he mentions in his journal, the landscape, the now-dried-up channel in the middle of Grand Turk. Whenever I mentioned the widely held assumption that Watling Island along the road had been Columbus' first transatlantic port-of-call, I'd be answered by dark, knowing references to the devious energies of the Bahamas' PR machine. No, no, I was assured again and again, it was definitely Grand Turk where Columbus first landed.

I'm not at all sure that this should be any cause for local pride, for one of the hard facts we know about Columbus' arrival is that it initiated a very efficient campaign of genocide. Before 1492, the Turks and Caicos were inhabited by the Lucayans, who'd come here some 900 years before from Venezuela via Haiti. As is usual with almost any matter concerning the Turks and Caicos, there are conflicting accounts about this, but one school of thought states that the Caicos part of the country's name is Lucayan. (The Turks bit is supposed to derive from the red flower of a local cactus that looks not very like a fez.) Another linguistic legacy was the Lucayan term for the practice of grilling meat over an open fire – *barbacoa*.

That's just about it as far as the Lucayan legacy goes, because, by the time the magnificently named Juan Ponce de León officially discovered these islands in 1512, the native population had declined from many thousands to one. That sole Lucayan was an old man who had somehow survived the newly imported diseases and the repatriation scheme whereby the Spanish took Lucayans back to Haiti as slave labour. Columbus himself had captured seven Lucayans as he passed through the Turks and Caicos. One of them he took back to Spain, where the godless savage was baptised in Barcelona, christened Diego Colón (the godparents were the King and Queen of Spain), prodded, petted and pointed at, and then employed as an interpreter on Columbus' next journey to the New World. What, I wondered, did Diego make of this alien abduction? It must have been every bit as mind-shattering as being whisked up into a flying saucer by tall, slim types with big, slanted, black eyes, and subjected to all manner of orificial probings.

The Lucayans sounded admirable. They fished, they grew fruit and vegetables, they weren't that keen on fighting, they were proficient astronomers (a settlement on Middle Caicos was laid out to correlate with solstices, the rising positions of Sirius and suchlike), and they liked their sport (the same settlement on Middle Caicos included a ball court). Unfortunately for them, they assumed that Columbus & co. were demi-gods, to be welcomed with food and drink and trust. That helps to explain why all that remains of their civilisation are pottery fragments such as I found on display upstairs in the museum.

The islands were completely uninhabited when some Bermudians arrived in 1678 to start raking salt – the islands' principal, in fact only, industry for nigh on three centuries. A pile of salt featured on the Turks and Caicos flag – or, rather, a pile of salt was supposed to feature on the Turks and Caicos flag, but a designer in Whitehall altered the white mound by inserting a couple of lines to make a door, the better to signify that this was an igloo. Such was the prominence of this country even during the height of imperial fervour in the 1870s.

The museum included a couple of exhibits concerning the igloo fiasco. Other landmarks of Turks and Caicos' history covered here were the visit of the Queen and the Duke of Edinburgh in 1966 (when the offending door on the flag was eventually removed to commemorate the occasion), the landing near Grand Turk, four years before the regal visit, of John Glenn, after he became the first

American to orbit the earth and . . . in truth, there wasn't much else, for it doesn't take long to deal with the history of the Turks and Caicos. In 1764, the French established a small settlement but were immediately kicked out again; 1799, the islands were annexed to the Bahamas; 1873, the islands were annexed to Jamaica; 1962, the islands were annexed back to the Bahamas after Jamaica gained independence; 1964, the final collapse, after a long illness, of the islands' salt industry, when the Bahamas built a salt-processing plant; 1974, the Bahamas gained independence and the Turks and Caicos had to go it alone and become a crown colony in its own right.

However, since 1974, the country has made up for lost time and generated more than its fair share of shenanigans. Politics here dates back to 1974 when Jags McCartney founded the Popular Democratic Movement and the future jailbird Norman Saunders the People's National Party. A year later there was the nearest the islands could manage to an insurrection when Jags and assorted followers barricaded themselves in the Junkanoo Club on Grand Turk and took a couple of people hostage – not that the hostages minded too much being kidnapped in a bar. There was a rumpus afterwards from one hostage when he was sent a bill for the drinks he'd had, but, apart from that, the affair ended peacefully and Jags was able to pursue his campaign for self-government legitimately when his PDM won the islands' first elections in 1976. Jags' battle with the imperial oppressor climaxed in 1979 when the imperial oppressor, in the form of Nicholas Ridley, told him that the Turks and Caicos would have independence whether he liked it or not, and here was twelve million quid to be going on with. Jags demanded £40 million. Ridley got angry. Finally, the negotiating skill of Thatcher's government was such that the Turks and Caicos received £12 million plus the assurance that they needn't be independent.

A year later, the Turks and Caicos returned to bug the British. Club Med promised to build a £50 million complex on Providenciales – if the British government supplied the readies to build a new runway and a road. Six million pounds were spent on a runway (where cracks immediately disfigured the surface), to the horror of the House of Commons, where MPs asked just why taxpayers' money was being splashed out to benefit a French firm. Jags, meanwhile, was killed in a plane crash, engineered, it was rumoured, by the CIA, and in the company, it was rumoured, of top-ranking American criminals. Just when the islands were threatened by political stability, Saunders got himself incarcerated and a British commission of enquiry found evidence of corruption throughout the islands, whereupon Whitehall suspended the local government and instigated a period of direct rule. And now, just when things appeared to have settled down again, Martin Bourke had thrown his spanner in the Turks and Caicos' creaking, rusting works. It seemed safe to conclude that the recent history of the Turks and Caicos Islands amounted to a shambles.

However, looking on the bright side, islanders weren't going short of gossip. And gossip was always high on the agenda back in the Turks Head Inn, where local (white) worthies gathered every night to sit around the big round table in the restaurant and relate tales of varying heights. Much of the chitchat formed an entertaining and, I am sure, libellous obituary of the governorship of the recently departed Martin Bourke – or Fat Martin, as some worthies called him. Here's to Martin, a good bloke. Say what you like but he wasn't stuck up like some governors here. The new guy was due in next week. Kelly from Bermuda. Supposed to be a hard-liner. Remember that time when KC stashed his hash underneath a bush and it was set alight? We got stoned just breathing the air. Incidentally, you-know-who was seen in Miami, deep in conversation with his main man. So expect a couple of night-flights from Colombia pretty damned soon. Hear what happened to that policewoman? Well . . .

The worthies found occasional rivals in the chaps who were staying for a night or two on business, although, from what I saw, business consisted of perching on a bar stool at the Turks Head Inn. These middle-aged, white, stogie-puffing businessmen weren't quite as bad as the pair on the plane from Provo, but they managed to make me feel unusually right-on as they compared notes about their favourite Puerto Rican brothels. One evening, the bar was bulging, as the worthies and the passing businessmen were joined by the three crew members of the freight plane that makes a weekly shopping delivery to Grand Turk. The trio were stranded, having unloaded crates of groceries to find that they couldn't start up the plane again; when they finally did succeed in cranking the aged machine into some semblance of life, they couldn't take off because the girl in the control tower had gone home.

Not too much had changed in the Turks and Caicos, it seemed, since the days when one of the Turks Head regulars, an amiable cove in his seventies called Barclay, had flown from island to island, delivering mail by flying as low and slow as possible, then simply dropping the packages on to runwayless ground. Before Barclay set up his own little airline here in 1969, journeys between the islands had to be made by sloop – thus, while the NASA personnel up the road were monitoring John Glenn's earth orbit, locals were having to set aside several days – four or five if there was a strong headwind – to travel by boat from Provo to Grand Turk.

Obeying Ritchie's First Law of Colonial Life – which states that, whichever pink bit I visited, I would have a better than evens chance of meeting an expert on Scottish football – I was befriended by a Glaswegian called Mike Cassidy, who, despite his addiction to cigarettes and his resemblance to Ray Illingworth, had played for Third Lanark and was still an avid Celtic fan. Nonetheless, one of his mates had been an ex-Rangers player, Sandy Leggett, who'd somehow landed on Salt Cay, married a local woman, Irene, and stayed there for thirty years. He'd died the previous year, but, Mike said, whatever I did, I should look in on Irene and say hello for him. Fortunately for Mike, he had also enjoyed the company of another Celtic fanatic – a previous governor who used to invite him round to the official residence for afternoons spent watching Celtic games via the government satellite. Fat Martin couldn't compete with such zeal for the Celts, but Mike had liked him well enough: 'He was all right. Although he fell out with me once, after the Queen's Birthday Parade, when the *Miami Herald* carried a photo of the T-shirt I was wearing for the occasion. The slogan was, "Grow Your Own Dope – Plant an Englishman". Fat Martin was not best pleased.' The resulting froideur had been a touch awkward, not least because Mike's wife Pat worked in the Governor's office.

Obeying Ritchie's Second Law of Colonial Life – which states that the non-diplomatic expats in Britain's pink bits tend to have intriguing biographies – Mike had graduated from professional football to become a mechanical engineer by trade and had made a living out here by mending anything and everything that was mendable. He'd been on Grand Turk sixteen years now, done up a house and bought some scrubland which, after several years' work with a machete, he'd transformed into his own eighteen-hole golf course. I should pop over some time for a game. And another thing – I should get in touch pretty damned quick with the number-two official and acting Governor, Roger Cousins, otherwise I'd be cold-shouldered by the powers-that-be, who, in the wake of Bourke's dismissal, might be a bit suspicious of any writer on the islands.

Mike was spot on. After two days of humming and hawing phone calls, I finally secured an appointment at the government offices. A short but thirsty walk up the road, I stumbled towards the Governor's expensively renovated official residence, Waterloo (it was built in 1815). I rested content with admiring one gable end of Waterloo, not on account of the 'Strictly Private' sign but because there was the rival attraction of the Governor's official car – a white taxi with a Union Jack on the radiator.

'Come in, come in,' said a jovial man with a greying beard as he motioned me into his office. 'Roger Cousins. Please take a seat. Right, before we start, I should tell you that you have been cleared by the Foreign Office.'

'What?'

'But only on the condition that our chat will be a general and off-the-record briefing. And that this briefing will be for your book and not for the purposes of any newspaper article.'

'What?'

'That is what I have been instructed to tell you.'

'But—' I was flooded with adolescent outrage. 'Free country,' I spluttered, 'British citizen . . . freedom of the press . . . every right to . . . public servant . . .' I may not have known what I was talking about, but I knew that I was now going to have to write an article about the Turks and Caicos and what the opening paragraph would be. As for the interview that followed, that was, unsurprisingly in the circumstances, bland. Governor's role, elected legislative council of thirteen MPs, aid programme from Britain of £20 million over three years, technical assistance provided by the Overseas Development Administration, blah blah blah.

It wasn't poor Roger Cousins' fault, and he did have me scribbling with interest at one point when I asked him why the Turks and Caicos was still a colony and he replied, 'I don't know,' but all this 'official clearance' and 'off the record' rubbish did make me wonder, not for the first time in the course of my travels for this book, if the Foreign and Commonwealth Office really knew what it was about.

Come to think of it, what was the Foreign and Commonwealth Office doing with and for the Turks and Caicos? How was that aid being spent? What technical assistance had the ODA provided? I couldn't see any sign of ODA projects, and neither could 'belongers' or expats, who would all answer my queries about Britain's technical assistance to the islands with a derisive laugh. Grand Turk was a picturesque but dreadfully run-down backwater which mysteriously had not benefited from having an exploitable low-wage economy, duty-free and offshore status, plus access to the European Community. (I was told that a Hongkong businessman had been scouting round the Caribbean to transfer his money to some offshore bank; he'd plumped for the British Virgin Islands because, in the absence of any information, he at least knew from their name that they were British. As for the Turks and Caicos . . . like just about everyone else on earth, he hadn't heard of the place.) More modestly, a couple of small factories producing high-cost items, even a bit of trade with the Dominican Republic or Haiti, would surely have helped. But there seemed to be no development here.

The best or only chance of a job for many people on Grand Turk and elsewhere in the island chain is in Provo, helping build or serving in a hotel. Wealth in the Turks and Caicos has always shifted from one island to another – once the economic centre had been South Caicos, then the salt industry had taken off on Grand Turk and Salt Cay, and now all the meaningful cash was being invested and spent in the tourist industry in Provo. When I asked the Director of Tourism, Earle Higgs, how much tourism now contributed to the national economy, he replied, simply, 'Everything.'

Earle's goal is to attract 100,000 people a year to the islands, but, as he readily admitted, the tourist industry is just beginning to develop here and the current number falls a good 20,000 short of the target. He wasn't panicking, though, sensibly reckoning that too rapid an expansion would pose far greater problems and would soon become self-defeating; tourists come here for the natural (underwater) attractions, which have to be treated with great care. He wanted to see diversification, so that the country could offer more than sunshine and great diving, and so that islands other than Provo benefited, but the statistics he handed me showed that any fulfilment of this vision still lay far in the future.

Those statistics also showed that almost all of the islands' visitors come from North America and hardly any from Britain, a fact which reinforced my impression that the British impact on the Turks and Caicos had been very slight. People drove on the left, the police wore British-style uniforms, the phone box outside the Turks Head was an old-fashioned number (bleached pink by the sun), the Queen's profile was on the country's stamps, Front Street had its Arclays Bank, and there was a smattering of freckly British expats here, but that – save for the scandalous contribution of the ex-Governor – was about the extent of the colonial influence. In 1974, the Turks and Caicos had applied for some sort of association with the Canadian government, which turned the request down, and in 1986 an opinion poll had stated that 65 per cent of islanders still favoured a link with Canada rather than Britain – and who could blame them, when Britain's acting Governor confesses that he can't see why Britain is holding on to the islands?

Britain's lack of involvement or purpose was all too evident in comatose Grand Turk. I had planned to spend most of my time on this island, since it was supposed to be the capital, but, following the advice of Earle and his deputy Ralph, I decided to move on. The arrangements were fraught and complex, but Ralph fixed me up with some sort of an itinerary. I'd leave early the next morning, spend a day on the petite island of Salt Cay, fly up to North Caicos for a couple of days, then end up in Provo. And there I'd stay, oh joy, at the Grace Bay Hotel. We celebrated with a lunch at a roadside café, then hitched a lift back to the centre of town from a cop car.

As Ralph and I were saying goodbye, the thin beggar who'd clawed me at the airport came shuffling towards us. I'd seen her since, staggering around the Turks Head Inn with an outstretched styrofoam cup, but this time she was more desperate and more insistent. She clung on to Ralph and kept howling her plea: 'Jess piece chicken gimme dollah jess a dollah jess piece chicken . . .' Quietly and kindly, Ralph calmed her down and placed something in her hand. Mumbling and stifling sobs, she shuffled off down a deserted, worn-out Front Street.

Exhausted after a night spent summoning up the courage to do battle with a rottweiler-sized cockroach, I sneaked out of the hotel as dawn was breaking and, miraculously, made it to Grand Turk's airport in time for the plane's departure at half-six. The morning air smelled cool and fresh, in sharp contrast to the visibly decaying plane, which smelled of its fish consignment three days before. By now an old hand at the small-plane game, I hunched down into a very damp seat, beside two old chaps and a young lad in a business suit, and whimpered calmly during take-off.

Fifteen minutes later, the plane swung down on to the runway on Salt Cay, where a pick-up truck was waiting to take us wherever we wanted to go on the island. I perched on my bags in the back and wondered if there could be anywhere on this dusty, silent outcrop I did want to go. After dropping off the two old chaps at a couple of nearby cottages – both could be graded as being halfway between shacks and bungalows – and the young lad at another cottage further along the road, the truck-driver suggested that he could take me to Brian's place.

'Can I get a cup of coffee at Brian's place?'

'Sure. If Brian's up.'

It was ten to seven. I hoped Brian was an early riser.

Not this morning he wasn't. Brian's place turned out to be a relatively substantial guest-house, equipped with two storeys, a corrugated-iron roof, a garden and, jutting out from the kitchen at the back, a little restaurant and a bar, where I dumped my bags. I nosed around in the kitchen, hoping against hope that I might bump into Brian, whoever he was, carrying a pot of freshly brewed coffee. I did bump into a hen careering about in the restaurant, where the only other occupant was a humming-bird which hovered around my head. Perhaps it was time for a daunder.

I strolled down the rough track to the slightly less rough road, which, I began to suspect (rightly), was the island's main street, now being used by an unsupervised herd of extremely thin cattle ambling off to my right. Brian's place was by far the most imposing building I could see. There were a few cottages dotted about, and a couple of long sheds. And that was all I could see of Balfour Town, Salt Cay's capital. I crossed the road, skirted a harbour containing one boat, and walked gingerly over a stone-strewn beach, where I killed some time gazing at the breaking waves. A jet-trail appeared in the sky. It was an incongruous reminder that elsewhere on the planet the late twentieth century was going about its business.

An hour later, I returned to Brian's place to find a pot of freshly brewed coffee waiting for me outside the kitchen. I was gulping down my second mug when a roly-poly, middle-aged, white chap with a bald, freckled head and more than a hint of the gingery skin that the sun loves to hate appeared from round the corner. 'I saw those bags,' he said, flopping over and shaking my hand, 'and, you know, I kinda guessed I might have company. You want some breakfast?'

Ravenous, I inhaled two eggs on toast while learning that my host was an American called Brian Sheedy and that he used to work in New York, creating audio-visual displays for corporate events. 'I'd been to Salt Cay many times before, but I came out here to live permanently eight years ago,' he said. 'I run this guest-house and a diving operation. This is a great place for diving.'

'I take it you're not suffering a high-season rush at the moment?'

'Not exactly. But I'm still busy. Got a lot of hay to gather this week.'

'I can't imagine anything less like life in New York.'

'Yeah. Not a lot of call for hay-gathering in Manhattan, that's for sure.'

Brian was soon busy enough because we were joined by two more human beings – a Welshman taking a holiday from the British Embassy in Cuba who had landed on Salt Cay's second incoming plane of the day, and the young lad in the business suit. The young lad was at something of a loss, for he had come here to perform an inspection for the Environmental Health Office and, having completed the task, faced a whole day waiting for the four o'clock return flight to Grand Turk. Quite why the Welshman was on Salt Cay for the day, he couldn't say himself. With all four of us not having anything to do, Brian offered to conduct a tour of the island. The other two said they were content to sit back and relax in the restaurant, which was just as well because Brian's tour vehicle turned out to be a two-seater golf buggy.

It was an inspired choice of transport for Salt Cay. The buggy's awning offered protection from the sun's glare, ventilation wasn't a problem since the bodywork didn't reach our knees, the little wheels coped very well with the island's pebbled tracks, and although the top speed must have been 6 miles an hour, that still meant Brian could reach just about anywhere in Salt Cay within ten minutes.

We bumped along to the airstrip, past several cottages whose walls were decorated with conch shells, then turned north under a blazing sun towards Salt Cay's magnificent folly, the trillion-star Windmills Hotel where the meanest room in low season costs $455 a night. The occasional haunt of stars of stage and screen, Windmills was currently in its customary state – completely empty. It was a lavish jumble of buildings with brightly painted turquoise and red roofs, and stood in lonely unused splendour on the edge of a beach of fine, white sand. It was easy to imagine ageing pop stars cavorting naked here with their oiled bimbettes. I was far more surprised by the unimaginary creature that watched us disembark from the buggy to snoop around. It was sitting on the top of a telegraph pole. Squinting up into the hot sky, I could make out dark wings and beak, a white breast and head.

'You see it?' Brian asked. 'That's one of our ospreys. They had a nest round here but it got blown over in the last hurricane.'

'An *osprey*! Jesus, when I was a kid, it was major news in Scotland when two ospreys turned up to make a nest. There were daily updates about them on the television. My dad took us on a two-day round trip to the Highlands so that we could look at the nest from a specially built hut about a mile away.'

'Strict security, huh?'

'God, yes. Those ospreys were guarded night and day by the paramilitary wing of the RSPB, and you've got them hanging out on telegraph poles.'

'Yeah, well, you'll see a few of them round abouts. You want to see Iggy?'

'Iggy?'

'Iggy our iguana. He and his lady friend live over the hill.'

We set off again, leaving Windmills to bask in its prolonged redundancy, and came to a kind of quarry. A yellow digger was sitting abandoned in the heat. And in the digger's shade there basked a small, green dinosaur.

'I think that's Iggy's girl,' Brian whispered. 'Get out nice and slow, tiptoe towards her, you might get a photograph. That's far enough. You get her?'

I did. As I write, I am looking at a close-up of a digger's front tyres, my thumb and a small, green dinosaur lumbering away from the camera.

The next wildlife spectacle was as surprising. We were bumping along the track leading back to Balfour Town, past a new but abandoned brick hut which was supposed to have been Salt Cay's airstrip terminal and was built on a site that the islanders assured the authorities would be subjected to the flooding which duly occurred. And there beyond the brick shell were some cows. Like the cows I'd seen in Balfour Town, they were extremely thin, and, I now knew from Brian, like them they were wild. Feral cattle. Their ancestors had belonged to farmers' herds in the distant past and, after the farmers gave up on farming here, had been allowed to make their own way in life. A hundred yards further along the track we came across a group of wild donkeys and a lone, slight bullock trying its best to look menacing.

When we returned to the island's hamlet of a capital, we looked in on Irene Leggett. She was a diffidently courteous old soul who smiled broadly when I passed on Mike Cassidy's best wishes and proudly led me on a tour of her house. I'd been half expecting to find her home covered in Rangers pennants and team photographs, but fortunately there was no Hun memorabilia, only a host of religious ornaments. Then it was back to the sightseeing as Brian gave me a tour of the remains of Salt Cay's salt-raking industry. In the eighteenth and nineteenth centuries, Salt Cay and Grand Turk were the world's largest suppliers of salt. Whereas the only reminder of those heydays on Grand Turk were the salinas frequented by the pelicans, here on Salt Cay the industrial heritage had remained untouched since the salt-rakers gave up and left the island to its drastic decline. Those sheds I'd already passed by the harbour had been used to store the salt. Over there lay a rusted winch, and there the remains of the short railway, and here were the irrigation trenches that led to the huge, rectangular salt ponds (each accompanied by a wooden windmill) which covered much of the island's flat centre. The basic idea was to fill the ponds with sea-water, expose them to the sun, and, after many months, rake in the salt residue. (The operation involved many more complicated filterings and irrigations, and it all made sense when Brian explained it at the time, but I'm afraid I've remembered only the bit about the basic idea.)

The next stop on Brian's tour was on the other side of the track. He veered off to a rotting warehouse and jetty, and then to Salt Cay's biggest building, a glaringly white, two-storey mansionette with green shutters and a distinctively Bermudian stepped roof. It was still owned by the Harriots, a Bermudian family which had once made a packet out of the saltworks, but now the house lay empty. In several places, notably under a wildly decayed shed, salt still lay in packed piles, waiting for boats that would never arrive. It was as if, eighty or ninety years ago, the salt-rakers had all packed a few suitcases and run off, leaving an unwitting memorial to Victorian industrial technology.

At the turn of the twentieth century, 900 people had lived and worked on Salt Cay. Now the number of adults living on the island was sixty-seven. 'During the eight years I've lived here,' Brian reflected, 'I've been to twelve funerals and not a single wedding.' There are, however, thirty-one children on Salt Cay, most of whom skipped around the buggy as we passed by the primary school, a neat little bungalow that boasted a fresh coat of yellow paint and a locally renowned reputation as the producer of bright, smart exam-passers. After some shy banter and one doomed attempt to hitch a ride on the buggy, the kids skipped off to start a chasing game on the raised paths that marked the boundary of each salt-pond. We bumped further along, past a series of empty, dilapidated houses. A dozen or so buildings or plots had been bought by expats for holiday homes, but Brian was the only permanent expat resident, and half the island's houses still lay fallow.

One of those empty houses caught my eye. It looked as if it had just been hit by a hurricane, but it was a matter of yards from the deserted and beautiful beach. Say ten thousand quid for the building and its patch of land, twenty thousand to do it up really well, shove in a generator and get a plumber in . . . install a fax and a modem . . . I could work, swim, sunbathe . . . go osprey-watching and . . . um . . . Well, it was a good daydream, no matter how silly.

Brian, by contrast, had had the wherewithal to make his own

daydream work. He had his guest-house, he had his hopes that one day the island's extraordinarily preserved industrial museum-pieces would be done up, and he had his diving. The clear, shallow, coral-strewn waters surrounding Salt Cay make for superb dives – so I am told – and Brian enthused about the marine life he'd seen, including humpback whales which pass by the Turks and Caicos each February on their annual migration. He had also made an underwater discovery. Just south of Salt Cay he'd come across the 200-year-old wreck of the HMS *Endymion* in a coral canyon busy with fish. The other highlight of Brian's diving tours lay on the seabed a stone's throw from the Harriots' house. It was a white marble tombstone commissioned by a smitten admirer to commemorate the death in November 1813 at the age of twenty of Jane Jones. Brian's theory was that the tomb marked the spot where Jane died, possibly during 1813's unsurpassably violent hurricane.

Only when Brian manoeuvred the buggy back up the track towards the guest-house did I realise that some of my facial muscles were aching because I had spent over two hours continually wide-eyed with astonishment and smiling with delight. And it seemed that the best part of the day was still to come, for I had seized upon Brian's offer to provide a mask and flippers. I'd never been snorkelling before and I swim like a cat, but the chance to see the reputedly wondrous coral reefs on Salt Cay's north coast was one I had to take.

Having rustled up some burgers and beers for lunch, Brian went off to discover when or if a plane could ferry me to North Caicos at any time in the foreseeable future. The Welsh diplomat, the young lad in the business suit and I chatted with a young German woman who was here for three weeks to study the island for some postgraduate degree. She was into her third week and clearly glad to see new faces. I said that I envied her the opportunity to stay here for much longer than the morning and afternoon I had allotted myself – a rash claim, it transpired, when Brian returned from an hour on the phone to Turks and Caicos Airways with confusing news.

'It's fairly straightforward for you guys,' he said, nodding at the diplomat and the lad. 'Seems there'll be a plane at four to take you back to Grand Turk. Probably. But as for North Caicos' – he raised his eyebrows and took a sharp intake of breath – 'that depends on Lovelace.'

'Who?' I asked. 'What? Why? When?'

'Lovelace owns Windmills. According to Turks and Caicos Airways – mind you, that's no guarantee – he's flying in today from America. He'll be at Provo in half an hour. TCA will fly him down here and I've asked them to take you over to North Caicos on the flight back. At half-four. Maybe.'

'At least that'll give me an hour's snorkelling.'

'Forty-five minutes to be on the safe side,' said Brian. 'Kit's in the hut down on the right.'

I said my farewells to the others and hurried down to the hut, dug out a snorkel mask and flippers, marched along the track and only then remembered that my swimming trunks still lay amid my smalls in one of my bags. No matter. Following Brian's directions, I left the track behind and began to wade through scrub towards Salt Cay's north-west corner. I climbed a hill, skirting some jagged cliffs where another osprey was perched on a rocky edge. The osprey examined me with disdain, then turned back to monitoring the sea below. Ten minutes later I arrived at the spot Brian had recommended and a minute after that, having checked that the nearest sign of life was still on Grand Turk miles to the north, I had stripped off. Because I am a Presbyterian (lapsed), this was the first time I had been publicly clothesless since I stopped breast-feeding. What a shame that this book doesn't carry photos; I'll have to leave the scene to your imagination. Suffice to say that I stood on that beach, six feet four of rippling muscle, naked, bronzed and magnificent. I took off my specs and put on the flippers. Maybe, I thought, as I tried to walk to the water, I should have waited to put the flippers on.

Not resembling in the slightest an upright pink seal wearing clown shoes, I made laborious progress towards the sea. Some folk memory told me to dip the mask in the water before putting it on. God knows what good that did, but it didn't stop me breaking the elasticated band that might have been supposed to go round my head. Reduced to paddling with one hand while the other held the mask, I dipped under the waves, enjoyed a blurry, specless vision of something brown, breathed in and choked on a lungful of seawater.

The next twenty minutes I spent in an unseemly, nude frenzy five yards into the sea, trying to extricate the flippers from sand or rocks, trying to breathe, trying to see some underwater marvels and failing in every respect. I did see a little, smudgy fish. And I didn't drown. And nobody was looking. So it wasn't all bad. Guiltily aware that I hadn't quite made the most of one of the world's most accessible and spectacular coral reefs, I gave up and flippered back to my clothes, towelled myself dry with my trousers, hopped about a lot to stop sea or sand getting into my shoes, and, once half-dried and half-dressed, put my specs back on to admire the fabulous scenery – the deserted beach, the bright roofs of Windmills in the distance, the tranquil scrub, the sea and, a couple of hundred yards to the west, the boat carrying two fishermen incapacitated by laughter.

I squelched back to Balfour Town and was placing the burst mask in an untidy and unvisited corner of Brian's hut when I heard a plane overhead. That'd be Lovelace coming in from Provo. I ran up to the guest-house annexe. The Welshman and the young lad were gone, but Brian was sitting at his bar, chatting to a local who'd popped in for a rum.

'No rush,' they said, as I reached the bar, puce-faced and panting. 'That's the plane for Grand Turk. Lovelace hasn't cleared Provo customs yet.'

'Any idea when his plane is due?' I asked, starting to become a little concerned.

'Nope,' said Brian.

'Will it be today?'

'Probably.'

I began to fret about my schedule, about the hotel room waiting for me in North Caicos. And then I thought, what on earth was there to fret about? The doomsday scenario was that I'd be trapped overnight on a fascinating, tranquil, tropical island. 'A beer please, Brian,' I said, and settled back to listen to him and the rum-buyer discuss the hay-gathering and the meeting at one of the four churches catering for Salt Cay's sixty-seven adults. The rum-buyer had heard that some people were flying in for the meeting at the Church of God of Prophecy. Maybe I could cadge a lift to North Caicos on that plane? Who knows?

Eventually, we all agreed that perhaps I ought to turn up at the airstrip to see what, if anything, was happening. Nothing, was the inevitable answer, but a woman in a TCA uniform who was sitting there was moderately confident that a plane going somewhere would appear soon, so I decided to hang around, on the off-chance. I said my goodbyes and thank-yous to Brian, just in case I did make it off the island, and began to hang around.

I was joined, after a while, by a young bloke who rolled up in a needless, well-appointed Dodge taxi to wait for the religious arrivals.

'That's some car you got there,' commented the TCA woman. 'How you get the parts repaired and so on?'

The young bloke shook his head in wonder. 'You know, I can go to Grand Turk, Fed-Ex my request and my money to the dealer in Chicago and a couple of days later the man'll be sending the parts to me.'

'And who you got to thank for that?' asked the TCA woman.

The young bloke closed his eyes and nodded. 'The Lord.'

'Praise the Lord!'

'Praise him!'

'Praise the Lord!'

'You know,' said the young bloke, 'there's some people who don't have the Lord in their hearts.'

'I know it,' said the TCA woman sadly.

'In the States and in Europe. Some people there have no faith.'

'Difficult to imagine.'

'It's a terrible thing.'

I tried to recall my own vague certainties – the Big Bang, evolution, living things are because they can be, God is either dead or congenitally unemployable – and realised that those ideas would strike my companions as pathetic and puny, and that since I'd lose any philosophical argument with them in humiliating fashion, I'd best do a lot of wise nodding. It was a useful revelation that immediately proved its worth, because the next plane that landed carried half a dozen young, smartly dressed, Bible-clutching members of the Church of God of Prophecy.

'We don't know when our time will come,' one smart chap was remarking to the Dodge owner.

'But it will come.'

'My brother, maybe it's his time now. He's in the hospital now, waiting for surgery. Appendix. And, you know, I'm praying for him.'

'My prayers are with you too.'

'Thank you. For prayer can change everything. Every time.' The smart chap broadened the range of his beatific smile to include me. 'Don't matter your colour, when you are down on your knees before the Lord, you can be black or white, don't matter, it's just you and the Lord.'

'Praise the Lord!'

Here we go again, I thought while nodding silently, but the praising was cut short by shouts from the other passengers in the taxi for the pair to hurry up. I shook their hands farewell and walked over to the plane. It wasn't, of course, going to North Caicos, but another one that swooped down out of the red sun ten minutes later, incredibly, was. I clambered in and on to the free seat, the co-pilot's, while my alarmingly young and laid-back senior officer started up the propellers, shoved on his headphones and flicked a few switches. The other four passengers were dudes who, as the plane rose into the air, cracked open cans of beer and howled banter with the pilot. We hung a left so sharp that my waist was level with the pilot's hair, then abruptly straightened out to head not for North Caicos but for neighbouring Provo.

It was dusk when we dropped off the four dudes on Provo and picked up six men who worked there and were flying back to their homes on North Caicos for the weekend. 'Come on, come on! Let's get a move on, let's go!' shouted the pilot as bags were flung into the wings and the new batch of passengers rushed in.

'What's the hurry?' I hollered to the man behind me.

'Ain't no lights on the airstrip at North Caicos,' he yelled into my ear as the pilot shut his door while accelerating for take-off.

Despite the rapid changeover, dusk had become darkness by the time we were finishing the short hop from Provo. 'See those lights down there?' roared the man behind me. 'That's my village. Bottle Creek.'

I looked down at a short row of street lights. 'So where's the airstrip?'

'Where you're looking.'

'I can't see a thing.'

'Don't matter. This guy knows where to land.'

He did too. He might as well have been blindfolded, but

somehow the pilot bumped down in the middle of the runway and drew to a halt beside a hut and a waiting taxi.

Four of us jumped into the car for a journey that taught me several lessons. One was that the islanders I had talked to before must have been speaking with tremendously moderated accents because, of all the words exchanged in an animated conversation in the car, I could understand one – 'man'. Another was that North Caicos was completely different again from Grand Turk and Salt Cay – it had lots of trees and vegetation, for a start, and it was much larger because the journey to my hotel took a good fifteen minutes. A third was that this island was probably more thinly populated than even Salt Cay, for we passed only half a dozen houses in that fifteen minutes. (According to the guidebook I consulted that night, North Caicos occupies an area of 41 square miles and has a meagre population of 2,000, but as many as 500 islanders work on Provo.)

The hotel was an unexpectedly flash affair, a single-storey series of rooms arranged around a very cultivated tropical garden. The hotel was an Italian concern called the Club Vacanze and was doing its very best to live up to its local soubriquet – the Club Vacancy – because I was the one guest. In fact, I soon found out that I was the one tourist on North Caicos. With the island's two other hotels shut and the Club Vacancy having a skeleton staff – a security guard and a couple of Italians swanning round the place – it dawned on me that I faced a slight problem: where could I find anything to eat? The taxi-driver came to my rescue. He was a genial giant named Cornelius and nicknamed Tiger (given his size, I decided to stick respectfully to Cornelius), and I will be forever in his debt, for he took me back down the road to the one place on North Caicos where I could buy food – a guest-house with a small restaurant, and a shop, and a motorbike-hire franchise, run by a can-do American called JoAnne and her partner, an islander called Prince. Thanks to Cornelius, JoAnne and Prince, I was soon fed, watered and supplied with a moped.

The following morning I managed to scrounge a cup of coffee at the Club Vacancy and set off on a scooter tour of the island. The contrast with my Bermudian moped experience could not have been greater because Bermuda has roads and traffic. All but two of the roads on North Caicos are dusty tracks littered with weeds, boulders and holes. It was on a particularly dusty and pot-holed track that I zoomed along, past swamps and lush green foliage, towards one of the Caribbean's many Sandy Points, on the north-west tip of North Caicos.

There was not a roadsign or another person in sight, and I possessed a map which, even with JoAnne's scribbled amendments, was uselessly inaccurate, so I happily took several wrong turns, zooming up ever-narrower tracks that ended in puddles or turned back on themselves. I reached Sandy Point by luck rather than cunning, parked the bike and gazed at a travel agent's wet dream. A small, empty white beach gave on to a shallow stretch of water that had just enough room to turn turquoise before running into another small, empty white beach on a little island, all of 200 yards away.

The little island was Parrot Cay, once the home not of parrots but of pirates. Calico Jack Rackham might have hung out here, buckling his swash with his much fiercer girlfriend, the cross-dressing, pistol-packing Anne Bonny. These days, Parrot Cay is home to what I guessed was a broken-down boathouse and, luxuriating in an uninhabited, tropical Eden, a multi-million-pound hotel. It had been built in 1991 but had somehow fallen short of a five-star rating, so the owners, in a huff, had refused to open it. Several changes of ownership had failed to see this idyllic hotel open; hopes were high that the latest buyers would get it going, but the precedents were not encouraging.

I knew from JoAnne how much progress had recently been made in North Caicos. When she arrived here in 1981, the island had no paved roads at all and no electricity. Plots of land were now being bought and several hotels had been constructed, but those hotels hadn't proved a success. Club Vacancy was the only one that had kept going, and islanders wondered just how and why, given that the establishment was often empty. It was all most odd. My scooter rides let me see that there are very few parts of North Caicos that are not heart-soaringly beautiful; one of the island's villages is called Kew, and quite appropriately, for much of North Caicos wouldn't look at all out of place in a hothouse. I revelled in the emptiness, not least on my hotel's long and beautiful and completely unvisited beach, or on the scooter, when I mucked about on empty roads, swerving this way and that, bellowing songs to the wind. But why was I the only tourist on North Caicos? Why did so many of the islanders have to commute to Provo to find jobs? Why had those few hoteliers who had cottoned on to the place struggled, then failed?

I appreciated how undeveloped the island was far more on my second day when I rode down late in the afternoon to find one of the two attractions listed in the guidebook – the remains of a slave plantation started by Loyalists who had fled America after the War of Independence. JoAnne's squiggle on my map indicated that the path to the plantation led off somewhere to the right after I'd passed through Kew. I drove down the long, straight road, entertaining myself by trying to ride with no hands, closing my eyes during a slow count to ten, generally acting the eejit. I was well behaved, though, passing through Kew, because everyone in the village was out and about – sitting on walls, standing in the middle of the road or just hanging around. These seemed to be the three available leisure activities in Kew, apart from attending one of the village's hundred or so churches. Village and villagers were not, it can safely be said, rich.

Past Kew, the road degenerated into another bumpy track which, after an interminable time, came to an end at a creek. There was a path to the right. I parked the bike and began to march up the path. This soon acquired a central reservation of plants, then a central reservation of undergrowth, before becoming all central reservation. Having fought my way through scrub and bush for another hundred yards, I decided to take stock. Some poisonous, man-eating creature was scurrying somewhere to my left. A humming-bird skimmed about my head. Another bird hooted in derision. The only sign I'd come across that I wasn't the first person in human history to have made it this far up the path had been a rotting Reebok – the one remnant of the last travel-writer who had come here. Dusk was falling. I tried to remember some handy hints on survival skills, but could only come up with the SAS tip that when you are suffering from hypothermia it's a good idea to place your feet in your partner's groin. With no little effort, I hacked my way back to the creek, where I was mightily relieved to see two fishermen.

'Excuse me,' I said brightly. 'Could you tell me if that's the path to the, ah, Loyalist plantation?'

'What you mean, man, Loyalist plantation?'

'Yeah, the plantation, um, started by the Loyalists.'

'The slave plantation?'

'In so much as, that is to say, deplorable and shameful, yes, the . . . plantation.'

'You're way past, man. Got another half-mile to go back to Kew, turn left, track's clearly marked. Too late now, though. Sun's going down.'

The sun had well and truly sunk by the time I reached the hotel. The last mile had been an awkward one to negotiate, since the bike's headlight had the strength of an oil-lamp. However, there were no visibility problems when I took my evening stroll down to the empty beach, which was regularly lit up by a spectacular display of forked lightning far out to sea. Actually, not that far out to sea. And getting less far out to sea by the minute. I returned to the hotel hoping to find someone who might give me any kind of food, for the alternative would be to make the twenty-minute journey to JoAnne and Prince's place, riding a metal bike, furnished with an oil-lamp, in an intense lightning storm, directly overhead, along an otherwise unlit, winding, pot-holed road.

I found one Italian whose extensive dumbshow established that the kitchen was closed, and that there was no chef and, crucially, no food in the hotel. I had eaten one modest sandwich all day. It would be an adventure.

A residual sense of dignity forbids me from reporting how I reacted during that journey, as insects performed a continuous kamikaze attack on my chest and specs, bike-consuming pot-holes reared up before me and the worst lightning storm I've ever witnessed cracked all around the sky, vast forks spearing the ground. I'll say only that, were I forced, under threat of expert and prolonged torture, to choose between repeating that journey or tap-dancing along the gun at O'Hara's Battery, I'd have to opt for a Fred Astaire impersonation 1,396 feet above the Mediterranean.

Alerted by my bike's roar and my own fearful yells, JoAnne, bless her, bless her, scurried out of her house, opened the restaurant for me, and gave me steak, chips and succour. Yes, if it's quality accommodation, food, bike-hire or souvenirs you're after on North Caicos, all at bargain-basement prices, make sure you head for JoAnne and Prince's place, Whitby Plaza, North Caicos, tel. 67301.

Recovery from the trauma of the lightning storm was swift – not so much because I possess wondrous mental and emotional fortitude, though obviously that did help, as because the following day I checked into the Grace Bay Hotel on Provo, and the Grace Bay Hotel proved every bit as plush as I'd hoped. I spent the afternoon working really, really hard while I sunbathed on the Grace Bay's exclusive patch of beach and waiters plied me with complimentary sorbets. Thence to my room – room! hah! roomzz – where I toured my temporary domain, as a Bushman might tour the *QE2*. Giggling the while, I sat out on my balcony to savour the super-executive-first-class-five-star ambience, the view of waves crashing discreetly on to the immaculate shore and the hope-you-settle-in bottle of choice champagne. I resolved to put up with it all.

After a ten-minute hop in the plane, I had found myself on an island distinguished by a new jumble of shopping centres, KFCs, villas and offices for property consultants. The arid beigeness of the undeveloped bits of Provo merely added to the effect; the landscape itself looked as though it would be finished as soon as some subcontractors had fitted it out with trees and fields. The contrast with the unvisited lushness of North Caicos could hardly have been greater had the plane landed on Tyneside. The uncultivatable island that the Lucayans knew as Yucacanuco and that almost every generation since the Lucayans had known as the dry wilderness called Providenciales had suddenly been transformed into Provo, the Turks and Caicos' equivalent of the Algarve.

Provo's transformation from barren no-hoper to zippy money-maker has been rapid. It started in 1966 when a pilot called Fritz Luddington noted the potential for development here as he flew over the island. The prospect from the air looked good, not least because an aerial view didn't highlight Provo's swamps and infertile ground. Fritz persuaded two colleagues to join him in his big venture and, by 1971, they had succeeded to the extent that they had built a rudimentary airstrip and basic roads linking the three small settlements. However, by 1971, Providenciales contained only one telephone, and even by the mid-1980s visitors could still marvel at the island's wilderness.

The construction of a Club Med in 1980 – with that bumbling help from the British government, which had funded the construction of the airport and roads Club Med demanded – kick-started Provo's tourist industry. Now hotels and restaurants line up along Provo's coast, which doesn't bear comparison with any Costa but does provide much-needed work and revenue.

And there is no more gracious and gorgeous establishment on Provo's coast than the Grace Bay Hotel. I stayed for two nights, one of which was taken up by a thorough investigation of Grace Bay's graciousness and gorgeousness, the other by coping with the effects of sunstroke. Dizzy, woozy and queasy, I padded round my roomzz, enjoying every ill minute. Towards the end of my convalescent second afternoon, I sat out on the balcony to enjoy the view for a final time. Excepting oases such as the luxurious grounds of Grace Bay, scrubby, beige Provo was no match in the picturesque stakes for anywhere else in the Turks and Caicos, for even down-at-heel Grand Turk had a somnolent charm, but thank goodness it existed, enticing some money into the country, providing some jobs, even if these meant workers camping out during the week in dormitories and flying home to see their families at weekends. At least something was happening here.

And in the immediate vicinity of my balcony and my roomzz, the Turks and Caicos had come up with opulence to add to the sleepiness of Grand Turk, the abandoned and enchanting Salt Cay, the empty and lush North Caicos. Yes, this was the life, I told myself. Then I recalled a wailing voice: 'Dollah, dollah, jess a dollah.'

Chapter Six

Five Hours in Edinburgh: Tristan da Cunha

Up and down. Up and down. And up. And down. And . . . up . . . and, oh dear, oh no, down. And up . . .

The ship had left Cape Town four hours before on its journey across the South Atlantic to Tristan da Cunha, 1,519 nautical miles to the west. Only five days to go. Up. And . . . down.

'Mind you,' said the retired South African sitting next to me in the ship's lounge, 'the swell could be much, much worse. Lord, yes, if the Cape rollers really get going. And if we come across gales like we had on the Cape last week, you'll be bringing up your breakfast, I can tell you.'

'Really?'

'Lord, yes. You'll be seeing your sausages a second time, I can tell you. And your porridge.'

'Hah,' I said in a relatively hearty way.

'Lord, yes. With a bigger swell, you'll be able to take a look and say, there goes my bacon.'

'Oh?'

'And the kedgeree.'

'Oh.'

'Lord, yes. And the fried eggs.'

'Excuse me.'

'Bing-bong. Good afternoon, ladies and gentlemen. Here are today's navigational points of interest from the bridge. The ship's position at noon today, Friday the 22nd of November, was latitude 34 degrees

16 minutes south and longitude 5 degrees 47 minutes east. The distance run from noon yesterday was 377 nautical miles, giving the vessel an average speed, in a twenty-five-hour day, of 15.1 knots. The distance to go to Tristan da Cunha is 901 nautical miles and our estimated time of arrival is 0600 on the morning of Monday the 25th. The nearest point of land at noon was Slangkopf Point on the Cape Peninsula, which lay 620 nautical miles to the east. The depth of water beneath the vessel was 5,250 metres. The wind at noon was westerly force five on the Beaufort scale and sunset tonight is at 19.34. Ship's clocks will be retarded one hour tonight to Greenwich Mean Time, so upon retiring please remember to put your watches back one hour. Thank you.'

Up and down. Up and down.

The Royal Mail Ship *St Helena* usually plies its way between Cardiff and Cape Town via St Helena, but it also pays an annual call on the British outpost of Tristan da Cunha, a volcano that is home to fewer than 300 people, halfway between the southern tip of Africa and the southern tip of the Americas. Unless you have a marvellous cartographical collection, you will probably find that Tristan features in your atlas only in those general maps of the world in the first or last pages. Tristan has no airstrip and is so remote that it can rely on visits from two trawlers three times a year and the annual call of the RMS *St Helena*, bringing mail, vital supplies and some luxury items such as bottles of gas or tinned peaches. Plus eighty-odd passengers, some of them St Helenians taking the long way home from the Cape, most of them adventuresome tourists – mainly retired folk who could afford the time and the money to indulge in this oddball cruise.

The first leg of the voyage, from Cape Town to Tristan, passed enjoyably enough, not counting the initial brouhaha in my cabin's vomitorium. There were quizzes and games and meals and more meals. There was a ceremony when we crossed the line of zero degrees longitude, when the otherwise genial crew did amusingly vile things with eggs, treacle and offal to gasping volunteers. Three whales swam by, announcing their presence by spouting thin sprays and a farewell flourish of fins. We sighted a grand total of two other vessels on the horizon: container ships from Brazil. And there were birds. By the fourth day of the journey, anyone pointing out an albatross gliding over the waves would be indulged with a polite half-smile, much as a first-time visitor to London might be treated on spotting a red double-decker bus. Albatross schmalbatross.

And all the while, the ship ploughed through the South Atlantic swell. Up and down. Up and down.

One thousand, five hundred and nineteen nautical miles west of Cape Town, the ship made its annual approach to Tristan. At half-past five, dawn was supposed to be breaking, but the weather rendered the event theoretical. A Falkland islander would have described the sky as overcast. I joined the crew and a handful of passengers on the bridge to peer out at grey-black clouds that filled the sky and a dark, swelling sea. Suddenly, a grey-black smudge appeared on the horizon. 'Tristan!' we shouted in chorus and pressed binoculars harder against our eyes. Below us, the ship's prow tipped and fell as it battled towards the shape, the first land we had seen since Table Mountain had receded into the distance five days before.

I stepped out from the warmth of the bridge and was hit by furious rain. It was melodramatically awful weather, even for November. And then I remembered, this was the southern hemi-sphere so this was the summer. As Tristan slowly emerged from the clouds on the horizon, the ship's prow tipped and fell even more as it fought against the wind that was gaining ever greater strength, whisking spray from the waves. The wind was now powerful enough to force me staggering backwards. The rain was starting to sting my face.

'Force nine,' said the captain, impressed. 'Gusting to a ten. It's just as well I'm wearing these.' He looked down at his mandatory rig of the day – white shirt, white shorts and white socks.

Gradually, we could make out, with binoculars and then without them, Tristan's grey-black cliffs turning black-brown. We knew that somewhere behind the clouds lay an island which, although a mere eight miles in diameter, rises to a peak of 6,760 feet, but those clouds allowed only the first thousand feet of those cliffs to loom out as we tipped and fell along its east coast. We wondered if that less forbidding bit of shore was the one called Down-where-the-minis-ter-land-his-things. A black patch appeared on the shore which could have been Sandy Point. Above the black patch there was a steep, green slope that, we agreed, might well be the Farm, the patch of land where the Tristanians have nurtured several trees and keep a small herd of cows, which they have to hunt because the place is inhabited by islanders only when they come here by boat for their holidays.

The ship rounded Ridge-where-the-goat-jump-off and skirted the southern coast. We now faced west but were still battling against a headwind. Another couple of miles and we rounded Deadman's Bay and skirted the western coast. We now faced north and were still battling against a headwind.

With the aid of binoculars we could see some buildings. Not houses, as we thought wishfully at first, but huts. And fields. So that was Potato Patches. The settlement would soon be coming into view. And there it was. Edinburgh. Or Edinburgh-of-the-seven-seas, as the hamlet of 294 people is officially known. Crew and passengers alike peered through the murk at the collection of tin-roofed cottages huddled underneath the volcano's cliff-face while the captain talked on the radio with Tristan's Administrator.

It was a short conversation. Waves were hammering into the harbour and landing by launch was impossible. The forecast for the rest of the day was awful. But the ship's schedule did allow for an overnight stay. We'd find an anchorage and try again the next day.

As had just been proved on our circuitous approach to Edinburgh, Tristan has no leeward side, so the RMS *St Helena* had to head south-west for twenty-five miles to another British property, the uninhabited Inaccessible Island. I had thought this a peculiarly uninspired title for any place in these parts – like christening some Caribbean outcrop Palm Tree Island – but as we neared the refuge of Inaccessible's southern side, I thought again. The ship was able to find a calm anchorage here because above it towered a sheer, thousand-foot, cloud-topped cliff.

Tristan and its uninhabited neighbours – Inaccessible, Nightingale, Stoltenhoff and Middle islands – are tips of a gigantic underwater volcano which erupted to break the surface of the Atlantic a mere million years ago, but Inaccessible's southern cliff looked as if it had been there since the days of the earth's first amoeba. The cliff was streaked by waterfalls and had been greened by clumps of grass. Small, weather-bashed trees suffered on the top. Somehow, such vegetation as there was added to the awesome, primeval quality of the sight before us. It was easy to imagine that, beyond the cliffs and underneath the heavy, swarming clouds, there flourished large and terrifying creatures as yet unknown to man.

Inaccessible has not, in fact, been properly surveyed, and just one attempt has been made to inhabit the island. Survivors of a wrecked East India Company ship had managed to keep themselves alive here for several weeks in 1821 while they constructed some sort of boat to take themselves across to Tristan, before two Germans, the Stoltenhoff brothers, had the truly barking idea to live on Inaccessible in the 1870s. They abandoned the project after some Tristanians snuck over and killed all their livestock. So the story goes – sometimes down in these parts hard fact, like the weather, proves to be less than reliable.

One of those less reliable facts concerns the first sighting of Tristan. Whichever ship first came across the island, it undoubtedly came from Portugal, for the Portuguese discovered that the best way from Europe to the Cape of Good Hope was to use the prevailing winds by aiming for Brazil, then swinging east. At any rate, Tristão da Cunha named the rock after himself when he passed by in 1506. The weather didn't permit him to land. Sealers and whalers did manage to step ashore in the eighteenth century, and the island and its forbidding neighbours were first surveyed in 1760, by Captain Nightingale of the Royal Navy. Tristan's first settler was an American, Jonathan Lambert, who declared himself its owner and emperor in 1810, but his fandangle didn't cause any diplomatic incident, for he was drowned in a storm two years later.

In 1816, Tristan was formally annexed to the British Empire along with Ascension after Napoleon was exiled to St Helena. The idea was to establish a garrison on the island, but it didn't take long for the Admiralty to realise that this expensive measure was quite unnecessary; if the French were going to attack St Helena, they would do so from the western coast of Africa, not from an inhospitable volcano 1,320 miles to the south. When the garrison was withdrawn in 1817, one of its members, Corporal William Glass, requested that he and his wife and two children stay on the island and make a go of living here.

With limited sources of entertainment, the Glasses produced a total of eight sons and eight daughters. They were gradually joined by castaways as well as by five women who were brought here from St Helena to provide brides for desperate bachelors. One of the castaways was the Dutchman Pieter Willem Groen, who was shipwrecked on Tristan in 1836. Glass and Green are two of the seven surnames in Tristan's indigenous population. The others are Swain, Rogers, Hagan, Repetto and Lavarello, the last two families being descendants of a pair of Italians who were shipwrecked here in 1892. The 1980s witnessed the upheaval of an eighth surname entering the island's community when an Englishman, Pat Paterson, married a Tristanian, Susan Green, and emigrated to the island.

Tristan's settlers survived surprisingly well for most of the nineteenth century. The one settlement of Edinburgh consisted of sturdy cottages fashioned from volcanic rock and roofed by thatched flax. When the weather allowed it, there was good fishing to be had in the surrounding waters. A couple of the island's lower slopes could support subsistence farming, and the crop grown down at Potato Patches provided a reliable if unexciting source of food. The population had topped the hundred mark by 1885 when calamity struck the colony. A lifeboat was lost at sea and fifteen men were never seen again. It took several generations for the island to recover. The next main event arrived during the Second World War, when Tristan, which had recently been declared a dependency of St Helena, came under the supervision of the Admiralty. HMS Atlantic Isle, as the colony was temporarily known, acquired a naval communications base, constructed with the eager co-operation of the islanders. When the war was over, a resident administrator was assigned to Tristan; his arrival and the introduction of money to replace the local currency (potatoes) were the two notable changes to the islanders' lives.

Until 1961. When, after a month of rumblings, tremors and widening fissures, the volcano erupted. The entire population of 264 people had to be evacuated, initially to Nightingale Island and finally to a military base in Hampshire, where they were subjected to considerable interest from the press and the investigations of psychological, sociological and medical experts. Having been treated as either specimens or curiosities, and five islanders having died in the meantime (from diseases they couldn't combat, from shock, from the humiliation of all those psychological, sociological and medical tests), the Tristanians got their own back. As soon as the island was declared safe again, after two years in exile, almost all of them rejected the chance to stay in Britain and returned home.

I went to a strangely motionless bed that night as the ship lay at anchor under Inaccessible's southern cliff, and studied all the instructions we had been given for going ashore. Setting foot on Tristan is no easy process in the calmest of weather, because the harbour is too small to take anything larger than a launch. Some passengers would not be allowed to get off the ship, being too old or too infirm to cope with the business of stepping down a steep gangway, or of clambering down the ship's side on a rope pilot-ladder, before judging the swell to cross on to a launch's narrow edge. Other dangers awaited on land; we had to avoid any nesting albatross, which would defend itself by projectile-vomiting (with an impressive range of fifteen yards); we were not to walk near any cliff edge, for the soft volcanic rock would crumble and we'd plummet into the sea; were we stupid enough to want to brave the cold, swimming was not advisable because of the sharks; on hearing the ship's whistle, we had to hurry to the harbour or we'd be staying on the island until a trawler arrived in two months' time, because storms can attack with such sudden ferocity here that the RMS *St Helena* might have to scoot away at a moment's notice.

I was woken at four the next morning. The ship was on the move. Once again, we tipped and fell towards the rock that loomed out of the darkness. Once again, we rounded the island, always into a headwind. Once again, we climbed up to the bridge to peer anxiously through binoculars at Edinburgh's lights and the waves that crashed on to the shore. I exchanged worried thoughts with Angela, another writer whose assignment was to make it on to Tristan, and we began to console ourselves that maybe there was still a story in travelling 1,519 nautical miles to find that the Tristanian weather, as it often does, had prevented a landing.

There really was no doubt about it. Conditions this morning were even worse. And the ship had to leave today. The captain lowered his binoculars and muttered to himself, 'Not a hope in hell.'

What was a problem for Angela and me was a dreadful blow to many of our fellow-passengers, whose lifetime ambition had been to set foot on this exotically remote island. And it was little short of a disaster for the islanders themselves, because the ship was ferrying badly needed supplies – vaccines, medical equipment, food and fuel – as well as mail and Christmas presents . . . And what about the five people on Tristan who were booked for the voyage back to Cape Town?

All was not quite lost. By extraordinary good luck, HMS *Endurance* was scheduled to be visiting the island today. A hasty conference on the ships' radio link established that some kind of airlift could be cobbled together, and a few essential supplies might be ferried over by helicopter.

The *Endurance* soon appeared on the horizon. As the two ships approached each other in the driving wind and the heaving sea, we watched a helicopter taking off from the *Endurance*'s deck, whirring then roaring over to us. Watching the helicopter desperately struggling to maintain its position fifty feet above us was scary enough. And the noise was as startling as the pilot's skill in keeping the machine fairly steady over a moving, dipping ship and against the gusting wind. A figure appeared at the helicopter's open door. Ludicrously, he was winched down, spinning slowly on to the tennis-court-sized deck, narrowly avoiding a smash into a crane. A fellow-passenger yelled into my ear the news that, in a recent Navy exercise, a cadet had fallen eighty feet from a winch into the sea and broken his back. Not for the first time in my life, I wondered how crazed a person has to be to enter the services, while the winchee stumbled on to the deck and was joined by several maniacal colleagues. The operation began.

Two helicopter trips and one roll of film later, I heard Angela's name being called over the tannoy. Then mine. We guessed that it was a message from the Administrator, Brendan Dalley – an extremely kind gesture, we agreed, amid all the stress of the airlift. We had guessed correctly but we were flabbergasted. The message from the Administrator was that the airlift's schedule allowed two passengers to be winched up into the helicopter which would carry us over to the island. He had nominated us.

We passed the captain as we were led to a room to be briefed. 'You pair look as if you're about to be shot,' he commented.

'I have to admit', said Angela in a quavery voice, 'I am completely terrified.' She turned, ashen-faced, to me. 'How about you?'

'Very scared,' I said, although in truth I felt calm. How very curious. In the course of my travels, I had been reduced to a quivering wreck by a moped, a cable-car, a hill, several small planes, a spot of lightning and a cockroach. Yet now that I was faced with doing something that was genuinely frightening, I was reacting not with wimpish, childish, neurotic, selfish cowardice but cool detachment. Gallantly, I led Angela into the briefing room where two chaps in brown jumpsuits jabbered safety instructions at us – unzip this, pull on this, don't on any account touch that, cross your hands like this, don't even think about doing it that way.

'Okay,' said one brown jumpsuit. 'You have a couple of minutes to get ready. Do you smoke?' he asked Angela.

'Nih-nih-no.'

'Have one anyway.' He smiled. 'Might be your last.' He turned to me. 'You all right?'

I gave him a thumbs-up because, all of a sudden, I had lost the ability to speak.

'Right you are. Get your cameras and pens and stuff then.'

'Hah-has anyone gih-got any whisky?' Angela asked.

I had to shake my head because I was too traumatised to grunt, far less explain that I did have an unopened bottle in my cabin but needed to spend my allocated two minutes alone and in a lavatory. For the first time since it happened, I remembered how I had felt when I was eight years old and staring at a yellow ceiling as I was wheeled towards the operating theatre.

Back in the briefing room, Angela and I were ushered into orange, rubbery survival suits, green lifejackets and helmets with big ear muffs. The brown jumpsuits led us outside. Angela asked to go first. Fine by me. With luck she might suffer a dreadful accident and the whole operation would have to be abandoned. She was led out to the middle of the deck, into the dangling winch and hauled up and up to the helicopter's open door. There was a long, long pause while the chap waiting there struggled to get a grip on her and the helicopter dipped and bucked in the wind.

My next memory is of a noose tightening against my chest – and a moment later something pulling me into the air. I stared at the silent applause of passengers and crew as I was pulled higher and higher towards the helicopter. Then someone grabbed hold of me.

Three minutes later the helicopter landed on a field. We were on Tristan da Cunha. What must have been half the island's population was waiting to greet us. They smiled shyly as we plodded towards them in our comical orange kit. I noticed the smiles broadening as I spent some time wriggling out of my suit. It also occurred to me that men and women were standing in separate huddles and that most of the men were decked out in blue overalls. One man, whose jeans and cream jersey already set him apart, stepped forward.

'Welcome to Tristan,' he said with more than a hint of a laugh. 'I'm Jimmy Glass.'

I was taken aback. So this was Tristan's elected head, the Chief Islander? I'd been expecting to meet a white-haired patriarch, but this great-great-grandson of Corporal William Glass was a fit, suntanned thirty-five-year-old with thick brown hair and a flourishing brown beard. Although he was the youngest Chief Islander in Tristan's history, Jimmy had won the election by a large majority two years before, and it soon became apparent why. A quietly spoken chap fond of indulging in an infectious high chuckle, he struck me as one of those men who would invariably be impressive in debate, know how to mend a bust whodoyoumaflip, never lose his cool. Jimmy's CV, I learned later, was as strong as I would have expected: he was now the head of the island's Natural Resources Department and its Conservation Officer, having acquired experience as a sea fisheries officer in the Falklands and South Africa; he was a qualified diver; he had recently designed a plaque and flag for the island, and he had once presented a paper at an international conference at Cambridge University.

While Angela and I tried to cope, after five days at sea, with swaying land, Jimmy set off at a disarmingly brisk pace past a row of long, cream-painted sheds that served as a store and depot and towards the Administration building. He showed us into the chamber where he and the eight counsellors meet every two or three months. Alongside the inevitable photographs of the Queen, there was an unusual chart. It showed the family trees of every islander who had ever lived. The chart did not take up much space on the wall.

Didn't this represent a far too limited gene pool? Surely a self-contained community of under 300 people, from seven families, would have acquired unthinkably scary afflictions? I soon had the chance to ask about this problem, for Jimmy had led us over to the island's medical centre and introduced us to Vaughan Miller, a young South African doctor, here on a four-month contract. When Jimmy wandered off for a moment, I hastily interrupted Vaughan's tour of the hospital's one ward, with its one bed, to quiz him.

'I suppose you could argue that, theoretically, 300 is maybe a little too few. But it's hard to say.'

'Don't you find dire mutations, chaps marrying their own mums and so forth?'

'No, no. There's nothing like that.'

All the Tristanians I saw and met certainly seemed in the peak of mental and physical health, and the only obvious physical feature they shared was a deep, weather-beaten tan. However, as Vaughan went on to say, unsensational genetic problems have arisen in the community and a few illnesses have afflicted an abnormal proportion of the population. Glaucoma is prevalent. Far more significantly, so is asthma, which was probably introduced to the island by two sisters among the first settlers. Half of the Tristanian population now suffers from the disease. Vaughan's store cupboard was piled high with Ventolin inhalers and his most important piece of equipment was an oxygen mask.

Several other pieces of equipment in the medical centre, including a new heart-monitoring machine, were reminders that the Tristanians' asthma epidemic may actually prove of lasting benefit. The equipment had been donated by a grateful research team from the University of Toronto, whose study of the community – ideal for the researchers, who could analyse a small, contained and completely documented gene pool – had brought the Canadians very close to identifying the gene that causes asthma. Fizzing now with optimism, Vaughan predicted that it wouldn't be too long before the gene was pinned down and a cure found.

Mind you, the man clearly possessed a positive outlook. When he showed us his little operating theatre, I asked what would happen if he himself needed to undergo an operation. He laughed. 'Remember that Tristan's got three nurses – Frances, Teresa and Beverley. But if it was something that I had to do, fix a broken leg or remove my appendix, maybe . . . I suppose I could give myself a lumbar injection and operate on myself. And there's always Derek Rogers. He's very good.'

'Who is Derek Rogers?'

'The vet.'

'I don't suppose you can risk doing much volcano-climbing, then?'

'No. Mainly because I'm on call all the time, so I have to be fairly near at hand. But the islanders have to be careful as well.'

Hence the fact that I didn't see anyone over the age of sixty on Tristan. When outsiders visit the island, the older folk keep to their houses, not because they are shy but because they are afraid of picking up a virus which might well devastate their unprepared immune systems. Hence also the invention of a sport unique to Tristan – football rounders. Just like normal rounders, Jimmy explained, except that sixty, seventy, any number of people could play, and the ball is kicked rather than batted away. A fun game for Tristanians of all ages, football rounders also serves as a safe substitute for normal football, which would be far more likely to cause torn hamstrings or broken limbs.

Football rounders is played on Queen's Day, one of the island's public holidays along wih Ratting Day – a jolly occasion, Jimmy assured us, when Tristanians do their bit to cull the rats that have in the past threatened to overrun the island. There are prizes for the largest number of rats killed and the longest tail, as well as, for the least successful haul, the booby prize of a toilet roll or similar.

By the time Jimmy walked us down to the harbour – where the waves which smashed against the concrete wall demonstrated the impossibility of landing by launch – Angela and I were exchanging puzzled frowns. Tristan, both of us were beginning to suspect, really was very sorted out. Our suspicions, and suspicions about those suspicions, and suspicions about suspecting those suspicions, grew as Jimmy showed us the harbour and the nearby factory, where the lucrative haul of crayfish is prepared and packaged on a fishing day. On such a day, the islander whose job it is to inspect the conditions will ring a bell (the 'dong'), the fishermen will leap into their boats and eventually return to a welcome party of women who greet them with coffee and sandwiches by the harbour and who then set to work in the factory.

If they wanted, the Tristanians could make a bomb out of the crayfish crop, but choose not to. 'We would be rich for four or five years,' Jimmy said, 'but then what would we do? What would our children and our grandchildren do?' Accordingly, the islanders impose an annual quota on themselves of 340 tons of crayfish. Jimmy told us about his patrols to check on ships that are granted concessions in Tristanian waters, and, much more surprisingly, the fines islanders impose on themselves for catching young or under-sized fish.

We only had a couple of hours left before the last helicopter would take us back to the ship, so we hurried up the hill for a rapid tour of the settlement – the post office, the long hut that is the Prince Philip Hall and adjoining pub, the little café, the outdoor swimming-pool, the Administrator's house and garden, where the Union Jack flapped violently, the almost completed Catholic church and the spotlessly clean Anglican church, St Mary the Virgin, filled with bright-green pews.

Popping into the store, we were met by more shy smiles from the women who were waiting anxiously for helicoptered supplies. The shelves and freezers weren't empty and the islanders are self-sufficient in eggs, milk, mutton, beef and, of course, potatoes, but Christmas was four weeks away . . . And the island had already run out of some things. While Angela and I toured the shelves of tins and cereals and shoes and clothes, a woman came in with good news – the margarine consignment was on its way. (We found out later that one of the reasons the islanders were facing shortages was that they had been cooking for two days in order to entertain all the other passengers who now wouldn't after all be arriving from the ship.)

As I chatted with some of the women in the store about their hopes that the helicopter would manage to ferry over frozen chickens for Christmas and presents for the kids, it occurred to me that I wasn't having any difficulty understanding them. That isn't what I'd been led to expect. I asked Jimmy if the people I was meeting, including him, were talking to me as they would to each other.

He chuckled. 'No, if we talked to you normally, you wouldn't understand a word.'

'Okay, say something in Tristan for me.'

He thought for a moment, then said something that could have been a recipe in Arabic for all the sense it made to me. He repeated the sentence very slowly: 'Ise goan down da Tater Patches demorrah mornin'.'

'Got it. And do you really use an aitch in front of words like egg?'

'Oh yes. Hegg. And you come from the houtside wull.'

One of the curiosities of Tristanian English is its inclusion of very odd words, some of them possibly derived from the Dutch of Pieter Willem Groen before he became Peter Green. Uncle translates to huncle and auntie to hahni but godfather is fardi and godmother is muddish. Another islander I asked about this, after she had been winched onboard the RMS *St Helena*, was the enchanting and unlikely grandmother, Pam Lavarello. She feared that younger Tristanians were losing some of their distinctive accent and dialect, just as they no longer knew the special accordion dances her parents and grandparents had revelled in. All I could do was reassure her that Tristan English was authentically unintelligible.

Television can't be blamed for any erosion of Tristan's folk culture because Tristanians can't receive TV. They do pass round videos, but there's not much danger of the islanders going square-eyed because they are too busy to watch much telly and there's a drawback in hiring videos from the library in Cape Town, where late returns are fined by the day. Nor is there any danger that islanders form video-derived delusions that life outside Tristan consists of men leaping from exploding skyscrapers or cute kids chumming with extraterrestrials, for Tristanians are eager listeners to the BBC World Service. I think to prove that point, Jimmy asked me what I thought about the protests in Belgrade and that plane crash in the Indian Ocean. After five newsless days at sea, I didn't know what he was talking about. It struck me that this was my chance to catch up on key events back home but, sad to tell, Jimmy couldn't recall the Raith–Kilmarnock result.

There was just enough time, Jimmy guessed, for us to visit his own house. We hurried further uphill, past tall hedges of flax and low, dry-stone walls constructed from black volcanic rock, past a succession of neat, scrupulously clean, tin-roofed cottages whose tiny, well-kept gardens held short rows of lilies, and arrived at Jimmy's place, guarded by a friendly collie and a mildly outraged sheep tethered to a wall.

We walked into a home that reminded me of houses I'd visited in the Falklands with its cherished spruce domesticity. Jimmy plied us with tea and lager and his wife Felicity, another quiet, smiley soul, plied us with delicious, home-made crayfish tart. Angela and I settled ourselves into the three-piece suite in the sitting room and, in between gulps and mouthfuls, continued to bombard Jimmy with questions because neither of us could quite believe what we were seeing on Tristan. Where was the hardship, the dire struggle to survive, the sense of absence and of sheer remoteness? As the interrogation progressed, our sense of disbelief grew. Not that we didn't believe Jimmy or the evidence of our eyes. It was just hard to accept how thoroughly admirable the community on Tristan really did appear to be. Everything we were learning about this fictionally remote island made it resemble a utopia, right down to the men wearing the uniform of blue overalls – with the one qualification that no creator of an idealistic allegory would ever have come up with football rounders.

Almost every Tristanian worker is employed by the Tristanian government – as a teacher, office-worker, carpenter, stonemason, whatever. Those who leave school at fifteen serve an apprenticeship of a year, learning various tasks, so specialities can be assigned according to ability and inclination. (Pupils who continue their education have to go to St Helena and then to a college in Uttoxeter.) When considering someone for a job, islanders also take into account the individual's financial needs and family circumstances, with the result that there is no poverty. The average wage is £150 a month, and the higher wages are not much more than double that, with the result that there is no elite. Although wages sound very low, the islanders don't pay any tax, all public services are free, they own their homes, and they are provided with a pension when they retire at sixty-five. They also catch or grow most of their own food, because, in addition to their government jobs, islanders work as farmers, fishermen, factory-hands, as the occasion demands, and in their spare time they tend the vegetable patches they all have. Islanders spend many of their 'leisure' hours doing odd-jobs, often for each other.

The economy works on a pooled basis, with all the revenue from Tristan's two sources of income – crayfishing and stamps – entering a central fund which pays for the island's infrastructure and the islanders' wages. Aid from Britain is required very occasionally and only for specific projects and never for the island's budget, which the islanders have managed so prudently that they have been able to build the safeguard of a reserve fund for the island, which has enough money to keep Tristan going for eight years, should the fishing industry meet some catastrophe. But, as Jimmy had pointed out, the chances of a catastrophe happening are slim because conservation is such a priority.

Our helicopter was due very soon. Angela and I scrawled down notes, finished our drinks, thanked Felicity and kept on pumping Jimmy for info, all at the same time. There might just be a couple of minutes to spare for a sprint round the school, so we trotted out and past the bewildered sheep, down the path lined by flax and low, black-bouldered walls, and ran into the school, where we scurried round with the head teacher, Marlene Swain. Wouldn't you know it, she was a marvel and the school was terrific – from the class of little ones who gaped at us before returning to their Christmas drawings to the bashful teenagers intent on working despite the racket of the helicopter which had just landed on the field outside. Searching for a criticism, I could say that the desks were old and the material on the class walls looked a bit dated (lads with side partings being chipper with frocked lasses and suchlike), but I would have to add that the exhibition in the assembly hall about Ratting Day was impressive, that the community library looked to be pretty well stocked, and that there are nine teachers for the forty pupils. Marlene was in the middle of a hurried explanation that Tristan Studies was an additional and obligatory addition to the national curriculum when the news came that Angela and I had to leave. Now.

We ran down to the field, where the helicopter was about to finish unloading its latest cargo of food and where a Wren handed us our comedy orange suits. Before I clamped on my safety helmet and muffs, I offered Jimmy profuse thanks and asked if I could take any messages for him or do anything in return for his kindness. With a slightly embarrassed chuckle, he handed me his radio ham's card and call sign.

'Isn't there anything else? Something I could send as a thank-you present?'

'No, no, don't worry.'

'There's got to be something. Come on, be honest, what do you really miss?'

He thought long and hard. Then he said, 'Fresh fruit.'

'Nothing else?'

He shook his head and chuckled again. 'No.'

After filling a poly bag with rocks – the only souvenirs I could think of grabbing for the other passengers who hadn't made it on to land, I plodded alongside Angela to the helicopter. The noise made conversation impractical, but I was glad of that because, as I turned to wave goodbye to Jimmy and all the other islanders who had come to see us off – the men in blue overalls, the women huddled in separate groups, everyone grinning and waving and not even thinking about complaining that most of their supplies were now on the way to St Helena – I felt a lump filling my throat and my eyes filling with tears.

I am fully aware that my time on Tristan amounted to five hours, that the community must have some disadvantages of which I'd remain unaware had my time amounted to five years, that if I forsook the houtside wull and tried to live here I'd soon find myself on a Cape-bound trawler, dribbling about pubs and restaurants and *Football Focus*, and that it sounds corny, but, just as Angela did and for the same reason, I felt extremely privileged to have been here. Meeting these shy, hard-working, self-reliant, profoundly gentle people, seeing how they lived in a community that truly did share and care – not because they were idealists but because it was the only way for them to survive and prosper together – had shown me humanity at its best. So yes, I treasure those five hours in the South Atlantic's Edinburgh.

Chapter Seven

Britain's Atlantic Alcatraz: St Helena

One thousand, three hundred and fifteen nautical miles north of Tristan da Cunha, the ship made its approach to St Helena. In the five days since Tristan we had seen not one ship. But there had been one moment of excitement when we took a detour to inspect a bobbing, tightly waterproofed cylinder – a discarded bit of ship's equipment, said the captain, coughing with embarrassment, because he knew as well as us that inside that cylinder was the kind of ship's equipment that could be chopped up into white lines and would keep the entire Royal Navy partying for a week.

Now, though, we had something to look out for. We were in the Tropics, and dawn was supposed to be breaking, but once more the sky was overcast. Bleary-eyed, I joined the clutch of passengers who were watching a Tristanesque lump of rock emerge from the gloom on the horizon. Two of that clutch of passengers were men from the island who had worked abroad for most of their lives and who now furtively rubbed tears from their eyes at the tall cliffs ahead of us – their first sight of their homeland for forty years.

Beachcombing is not a popular activity on St Helena for the very good reason that there is almost no beach. The one feasible harbour is at the capital, Jamestown. Because the rest of the coastline consists of impregnable cliffs, St Helena made an ideal island prison for its only famous resident, Napoleon Bonaparte, who was incarcerated here from 1815 until his death in 1821. Even better for Napoleon's captors, this Atlantic Alcatraz was also handily situated – 1,150 miles from the Angolan coast, 1,800 miles from Brazil. St Helena's nearest neighbour is Ascension, 700 miles to the north. Hence its world-record status, to repeat the pub-quiz information of the first chapter, as the bit of land furthest from any other bit of land. Such is St Helena's isolation that the Portuguese managed to keep the island a secret, after they discovered it in 1502, for the best part of the sixteenth century.

St Helena's public profile is not much higher these days, being known, if at all, only as the site of Napoleon's imprisonment. I used to picture him in solitary exile on a rock the size of my bedroom, his uniform tattered, his hat at his feet beside a tea-chest of rations. The lingering influence of that childhood image, in addition to the recent memory of Tristan's Edinburgh, probably explains the shock I felt when I glimpsed a clutch of bungalows atop a cliff. 'Half Tree Hollow,' said a 'Saint' leaning next to me on the ship's rail. Then he said, 'Jamestown,' with an air of proud glee and pointed towards a harbour full of little fishing boats. The ship swung slowly round to reveal a straggle of buildings wedged at the bottom of a V formed by two steep, brown hills.

After a daft bureaucratic rigmarole conducted by four immigration officials who bequeathed me a sheaf of permits and papers and, with no little ceremony, another stamp on my passport, I teetered down the gangway and stepped over to a launch that bobbed across to the harbourfront. I jumped on to the wharf and once again staggered with my sea-legs along a swaying road to join the queue of passengers busy keeping their balance in a long shed. Here an inexplicable army of immigration officials smiled at us pleasantly and advised that we wait for the bus to take us three hundred yards into the heart of Jamestown.

The heart of Jamestown appeared to have suffered a stroke. The main artery, Napoleon Street, was deserted, save for a woman standing outside a hardware store and a group of passengers from the ship. They were walking up the street as if they were on a reconnaissance party from the Starship *Enterprise* checking out a suspiciously abandoned settlement. Jamestown itself looked just like the kind of stringently budgeted filmset that reconnaissance parties from the Starship *Enterprise* often found themselves checking out. There were a few vaguely Georgian buildings, notably the bright-blue Wellington House Hotel – leftovers from a TV adaptation of

Moll Flanders that jostled unconvincingly with the verandahed, tin-roofed frontiersville look of the cream post office and the worryingly rickety Consulate Hotel. Some of the vehicles that were parked aslant down the centre of Napoleon Street definitely had no place in this production, having been imported long ago from an early episode of *Z-Cars*. God, I hadn't seen a Ford Consul since I scorned short trousers. And Anglias! Those wee triangular windows with stiff catches!

The time-warp continued in the Consulate Hotel, where I checked into a room in a provincial boarding-house of the early 1950s. I parted the furry cream curtains and appraised the view – the reconnaissance party was still swivelling slowly around on Napoleon Street below, where they had stopped underneath a pair of old trees – the same trees where, in 1827, those five Saint women had waited to be taken to Tristan as spouse material (in exchange for some potatoes). A series of sun-bleached tin roofs led off to the left and ended all of a sudden when they came up hard against a red-brown cliff. A road had been cut into the side but there was another way up to the top – Jacob's Ladder, a laughably horrific set of 699 steep steps. I went out to have a closer look at the construction. Even with my battle-hardened experience on the helicopter winch, I managed to climb ten steps before returning (backwards and with my eyes closed) to ground level. I was told that a Saint called Paul Thomas can make it up to the top in three minutes, but any Saint above the age of five can make the downward descent in a minute less than that, using the locals' traditional sliding technique – lying face-up across the railings which rise on either side of the steps, extending the arms behind one railing, crossing the ankles round the other. Apparently, in bygone days of yore, little boys would do this to carry plates of soup from the cookhouse at the summit to the sentries below, balancing said plates of soup on their stomachs.

With a heavy heart, I had to accept that I wouldn't have the time to slide down Jacob's Ladder. First item on my packed agenda was a tour of the island in a car that made the Anglias and Consuls look like newly minted BMWs. Colin Corker's charabanc was a 1929 Chevrolet powered by an engine that dated from 1945 and sounded very much of that vintage, particularly when it was faced with a sharp uphill incline. This happened quite a lot because sharp uphill inclines accounted for 50 per cent of the journey, the remaining 50 per cent being sharp downhill inclines. There is one flat patch of land on St Helena that might just serve as an airstrip, given a hefty amount of construction work and should the island ever receive the money or the permission from Britain to acquire one. Games of cricket have been played on one plateau inland, despite the difficulty experienced by fielders on the boundary; during one game, a fellow at long-on flung himself at a high six and off the plateau, the result being recorded in the scorebook as 'Retired, dead'.

First stop on the charabanc tour, a couple of miles inland from Jamestown and, it seemed, the same distance above the town, was the Briars, the house where Napoleon lived for his first six weeks on St Helena. The house was strikingly pretty with a superb view across the hills to the sparkling blue sea, but Longwood, Napoleon's permanent prison, beat it into a cocked hat. A French flag flies outside Longwood, the building is administered with French money by a French consul and the house and garden are in French territory. This spot of St Helena that is forever France is spacious, elegant and pangfully beautiful. You would not have guessed this from the accounts of many French historians, who had Napoleon cooped up in a hovel. But I suppose he was used to grander accommodation than a well-appointed house surrounded by a gorgeous garden and marvellous scenery. The Duke of Wellington appreciated Napoleon's former lifestyle when he chanced to stay at his adversary's old place – just when Napoleon had arrived on St Helena and been quartered in a room in Jamestown where Wellington had stayed himself. The irony was not lost on the good Duke, who made a clumping jest to an aide: 'You may tell Bony that I find his apartments at the Elisée Bourbon very convenient and that I hope he likes mine. It is a droll sequel enough to the affairs of Europe that we should change places of residence.' Boom boom.

The ex-Emperor's next residence lies a mile away from Longwood, at the bottom of a damp, wooded hollow. As I squelched towards the empty tomb, I wondered why he had chosen this particular spot. Because it was appropriately sepulchral? One account states that he ended up here, in the Sane Valley, after he expressed a desire to be buried near the Seine, but I stuck to my own theory that he selected this place because here there is no view of the sea which imprisoned him.

The choice was such an odd one given the wonderful sites Napoleon could have chosen for his grave, because St Helena's landscape is astonishing. Behind the wall-like cliffs lies a countryside as diverse as it is spectacular. When the charabanc had chugged laboriously above the barren slopes that hem in Jamestown, cactus and aloe appeared on the hillsides, then just as abruptly gave way to wild flax, which was suddenly replaced by eucalyptus trees, thorn trees, pines, hibiscus. As the charabanc approached each tight turn, nudging closer and closer to the stone wall that protected it from a long plunge straight down, I could never guess what lay ahead. One moment we'd be in the middle of Arizona, the next in the Dordogne, and a minute later we'd have swung into some part of New Zealand. And in the background would usually be a view of hills and escarpments that could have modelled for what I had always thought until now were completely unrealistic Renaissance paintings.

Dotted around this grand landscape were some country houses that rivalled Napoleon's tasty farmhouse, but best of all was undoubtedly the Governor's residence, Plantation House – a charming two-storey Georgian number done out in bright white walls with bottle-green shutters and with a large lawn that is home to Jonathan, a tortoise estimated to be somewhere between 130 and 260 years old. But most of the houses scattered inland were neat though noticeably unprosperous cottages. There were no third-world shacks, but the prefabs which served as a small primary school and centre for mentally handicapped children at Longwood came close. And the new homes of Half Tree Hollow, an area separated from Jamestown by the cliff adorned by Jacob's Ladder, had the misfortune to be built on a hillside so barren and ill-appointed that the residents were hard pushed to make the area look anything more than the sort of trailer park in American movies where Harry Dean Stanton stars as a forlorn alcoholic.

The charabanc had had to miss out a good deal of St Helena's 47 square miles, but since it would have been trounced in a race by Brian Sheedy's golf buggy or a strolling grandparent, the charabanc still took five hours to complete its tour. So as soon as I was dropped off back at the Consulate, it now being seven of a Saturday evening, I went out on the town to see what was cooking. Things seemed to be already hotting up at an old pub called the Standard. The one room looked like the kind of saloon bar where you're considered a poof if you've got both ears, but the dozen customers regarded me, if at all, with not a trace of hostility, merely some puzzlement since I hadn't been propping up this bar for the past two decades. Reggae music hammered out of a ghetto-blaster with such force that I ordered a can of Castle lager using only my index finger. The décor was odd. A crayfish in a glass cabinet. An exhibition of unlikely banknotes. A poster for Oxford United's Milk Cup victory in 1986.

I fell into a conversation that was slightly limited in scope, restricted as it had to be to exchanges of smiles and thumbs-ups. The bloke i/c the ghetto-blaster, realising that the volume level was ridiculous, promptly doubled it. Having discreetly checked to see if my ears were bleeding, I swigged the last of my lager, bade my bar pals farewell with a raised palm and escaped to the Consulate Hotel. It was far busier than the Standard but, inevitably, far quieter. Hundreds of Saints and scores of passengers and crew from the ship mingled in the bar and the courtyard. It wasn't difficult to tell who belonged to which group. For one thing, all the visitors were white, whereas the Saints' skin varied in colour from milky coffee to espresso, while their facial features offered an intriguing and often extremely attractive mix – many Saints looked, to my eyes, Burmese, others Malaysian, and several could have passed for Polynesians or even Zulus. (There once was such a thing as a born-and-bred white Saint, but there are no longer any natives of, in the telling local phrase, 'high colour'.) But, more subtly than lack of melanin, it was prosperity that made us visitors conspicuous.

While I sat in that courtyard and drank several cans of South African lager, I puzzled over a variety of questions that had been floating around in my head ever since I had stepped uncertainly on to this island. Why was there so little to buy in the shops? Why were so many of the homes I'd passed by in the charabanc cheaply constructed? Why had I seen so little farmland in such an extra-ordinarily fertile, if daftly hilly, countryside? Where was the local industry? Why was St Helena so thoroughly, shabbily *poor*?

I was woken the next morning by harsh chirruping and cursed Miss Phoebe Moss, who, in 1885, freed five mynah birds on the island, which is now overrun by the little bastards. I went out for a walk, down Napoleon Street to the old, stone-built church, looked in at the neighbouring prison, crossed the road to the police station, peered in at the shut museum, noted the floral display in the public gardens, inspected the stairs that led down from the older houses to the basement (the sometime slaves' entrances), idled in front of the hardware store, idled up to the market for a coffee at Dot's café, found the market wasn't open, and, for want of anything else to do, idled back down to the Consulate. Everything was shut. I hadn't seen a soul. Fair enough, it was ten o'clock on a Sunday morning, but there was the big event of a ship being in town – yet Jamestown looked as if it had been hit by a neutron bomb.

I sat down on the steps outside the Consulate and surveyed the surrounding emptiness. Salt Cay had had the same air of having been abandoned, but it had retained a magical quality completely absent here. I gazed across at the post office which, like everywhere else, was shut for the day, although out in the harbour there was a ship full of rich tourists anxious to part with their money for stamps or, come to that, any souvenir other than the plastic plant pots and nylon shirts that seemed to constitute the island's entire stock of consumer goods. And while I gazed, I finally gave in to the depression I'd been fighting. For the first time in my travels throughout Britain's far-flung outposts, I felt miserably homesick. Correction – I yearned to be anywhere but here, stuck in a ghost village on a speck in the middle of the Atlantic, where the only escape-route was a two-day journey by ship to Ascension or a four-day journey by ship back down to Cape Town. Six thousand people live on St Helena and, for the life of me, I could not see how. I began to appreciate Napoleon's strength of character in lasting all of six years on this island.

Appropriately for a country best known as a prison, St Helena's first inhabitant was another penal victim. Fernando Lopez was a dis-graced soldier whom the Portuguese punished for desertion in India by cutting off his nose, his ears, his right hand and the thumb on his left hand before dumping him on St Helena in 1513. He survived on his own for ten years, evading many attempts by Portuguese mariners to find him and give him food, until he was joined by a shipwrecked slave boy from Java. Unfortunately, the two castaways didn't get on. In fact, they hated each other – so much so that, when the next Portuguese ship called in, the boy told the crew where poor Fernando was hiding. He was taken back to Lisbon, a star, and to Rome, where he gave his confession to the Pope, who granted him a wish. Fernando requested that he be taken back to St Helena. He returned to live here for another twenty years, his only companions his pet poultry.

St Helena was annexed by the Dutch in 1633 but they didn't occupy it, thus allowing the British, in the shape of the East India Company, to take control of the place in 1659 and to use it as a supply station for their ships. When Napoleon arrived here, the island had to be leased by the East India Company to the government. St Helena had been visited by celebrities before – Captains Cook and Bligh stopped off here and Edmund Halley had built an observatory here in an ill-starred attempt to observe the transit of Mercury (he was denied by fog) – but the arrival on this remote colony, at a few days' notice, of the most famous man in the world, and his entourage, and a garrison of several thousand troops transformed St Helena into a bustling, significant, talked-about place.

Then Napoleon died. Bereft of glory, St Helena pootled along, cheerily unaware that in one of the future's dark alleyways catastrophe was waiting, patiently tapping a palm with its cudgel. In 1834 control of the island was permanently transferred from the paternalistic and generous East India Company to the British government. The new crown colony became poor overnight. By the time it had begun to recover from that first mugging, St Helena suffered another bad blow in 1869 with the opening of the Suez Canal. The shipping route down the African coast was already in a bit of a decline, but the Canal consigned the island to be a mid-Atlantic anachronism.

Seven thousand people lived on St Helena at that time – British soldiers and officials and the descendants of workers brought in here by the Company from the East Indies, of Chinese labourers and of slaves from the African coast and Madagascar. This racial hotchpotch did find a couple of sources of employment and hope when the island was used as an imperial cable-relay station and then for the growing and processing of flax. Impoverished as it was, St Helena survived until the mid-1960s, when it received another blow. This time the devastating uppercut was delivered by the British GPO, which in 1966 changed from using flax to synthetic twine for bundling letters. It took one Post Office memo to knock out St Helena's economy.

And, as I could readily appreciate while I walked around a grimly tranquil Jamestown that Sunday morning, St Helena has never recovered from that single swipe. I know that sounds like a glib exaggeration, so I'll quote part of a recent speech given to the island's Legislative Council by the man I was due to meet at noon, Councillor Eric George; pondering the current state of the St Helenian economy, he stated, 'We have no economy.'

Belying his words of doom and gloom, Councillor Eric George turned out to be a tubbily avuncular chap, possessed of a round face that was made to gleam and twinkle. Eric also evidently possessed great qualities of resolve as well as affability; in 1954 he overcame immense problems and official apathy to set up the island's electricity network, and over forty years later, here he was, leading the island's fight for survival.

As Eric handed me document after document and we discussed the island's troubles, it became depressingly apparent that St Helena's bleak present looks set to evolve into a bleaker future. With hardly any private enterprise or indigenous industry, the island is almost entirely dependent on the aid it receives from Britain. This aid amounts at present to £8.5 million, but £5 million of that is spent directly by the British government – subsidising the RMS *St Helena*, for example, funding the ventures of the Overseas Development Administration – and over half of that money re-enters the British economy, so that part of the aid package functions rather like a toff handing out a fiver only to demand a double scotch in return. The Saints get to spend and benefit from the remainder, but that £3.5 million was about to be cut by half a million, and a good slice of the money would have to pay for the growing number of unemployed. There are 3,000 people in the island's labour force but, Eric explained, a thousand of those work in Ascension and the Falklands, usually in menial jobs and on contracts which condemn them to pensionless retirement. Of those who remain on the island, 200 were jobless (with the figure likely to double in the following four months) and 120 were on a government work scheme, earning £25 for a three-day week. Unemployment benefit was £12.50, £5 if the jobless person could be classed as a dependant. For those who were in work, the average wage was £50. One of the best job opportunities for Saints was on the RMS *St Helena*, which can therefore boast one of the world's most intelligent and multi-talented crews; my cabin steward, for example, was an ex-policeman who had grasped the opportunity to double his earnings – to £5,000 a year.

The British government's cunning solution was to encourage a private sector that didn't exist by introducing cutbacks in public spending. The result was that, in recent months, an eminently peaceful island had seen a protest march by teachers and another demo when, in an unprecedented move, ninety people occupied the Governor's office. Eric had led the protest of the island's elected councillors, seeing his motion condemning the British aid pro-gramme passed unanimously. In reply, Baroness Chalker at the ODA had offered the serene reassurance that 'The ODA's aid programme for St Helena gives both St Helena and the UK value for money.'

On both the ship and the island, there were many, many discussions about St Helena's plight, mainly because Saints were sobbingly grateful to have any chance at all to talk to non-Saints about what was going on in their island. Wondrously good-natured as they were, devoted to Britain and proud subjects of a Queen they worshipped, Saints were becoming frightened, rather than merely very worried, and angry, rather than merely completely bewildered, by what the British government was doing to them.

I was to learn more about what British governments have done to St Helena after my meeting with Eric George, when I listened to three prominent islanders over a Sunday lunch hosted by George Stevens, the manager of the Cable and Wireless operation (the only significant private-sector employer, bar a couple of shops). It was an idyllic setting, next door to Napoleon's first gaff at the Briars and with a stunning vista of ravines, cliffs and sea. As we basked in the December heat and George's stereo played Christmas carols in the background, the conversation developed into an equally surreal account of life on the island.

Far from wanting to scrounge, Saints had to rely on British handouts because every initiative the Saints had come up with had been blocked or cocked up by the British administration. Not for want of advice either, for St Helena has been inundated by ODA experts. As one islander said, 'If every consultant that came here planted a tree, we'd have a new forest.' I thought back to the contempt the ODA employees had inspired in the Turks and Caicos, to Jimmy Glass' fierce concern that the Tristanians remain self-sufficient or else the ODA would be called in and dismantle the unique and inspiring economy he and his compatriots managed, to Jimmy pointing in disgust at the ODA's great contribution to Tristan – the extension to the harbour wall, which was worse than useless because the islanders' own expert advice had been ignored.

I later found the reason for one potential moneyspinner for St Helena being stamped on; a plan to set up a 'St Helena' lottery on the Internet (whereby the island would receive 1 per cent of the proceeds merely for lending its name to the scheme) had been vetoed by Whitehall because existing legislation wouldn't allow it. But why didn't St Helena have a bank? Why had it taken the British administration so long (nearly two years) to respond to the Bank of Nova Scotia's proposal to set up in business here that the Canadians got fed up and threw the plan in the bin? Why was a Brit not being allowed to set up a hotel here? Why had a German entrepreneur been prevented from setting up a local brewery? Why had the subsequent venture by the ODA been to set up a brewery which brewed bitter, when market research, consisting of three minutes propping up the bar at the Standard, would have confirmed that Saints drink lager? Why was the land allocated for new housing concentrated on the hostile, arid slopes at Half Tree Hollow, and why had no proper infrastructure been provided there? Most puzzlingly of all, why was a country which had been described by early explorers as 'bountiful', 'an Earthly Paradise', which had once grown all manner of fruit and vegetables and coffee and cotton, now importing 95 per cent of its goods? Fruit trees whose distant relations had once provided South Africa with the start of its citrus crop languished untended, cotton grew wild by the roadside, and all the prime farmland was in the hands of the ODA, which had mucked around for years and years and years and come up with absolutely bugger all.

More shocking still is the fact that Saints can't protest about this state of affairs because Britain presides over a country which does not have a democracy and where there is no free press. Yes, Saints can vote but only for a council which has minimal influence and which is subservient to the non-elected governor and chief secretary who possess, to quote the admission of a high-ranking member of the Foreign Office, 'virtually unlimited power'. As for the local media, that consists of a government-funded newspaper and a government-funded radio station; since it is against civil-service regulations for government employees to criticise the government and since almost every employee on the island is employed by the government, the result is state censorship. To show that this is censorship carried out with great zeal, a Saint told me about the occasion when he gave a television interview under the watchful eye of John Perrott, the Chief Secretary, who on another occasion reminded a radio broadcaster that if he deviated from an approved script he'd be sacked. Terry Richards, the General Manager of the island's Fisheries Corporation, gave me several letters of protest he'd written to the *St Helena News* that had been refused publication; he wasn't a government employee but had been, technically, appointed by the Governor, who dressed him down for his effrontery and threatened to sack him.

Much though I wanted to, I can't cast the present Governor, David Smallman, as a moustache-twirling villain. His is a thankless task, implementing Whitehall's cutbacks, struggling, as all his predecessors have done, against the ignorance and indifference of the Foreign Office. The truth is that no British government has bothered about St Helena since 1815 and they haven't needed to because the Saints can't vote for an MP. Nor do Saints have British citizenship. The church – that rare phenomenon on St Helena, an institution free from government – is leading the campaign to have Britain recognise Saints as full British subjects, as guaranteed by a Royal Charter of Charles II. Instead, the British Nationality Act has granted Saints dependent territories citizenship, which denies them any right of abode in the UK and has, effectively, imprisoned them.

After one of the most amiable and depressing Sunday lunches I have had, George Stevens drove me down to Jamestown. We looked in at the church, where a special seaman's service was being held in honour of the ship. Afterwards, the congregation shuffled out to watch one of the parades that the Saints love to indulge in. To a thumping drum and a tootling of bugles, down Napoleon Street marched the Scouts, the Guides, the Cubs and the Rainbow Guides. There was Eric George in his Scoutmaster's uniform. And Terry Richards, woggle askew. And George's six-year-old granddaughter April, heart-breakingly pretty and proud in her Rainbow Guide dress. Across the road Governor Smallman and Captain Roberts from the RMS *St Helena* were waiting in immaculate white uniforms. The two dignitaries snapped a salute as, to thumps and tootles, the Saints went marching in, Scouts and Guides and Cubs and Rainbow Guides all faultlessly in step.

For the second chapter in succession, I felt a lump filling my throat and my eyes filling with tears. In St Helena, however, I felt not humbled but humiliated, not privileged but mortified. This sweetest of British ceremonies, enacted by people who knew they were British although Britain wouldn't acknowledge it, whom its colonial power was treating like scum, could only make me feel profoundly ashamed. Nor could I find any comfort in the thought that my feelings echoed those of earlier visitors to St Helena. In 1985, Simon Winchester described the 'poor decisions, ignorance, insouciance, obstruction and unkindness' of Britain's treatment of St Helena. In 1980, the Conservative MP Sir Bernard Braine had produced a damning report which concluded that St Helena was suffering 'enforced dependence'. In 1958, another MP, Cledwyn Hughes, had been scandalised by the state of the colony. Philip Gosse, the eminently nice, optimistic, tactful historian of St Helena, had been driven to outrage by the islanders being denied the right to express their views or own land or be granted a dynamic, go-ahead governor; Gosse expressed his outrage in 1937. All I can do is repeat the fact: what Britain has done with St Helena is a scandal.

I think it is also an instructive scandal. I can find one commendable feature of the policy of successive British governments towards its remaining overseas possessions – the guarantee that it will respect the right to self-determination, that the colonies will be colonies as long as they want to remain so. But that is the one bright exception to an otherwise dismal rule. Six EC countries retain overseas territories and five of those countries have granted full rights of citizenship to the people born and bred in those territories. In Dutch Aruba, French Guadeloupe, the Danish Faroe Islands, Spanish Ceuta and Portuguese Madeira, the same laws and rights apply as in Amsterdam, Paris, Copenhagen, Madrid and Lisbon, and people possess passports that allow them to travel freely to and from the overseas territory and the parent country. As I write, the only British colonies which have been granted full citizenship are Gibraltar and the Falklands. As it happens, these are Britain's two remaining colonies where all the inhabitants are white. Every other colony is waiting, more in hope than expectation, to see if the appalling British Nationality Act will be amended after the loss of Hongkong.

But the omens are not good. In fact, such is Britain's track-record in its dealings with its colonies that Saints might almost think themselves lucky. They have been denied the two prerequisites of a healthy and prosperous society – a fully functioning democracy and a free press – and they have been trapped, by meaningless passports and poverty, on an island in the middle of nowhere, but they are a damned sight better off than the people who used to live in British Indian Ocean Territory. This straggle of coral islands south-east of the Seychelles was once home to 1,150 people – until, without any consultation far less consent, Britain moved them to Mauritius, where they were flung into a ghetto and on to the dole. The islands were turned into a military base that Britain generously shared with the United States, and the United States generously waived its £7 million bill for the research and development of the Polaris nuclear submarine.

Lest anyone think this a glitch in an otherwise admirable post-imperial policy, some recent examples of decolonisation should also be taken into account. Britain pushed Dominica towards independence in the mid-1970s, without a referendum, and in the knowledge that the country would be in the hands of Patrick John, a corrupt, violent autocrat. Britain made Brune! independent in 1984, without consulting the inhabitants and against the wishes of the ruling Sultan. Britain granted independence to Grenada in 1974, in the certainty that it was consigning the island to the corruption and tyranny of Eric Gairy. There is also the humiliating case of Britain offering £80,000 compensation to the Banabans for having allowed phosphate mining to transform their Pacific island into a lunar wasteland; when the

Banabans took the British government to court, they lost on a technicality, but the High Court judge commented that Britain should still make proper amends because that was clearly its moral duty.

But when was a British government last guided by any principle other than those of not spending money or of staying in power? Britain has a clear moral responsibility to its colonies and St Helena shows how Britain has failed that simple morality test. Successive British governments, under no pressure save that of mere principle, have done as little as they can to fulfil their responsibility and have treated the place with apathy, ignorance or downright hostility.

The morning after the parade, while I packed my bags, checked out of the crumbling Consulate and walked down to the wharf, I reflected that those colonies which have achieved prosperity have done so without or despite British involvement. Tourism and offshore finance have paid for an effectively independent Bermuda. Gibraltar has managed to survive despite Britain's rapid closure of the dockyards, which had been the colony's economic mainstay. Tristan da Cunha has gone it alone and done its very best to preempt any British meddling. It took the disaster of a war for Britain to pay any attention to the Falklands. The Turks and Caicos Islands are a charming shambles. And St Helena is, to quote a previous visitor, 'an imperial slum'.

I had met a lot of people I liked very much on St Helena, but as I stepped on to the launch I could feel my shoulders slump in misery and relief that I was leaving. Then I bowed my head too, as I wondered what kind of future April could expect under British management.

A year after starting out, I was about to finish my imperial tour. What answer would I give to George V's deathbed enquiry: 'How is the empire?'

'Well,' I could say, 'it still stretches far and wide and it contains beautiful, fascinating places full of truly fine people . . .'

But the dots in that reply would beg another question.

'And?'

'. . . To be honest, your Majesty, it's not very big. And it's a disgrace.'

DATE DUE

28 DAY

JUL 01 1999	NOV 27 2004
JUL 13 1999	
AUG 10 1999	DEC 11 2004
AUG 11 1999	
AUG 26 1999	AUG 02 2007
SEP 14 1999	FEB 01 2008
OCT 20 1999	DEC 07 2008
NOV 03 1999	FEB 22 2009
DEC 06 1999	
APR 12 2000	
APR 10 2001	
OCT 09 2002	
SEP 19 2003	

BRODART

Cat. No. 23-221

Mechanics' Institute Library

3 1750 03251 6844

942
R58   Ritchie, Harry.
              The last pink
           bits

WITHDRAWN